PENGUIN BOOKS

MAKING SENSE

Ellen Goodman, columnist and associate editor at *The Boston Globe*, writes a column that is syndicated by the Washington Post Writers Group and appears in over 420 newspapers across the country. She was awarded the Pulitzer Prize for her columns in 1980, and the Hubert H. Humphrey Civil Rights Award in 1988 for dedication to the cause of equality. A frequent commentator on both television and radio, Goodman is the author of *Turning Points*, *Close to Home*, *At Large*, and *Keeping in Touch*. She lives near Boston with her husband, Bob Levey.

MAKING SENSE

SENSE

ELLEN GOODMAN

PENGUIN BOOKS

PENGUIN BOOKS
Published by the Penguin Group
Viking Penguin, a division of Penguin Books USA Inc.,
375 Hudson Street, New York, New York 10014, U.S.A.
Penguin Books Ltd, 27 Wrights Lane,
London W8 5TZ, England
Penguin Books Australia Ltd, Ringwood,
Victoria, Australia
Penguin Books Canada Ltd, 2801 John Street,
Markham, Ontario, Canada L3R 1B4
Penguin Books (N.Z.) Ltd, 182–190 Wairau Road,
Auckland 10, New Zealand

Penguin Books Ltd, Registered Offices:
Harmondsworth, Middlesex, England

First published in the United States of America by
The Atlantic Monthly Press, 1989
Published in Penguin Books 1990

3 5 7 9 10 8 6 4 2

The articles in this book have been published
previously in *The Washington Post*.

LIBRARY OF CONGRESS CATALOGING IN PUBLICATION DATA
Goodman, Ellen.
Making sense/Ellen Goodman.
p. cm.
ISBN 0 14 01.3897 8
I. Title.
AC8.G7623 1990
081—dc20   90–7374

Printed in the United States of America

ACKNOWLEDGMENTS

EVERY YEAR, I hear from a student or two who wants to observe a columnist at work. I cannot imagine a more thankless task, and I try gently to discourage this.

Watching a writer work is like watching ice melt. All you learn is that eventually there's a puddle of water on the floor. Writing is internal. It takes place in your head more than your fingers. It is a lone if not lonely sort of task.

But there are a number of people who understand and are a part of this life and very much deserve my thanks.

My husband generously listens to me stumble through the germ of an idea or two early in the morning. More than that, he suffers through the distracted, grimacing, anxious moments before that idea takes form.

My daughter has also allowed me to plumb some pieces of our life together. She has, with good humor and love, withstood my maternal perspective of that life.

My sister Jane Holtz Kay, my friends Otile McManus and Pat O'Brien surely recognize our long conversations reconstituted on these pages. So do many others—companions on planes, over dinners, in strange and familiar cities. I thank them for the informal reporting they find here.

I also want to thank Celia Lees-Low, the person who comes closest to watching this writer at work. She is the one who finds the missing fact, telephone number, airplane reservation and keeps this rather fragmented life on track. She is also my friend.

Over a dozen years, I have more than appreciated Bill Dickinson at the Washington Post Writers Group. He and Anna Karavangelos are the most tolerant of editors.

Esther Newberg, agent and Red Sox fan, shepherded this collection and even named it. A thank you to her and a final one to my editor, Ann Godoff, who made the process of putting this together fun.

CONTENTS

PART THREE
BIO AND OTHER ETHICS

PART FOUR
KEEPING IN TOUCH

PART ELEVEN
IN A FAMILY WAY

PART TWELVE
AT LARGE

Introduction

THIS BOOK marks an anniversary of sorts. With these words, I am putting the finishing touches on my twenty-fifth year as a journalist.

I could say that I have spent a quarter century in the newspaper business, but "quarter century" sounds like something that should be chiseled in granite rather than typed in green letters on a computer screen. Twenty-five years is imposing enough when calculated in daily editions.

Newspapers are as transient as the day. They chronicle the events from one dawn to the next. They tell what has happened in the last twenty-four hours. But I have spent most of my career in the corner of that world, trying to wrestle meaning out of those daily stories. Trying to make sense.

Making sense is not like making bread. There is no cookbook to study, no recipe to follow. When I set out there is no certainty about the end result. Will it rise? Will it taste the way I imagined it? Will there be enough to share? The attempt to make sense of the personal and public world in which we live is a high-risk business.

The starter dough for many of these columns is in the daily news. A Washington woman has a forced cesarean. A safe-sex club opens in Michigan. An unwed father asks the Supreme Court for visitation rights. The texts of the times contain at least one necessary ingredient for this work. They tweak my curiosity.

Most of these columns began with a question: Why? What's going on here? I write to figure that out for myself and others. Why has character become the dominant political theme of the past four years? Why are we less concerned about public morality and more about private ethics? Why do we head into the 1990s still wrestling with the sixties?

The columns collected here are my attempts to chronicle and understand changes like these. To put them in context, my own and my country's.

Indeed, this has been a remarkable time for any apprentice sense-maker. The color scheme of the era has turned during this period from Reagan Red to Bush Blue, a less dramatic hue. The Cold War has finally subsided, but new struggles burst into consciousness like terrorism exploding in the sky.

Much of the change in our everyday lives has come in low-tech and high-tech costumes. Our world seems to be filled with an increasing number of user-unfriendly machines we must deal with—to get money from a bank wall, or to turn on a washing machine. Such non-sense is happily a part of this record.

In our everyday lives, a cacophony of researchers has turned modern health into a long-running soap opera. Each week we get a new installment on the dangers of food and the delights of exercise, while the trend-watchers tell us the fastest-growing cult is producing a bumper crop of couch potatoes.

The columns here also explore the new choices science offers—in vitro fertilization, tests for Alzheimer's—and the new decisions people must make. Technology forces us into new ways of thinking about life and death. It even makes us rethink a word as fundamental as *mother*. Who is the mother of a child created from one woman's egg, nurtured in another's womb, adopted by a third?

Items such as these come crashing to our attention in the news. But the longer, slower changes in society and in relationships also deserve room in our consciousness.

I have long charted the social evolution that carries the label of the women's movement. In this new batch of columns, women who once aspired to the image of superwoman now worry about becoming superdrudge. Those who wanted to have it all now ask whether they have to do it all.

There are men and women seeking the kind of success you can't dress for: a balance of work and family. More than a few working mothers here are wondering about the fast track and asking whether the mommy track is a solution or a derailment.

Along with these ingredients are the personal observations that spice my attempts at making sense. I am not just an observer but a part of this work, these times. I know, firsthand and first person, about the one commodity in greatest demand and shortest supply: time. I also work, after all, from the perspective of writer, mother, daughter, wife, and now mid-life observer of generations.

Since the last time I put my columns between hard backs, my daughter has become a woman. As accomplice to her growing up and away, I delivered her to that way station called college and accepted the transition to another stage of life. For both of us.

In the middle, I am very conscious of the relationships between generations. Very conscious of time lines. It comes with the twenty-fifth anniversary.

I am told these columns have a very strong flavor of America. If so, they are as American as the instant fame of Oliver North and Jessica Hahn. As American as the attention given First Ladies and Clint Eastwood's raised consciousness. As American as Madison Avenue selling condoms to women. As American as lemon chiffon pie at my family's annual Thanksgiving gathering.

Finally, in an era of great divides, many of these columns seek common ground. They are infused less with a set political perspective than with a set of values. I leave the manufacture of great "isms" to others. I prefer to use my tools in these modest attempts at making sense.

PART ONE

AMERICAN SENSE

*The more splintered Americans are, the more
separated in our private homes and ideologies, the
more we yearn for shared community, shared
enterprise, shared values.*

RUNNING SCARED

LET ME SEE if I've got it straight now. My neighborhood health tipsheet, the *New England Journal of Medicine*, reports this week that rigorous running may be bad for the hormones. Go for the really long distance and it isn't just the old shins that may splint. You could end up infertile, with thin bones and a lousy immune system. But when it happens, or so I'm told, your heart will be in great shape.

The week before, the *Journal* warned that a mere three drinks a week could increase the risk of breast cancer. But the same few pops, or so I've read, are supposed to lower the cholesterol level.

I'm not sure whether to be grateful for these accumulated pieces of knowledge or not. What have I learned? Run too little and die young of a heart attack? Run too much and die, without offspring, of some bizarre infection? Drink your way to breast cancer? Abstain all the way to the coronary unit?

I think it has become impossible for Americans to keep their health IQ updated. We are all suffering from an information glut, research overload. But worse than that, we have accumulated a midriff bulge of confusing and contradictory health advice.

Sugar, we have been told, causes cavities, but saccharin may cause cancer and aspartame may cause seizures. The sun apparently gives you vitamin D and also wrinkles. Stay out of the summer rays and you get depressed, stay in and you get skin cancer.

Coffee has been on and off the list of endangering species. People now wake up at 4 A.M. wondering whether their decaf was water-processed. We have been told to stop eating beef and start eating fish, but also watch out for mercury poisoning.

(Are you running with me? Not too far, I hope, or your hormones will get you.)

Then there is oil which is bad for you, except for olive oil which is good for you, except that it adds calories which are bad for you. Everybody says it's healthier to be thin than fat, but it's important to have some extra pounds in case you get sick.

Losing weight itself is just a matter of cutting down on calories, except that cutting down on calories slows down the metabolism that burns the calories. Cheese, by the way, is high in calcium but also high in fat. If you are going to eat the stuff you need, then you have to work it off. This leads directly to aerobics, which trims the waistline and wrecks the knees.

The way I read it, what's good for the bones is probably bad for the arteries. What's good for the heart is probably bad for the back. And just reading this news raises everybody's stress level, which is dangerous in itself and must be reduced by exercise. But not too much exercise or you'll become infertile, and if you don't have any children you'll increase your risk of breast cancer.

This cacophony of reports from researchers has turned personal health into a modern soap opera. *(General Outpatient? As the Body Turns?)* Something new comes up every week. It's enough to make anyone long for the days of the four basic food groups.

This is not just the result of a research boom. It's an offshoot of living in the era of subspecialties. The hip bone may be connected to the thigh bone, but not in the lab. Many of the researchers who deal with organs as near as the liver and kidney are fairly detached from each other.

There's a tendency to study single diseases and small body parts instead of lives. The group concerned with the maintenance of the lungs doesn't always "do" ankles and the cancer-prevention team isn't "into" cardiovascular disease.

As the last generalists, we, the owners of whole bodies, are supposed to think of ourselves as nothing more than the sum of parts and potential diseases to be taken care of with separate regimens. A bit of fiber to stave off colon cancer, calcium to keep the spine straight and don't forget the dental floss.

Our running research team at least prescribed a compromise: moderation, something between the life-style of a couch potato and that of a marathoner. But somewhere out there (you can count on it), there is a researcher deep in a lab about to prove conclusively that moderation is absolutely hazardous to your health.

HOUSE-RICH, HOUSE-POOR

THEY WERE TALKING about real estate. It is, to be frank, one of their favorite subjects.

Each of them had a story to tell. One had bought a house in 1973 for $40,000. It had just been valued at $265,000. Another had a neighbor who sold her house, tripling her money in ten years—the right ten years. A third figured carefully the inflated value of his home into his retirement plans.

They did not brag, these couples in late middle age, of having had any special prescience about a real-estate boom. They had put money down on a house in the sixties or seventies and won the jackpot of the eighties. There were no oil wells in their backyards, but the homes had made a more spectacular return than any gusher.

They simply rode the real-estate boom to a certain measure of paper profit. The houses they chose to live in were also investments to live off. They were now middle-income and house-rich. So conversations like these make them feel good or at least lucky.

But then the subject turned to their children, grown children. Could their children afford to buy the houses they had grown up in? A second set of stories poured out, more troubled than the first.

They had working children wholly unable to save a down payment that might equal the parents' entire first mortgage. They had married children who needed two jobs to afford what they had supported with one. Most of their offspring were double-income and house-poor.

To this eavesdropper, there was no news bulletin in this exchange. These days the economic gap between generations is built on the private turf of real estate. A space has grown between those who have houses and those who do not.

More people over 65 and fewer people under 35 own their own homes. In 1977, 11.5 percent of new home buyers were in their early twenties. In 1987, only 4.2 percent of these buyers were that young. More than half of new mortgages depend on second incomes.

The gap grew through the vagaries of supply and demand. Over the past fifteen years, incomes fell behind inflation and houses sped ahead. Tax breaks have gone to those with mortgages, and so-called tax revolts made generational differences even more striking. In California, famed Proposition 19 froze property taxes at 1978 rates—but only for those who already owned homes. A new neighbor now may pay vastly more than the older couple in an identical house next door.

There are other very real effects of real estate on these two generations. Generations find common ground in the family. There, the house-rich middle class increasingly is called upon to help its house-poor children.

I am told that standard equipment for any mortgage lender's office includes at least four chairs: two for the couple, two for their parents who help bankroll the sale. As many as half of first-time young buyers are getting help from their parents.

If I am to judge by my listening sample, these elders feel both duty-bound and willing to share their good fortune. But another of their favorite conversations echoes concern about the long-term dependence of "kids these days."

The "kids" of 25 and 30 have in turn become awkwardly conscious of the way that real estate has solidified the two-class structure. The have and have-nots of their own age are often those who either have or have not parents with home equity. Those who will have or will not have their legacies.

I don't want to turn a real-estate boom into a sociological bust. The windfall is a large component of an older generation's improved economic status. Their independence is a boon to their children as well.

But it is also a major reason why the scales are tipping, why grandparents often live better than grandchildren. It's why there is a need to build more affordable housing, tax more of the capital gains that came to those who rode the real-estate boom and allot the money to help families buy into the market.

Rising real estate makes for great conversation. I can attest to that from my listening post. But a younger generation is being left out of the lucky dialogue. It looks as if the family homestead rests on very shaky ground.

A TWO-TRACK TEETOTAL

S O MUCH FOR the battle. Tower has been toppled. The would-be Secretary of Defense couldn't defend himself successfully. He will go down in the annals of military history as a man defeated by the troops of New Morality.

Gary Hart and the A-word. Douglas Ginsburg and marijuana. John Tower and wine and women. Is there now a sin screen to public office? Has the country turned right and righteous?

The reports from the siege of John Tower were extraordinary. A true confession of adultery: "As a matter of fact I have broken wedding vows." A pledge of sobriety: "I hearby swear and undertake that if confirmed . . . I will not consume beverage alcohol of any type or form." More than one enemy reported Tower in the act of "womanizing." More than one saw the man pickled. He was even accused of the vice of avarice.

Now the Tower defeat raises the question again. Is this a teetotal society choosing leaders the way they might choose a designated driver? What has happened to change our rules?

Up through the 1950s, most men in public life (and they were mostly men) were covered by a kind of double standard. They were expected to hold up the traditional flag of piety in public. But they were allowed to hide behind the flag of privacy in their personal lives. A subclause of the gentleman's agreement assumed that there was little connection between the private and public man.

The generation of the late sixties condemned this double standard as two-faced. They didn't care what anybody did as long as they didn't lie about it. They were open-minded about every "sin" except the sin of hypocrisy. As for sex, drugs and rock and roll in high places: Who cared?

And now? The late 1980s has seen a new set of allies emerge out of the most unlikely old enemies. A coalition of brimstone and Perrier. It's the coalition that doomed John Tower.

Today, the Bible Belt brigade calls womanizing an evil. The Rolling Stone regiments describe it as tacky or exploitive. For one, it's a sin of the flesh; for the other, a breach of equality. The fundamentalists may regard boozing as a sinful activity. The new age describes it as self-destructive. But they both vote against it.

The old-time sin watchers always judged the private behavior of public people on religious grounds. Now the new-timers judge the private behavior of public people on the grounds of psychology or character. What we are seeing, as baby-boom watcher Ralph Whitehead, Jr., puts it, is an unexpected merger of "the Puritanism of the Bible Belt and the sadder-but-wiser abstemiousness of a younger generation."

The signs of abstemiousness are all around us. In this month's *Glamour* magazine, two young women wear T-shirts bearing the slogan of their generation. One says Abstinence. The other says Moderation. The Calvin Klein perfume ads once featured sexual proponents of Obsession. Now they promote parent-and-child images of Eternity.

It is easy for a generation that has given up cocktails at night so they can work in the morning to make a link between alcohol and job performance. Especially for a Secretary of Defense who is literally never off work.

Repentance is also ripe among this secular crowd. You cannot read a magazine or watch a talk show without confronting the dramas of people who have freed themselves of addictions, drugs, smoking, drinking. Hallelujah! If John Tower's pledge to stop drinking failed to impress this new audience, it was because he coupled it with denial rather than confession.

The old moralists may worry about damnation. The new ones worry about health, mental and physical. They each judge the people in public life according to their values. In this controversy, Whitehead says, "The 'dries' may think of Tower as a hopeless wet. The young may think that if you haven't moved out of fossil fuels and into your own endorphins, you aren't smart enough to run the Pentagon." Wet or dumb, they both judged Tower lacking.

The rallying cries of this bitter Senate fight came over words like *fitness, judgment, character*. More than one senator warned the others that they were raising the moral ante, the standards by which they too may be judged. They can count on it.

The handwriting on the wall is written in two very distinct styles. But it's writ large enough for everyone in public life to see.

MARCH 1989

Safe Sex and the Singles Club

THERE IS a new club in West Bloomfield, Michigan. You might call it a health club although it doesn't offer barbells, treadmills or aerobics classes. All it promises is a membership that is AIDS-free. They call the club Peace of Mind.

There is a new dating service in Manhattan. They don't check your pedigree or your credit rating. What they insist on is an AIDS test. It is named the Ampersand Singles Club.

There is another dating service in Vermont that demands tests, and a fourth in Massachusetts, and I am sure a fifth, sixth, sixteenth. What they give members in return for a hefty fee is admission to a population of the certifiably clean, people who carry a card symbolic of their status in the dating world: AIDS-free status.

This is what's happening in the second phase of the AIDS epidemic. The hottest item in the marketplace of supply and demand these days is safe sex. So, a new breed of anxiety entrepreneurs have come out hustling and a new breed of the anxious are buying.

Just a few years ago, the people looking for love developed their own code in the personal ads. SWM for single white male, DF for divorced female. Now, the most desirable credentials are AF, AIDS-free. They are in pursuit of guarantees, certified safety.

It's part of the same anxious pattern that has escalated along with the numbers of people infected with the virus. Early in the AIDS epidemic, there was serious debate about quarantining carriers. That impossible notion has now been relegated to the LaRouche fringe. Today the healthy want to quarantine themselves.

And among them are those who want, as one entrepreneur put it, "romance without risk." They want, in effect, to save the sexual revolution in its 1970s form.

But sex just doesn't come carefree anymore. A few weeks ago, in a conversation in San Francisco, Dr. Mervyn Silverman, president of the American Foundation for AIDS Research, put it succinctly: "This is a disease of consenting adults. You have to *place* yourself at risk. If everyone was educated, if everyone listened, you could stop the spread of the virus tomorrow. I can't do that with the flu."

For all that's been said in the past year about "safe sex," there is only one kind that is foolproof: sex with someone who is uninfected. What "peace of mind" does the Michigan club offer for its deluxe-plan price of $649? Only what potential lovers can get on their own for the price of a test.

What they are really proferring is the notion that people don't have to change their behavior at all: the illusion that an entire world of singles bars and single nights can be quarantined off, protected from threat.

At Peace of Mind, those who pass the entry exam not only get a list of local bars where members hang out, but a stickpin with the club's insignia and an ID card. These badges become a magic talisman members may use to protect them from having to ask intimate questions, to wait, to make commitments or, for that matter, use condoms. They promise to protect pockets of promiscuity. Save the seventies.

All this would be nothing worse than sleazy and exploitative business if it were not also dangerously wrong. The AIDS test itself doesn't say what's happened in the past three weeks, or perhaps three months. It takes time for antibodies to appear.

More to the point, it doesn't protect a person from what a partner did the day after the test. A club may test every six months, even four, but unless it tracks members and draws blood with the vigilance of the FBI, it's no more risk-proof than the rest of the world. Indeed, whatever anxiety people have about the promise of one partner to remain monogamous can only be multiplied about the pledge of an entire membership to be true to the club.

In the end, the promise of an AIDS-free zone is intrinsically dishonest. The most enterprising entrepreneur cannot create a risk-free club any more than the most committed bureaucrat could create an AIDS-free community or country.

What we can do involves a more fundamental and individual change. We can only stop the spread of AIDS at the border of our private lives. It is far safer to maintain our own admissions standard. Call it responsible behavior. Membership in that club is absolutely free.

JEALOUSY AT WORK

I HAVE HAD the cartoon in my desk for months now. A lone businesswoman is standing before a table full of suited men. One of the men asks her this question: "If you have a baby, will you like it better than us?"

It is a wonderful moment, comically inappropriate, ripe with possibilities. In real life, after all, the word *like,* or surely the word *love* is kept out of the boardroom. In real life, no boss or panel of partners would air their anxiety about the alienation of a coworker's affection.

Indeed, we are not expected to feel as strongly about our colleagues or even our jobs as we do about our families. In all the talk about work and family conflicts, we couch our concerns in much more objective terms. We talk about practical struggles over hours and obligations. We talk about parental guilt and workplace inflexibility, about stress and stretch, time and tensions.

But maybe in all this, we have missed something the cartoonist saw. A hidden emotional component to the work/family dilemma. A component called jealousy.

One woman who chuckled at the printed image admitted that she has often felt like the central character in a ménage à trois, a love triangle. Her double life of working mother remained as difficult to arrange as that of a married woman finding time in her Filofax for an affair.

Leafing back to six years ago, when her baby was born, she remembers how a boss put her through a series of small tests. At the time she thought that he was testing her commitment to work. Now she wonders if he was testing her commitment to him. Once she had her baby, did she like the baby more?

I suppose that sibling rivalry is a better model for this sort of jealousy. A friend says she never understood her manager's behavior until she had two children of her own. Her eldest daughter acted up like clockwork, whenever she fed the newborn. Her department head just as regularly arrived with problems as she headed out to the baby-sitter.

The same man who had been genial when she needed time off for study or medical care was visibly disapproving when she needed time off for motherhood. He kept track of the claims of his small rivals with the arithmetic precision and the suspicion of an elder child. He didn't want to share her attention with the (other) children.

We have ignored the psychological model of the work force for so long that it's easy to exaggerate it here. Most bosses, male and female, have a company goal, a production quota, work to be done. That is their priority. Whatever distracts workers makes the company less (in the word of the hour) competitive. But even that word resonates in our personal lives.

Have you seen the television ad that shows a swimmer thinking of work as she does her laps? She is an employer's fantasy of a single-minded employee whose brain is on the job even when her body is submerged.

Do you remember that moment in the movie *Kramer vs. Kramer* when Dustin Hoffman was describing the joys of fatherhood to his boss and his boss fired him? In *Baby Boom*, Diane Keaton's superior replayed that scene when Keaton fell in love with a baby. She lost her place because she'd "gone soft."

Are these strictly business decisions? Are those in charge carefully calculating the cost of chaos and confusion? Or is there a jealous soul wondering: "What about me? Don't I come first anymore?"

We think of the two parts of our lives separately. We subdivide them neatly into the personal and the professional. We think of the conflict between family and work as one between people and tasks, relationships and obligations.

But it isn't really like that. Most of us have two personal lives: one at home and one at the office. We have two sets of relationships. There are many employers, of course, who feel comfortable with these shared loyalties and try to build bridges over the gaps.

But it isn't only bosses in cartoons who worry that a working mother will neglect them. Under many a proper business suit there is a little green-eyed monster who sometimes sees families as not-quite-sibling rivals.

MARCH 1988

AGING GRACEFULLY

"I DON'T INTEND to grow old gracefully. I intend to fight it every step of the way."—Anonymous, 1988

This quotation may never make it into Bartlett's. The author is not a poet after all, but an unknown copywriter, maybe a committee of copywriters, who seek inspiration at the well of Oil of Olay.

Nevertheless, it stuck into some groove in my own brain, like a song that you don't like and can't expel. I cannot open a women's magazine without seeing this sentiment emanating from the well-contoured mouths of a rotating cast of models. "Growing old gracefully" is apparently out of fashion. It's an admission of a defeat rather than the story of a success.

What am I to make of this message? The Census Bureau just announced that the average age of Americans is now a notch over 32 years old. The first of the 75 million baby-boomers have passed forty. Their mid-life is marked by the emergence of all sorts of products to help them "fight it every step of the way."

There are more than the usual number of unguents and elixirs that promise to rub the age out of our skins and preserve our energy. There are more than the usual products to cover gray hair and fill in the face lines. There are more than the usual admonitions to leg-lift a path to eternally youthful thighs.

Add to the list Minoxidil for the bald, Retin-A for the wrinkled and liposuction for the middle-aged spread. Those of us who once had two scant choices—aging gracefully or foolishly—are now offered a much larger arsenal of weapons for the battle against looking our age.

Men who could accept their baldness or risk the ridicule of a toupee now have the chance of growing hair again. Women and men who had to accept their crow's feet or risk the knife to retrieve their younger, tauter skin can now chemically iron their wrinkles.

In modest ways, aging has begun to look like a personal choice. How far are you willing to go to stay the same?

When women over 40 get together these days, there is often some bashful conversation about Retin-A. Would you use it? Would you? Among my friends, one has had a vial of this potion for months now, unused. It's a security vial in some running internal debate she has about wrinkles versus side effects. And about aging gracefully.

Women of a certain age wonder. Is Retin-A, like eye-liner, a cosmetic chemical that merely makes you look your best? Or is it a first seductive step in some unappealing chase after youth that conjures up the image of an octogenarian with platinum hair and scarlet nail polish and her third face lift?

What of the other choices? Are they the acceptable tools of self-improvement, or are they proof of self-hate? If you don't color your hair and firm your thighs, are you letting yourself go? If you do, are you fighting—gracelessly—against the inevitable, the natural?

If I had a role model of an older woman, she would look a lot like Katharine Hepburn or the artist Georgia O'Keeffe. She would not look like Zsa Zsa Gabor. I note approvingly the gray strands in Kathleen Sullivan's hair. I have been struck by the strong images of women in *Lear's,* the new magazine "for the woman who wasn't born yesterday."

But I don't know how Katharine Hepburn feels when she looks in the mirror or whether the women in *Lear's* harbor small vials of Retin-A in their drawers. There is an ad in that magazine that admonishes: "Take control of your skin's age."

Clearly the money is in youth products. There is no way to sell self-acceptance. There may be a profit in the natural "look" but not in nature.

As we are offered this expanding array of weapons, we increase our defense budget. And with each item, with each choice, how much harder it becomes to negotiate a peaceful coexistence with our own age. How much harder it becomes to age gracefully.

APRIL 1988

OF LIBERTY AND
COMMUNITY

THEY ARE GOING to make a spectacle of her. You can count on that. By the time Nancy Reagan cuts the ribbon around Lady Liberty's toga and 5,000 homing pigeons are released into the Manhattan air, they will have popped all the corks in the champagne cellar of American extravaganzas.

No poor huddled masses will be imported to New York's harbor this weekend. Count instead a thousand banjo players, a parade of tall ships, a tug of war by NFL All-Stars, a massive citizenship ceremony for 15,000 immigrants. Four days worth of whiz-bang celebration for our national totem. Four days of glitz pride for the twin pillars of our secular creed: Liberty and Independence.

I have no snobbish objection to this super-Fourth. It is true that I will take my own holiday in miniature on a Maine island where the homemade parade of pickup trucks and family floats makes one rambling circle by the community center and the schoolhouse before it disbands. But I am not immune to goose-bump patriotism, even when the goose bumps are mass-produced.

Still, looking over the schedule for this David Wolper production of Americana, it occurs to me that this is how the American people get together nowadays. In well-marketed mega-events.

We collect under a banner cheering some denominator as common as fireworks and national anthems. We rally around a symbol with as many meanings as a Delphic oracle. We come together to celebrate something in short supply: togetherness, and the ability to act in union.

What do I remember of that other David Wolper mega-event, the West

Coast torch, the 1984 Olympics ceremony? The echoes of "USA! USA!" Across the country there was a shared pride in Number One-ness. We could unite in celebration of something no more controversial than running and jumping.

Last summer, when the Live Aid concert played for Africa, much of the pleasure was in its joint enterprise. The stars who recorded "We Are the World" announced with proud surprise that they were able to "check their egos at the door" and join the chorus for a cause.

And on May 25, when five million people joined Hands Across America, many experienced a high from just the sensation of linking up with others. If only for a few hours. If only in a brief togetherness binge.

Behind each of these orchestrated mega-events there has been a real desire to share, to break out of the single cell of self. There is a longing for the feel-goodness of community. For the goose bumps.

It may be odd to read that same longing into this weekend special. We are celebrating, after all, a statue of Liberty, a day of Independence. In many ways, those are our most appropriate symbols. We are a nation of leavers. The immigrants who passed through New York harbor were people who left old communities for new opportunities. One American generation after another, moving west, has chosen that pattern. We still do.

For many of us, liberty isn't just the freedom from repressive authority, but from any authority. Independence isn't a declaration, but a centrifugal force. We often choose isolation, even loneliness, rather than the obligations that come with commitment.

The more splintered Americans are, the more separated in our private homes and ideologies, the more we yearn for shared community, shared enterprise, shared values. The mega-event fills that need, at least briefly. It gives us the quick hit of emotion, the momentary sense of belonging, without demanding much in return.

We can check our egos at the door of a mega-event and pick them up again on the way out. We can link hands for hunger and go home for dinner. We can take a holiday from our individual lives to be members of a nation, and then take back a souvenir for our private collection.

Maybe it is enough that we celebrate together. Maybe it's enough to have a 500-piece marching band, 300 Jazzercise women and 200 Elvis Presley look-alikes on our television set parade.

But most of us were taught that Liberty is more than a weekend affair, and patriotism is more than a tourist attraction. Even today, in the era of the mega-event, in the shadow of the Statue of Liberty, America needs more of its citizens than a case of the goose bumps.

JULY 1986

SIN, SALVATION AND A
GOOD SHRINK

WHEN JIMMY SWAGGART fell from grace, the event resounded as loudly as a golden idol hitting a marble temple floor. The fall, like the rise of this evangelical, made for high televised drama. At its peak, he cried out, "I know that so many of you will ask, 'Why? Why?' I have asked myself that 10,000 times through 10,000 tears."

Swaggart had preached mightily against sin, unforgivingly against weaknesses in his brother preachers and bitterly against pornography. "Pornography titillates and captivates the sickest of the sick and makes them slaves to their own consuming lusts . . . ensnares its victims in a living hell," he once wrote. It appears now he knew a good deal about that living hell.

But it wasn't just Swaggart's flock that asked "Why? Why?" as they found out the details—the motel strip he cruised regularly, the $13-an-hour motel room where he is said to have paid a prostitute to perform pornographic acts, all in the shadow of a billboard that reads, "Your Eternity Is at Stake." The most cynical and secular people I know seemed somewhat bewildered. Listing the sex-scandal ministers alphabetically from Jimmy Bakker to Marvin Gorman to Jimmy Swaggart, many of them asked, "What's with these guys?"

In the weeks that followed, I watched two distinct sets of answers to that question and to Swaggart's "Why?" emerge. They reveal a split in American society that runs deeper even than the split in Swaggart's life. A split between those who analyze human failings in the terms of psychology and those who analyze them in the terms of scripture.

To the millions who worship in Swaggart's church and through his televised ministry, the minister lost a round in the battle between God and the Devil. To the secular millions who've absorbed psychoanalytic terms into their everyday vocabulary, he lost in a battle between the superego and the id.

To the first group, he was a sinner. To the second group, he was screwed up. The first group described a struggle between the forces of light and darkness. The second described the subconscious urges that led to the motel strip where he was caught by his arch-rival.

These two American cultures spoke in their own distinct languages. Even words like *healing* and *counseling* have different meanings in their dictionaries. If, for example, Jimmy Swaggart's wife had written to Ann Landers that her minister-husband had an obsession with pornography, she would have been directed to "seek help." But it would have been a very different sort than the "counseling" prescribed by the Assemblies of God. As distant as prayer is from psychotherapy.

The fundamentalist and therapeutic cultures in this country are not always crisply divided. Confession has much in common with what Freud called "the talking cure." One group's soul is the other's psyche. Most of us are at least somewhat bilingual. The therapeutic language has infiltrated fundamentalist speech, the words of a moral code are rampant in a secular world.

Fundamentalist Tammy Bakker described her use of contributions for personal shopping as "therapy." More than one secular supporter judged Gary Hart's behavior as both a character and a moral flaw, two parts stupid, one part wrong. At their edges, feel-good fundamentalism and feel-good therapy offer the same promises.

But between the hard-core groups, there are more than differences of vocabulary. There are conflicts as great as one's focus on the afterlife and the other's focus on the here and now. Swaggart himself railed against psychology as a modern devil. There are therapists, in turn, who accept everyone and everything except religious self-righteousness.

The gap is particularly great in regard to sex, the centerpiece for the Bakker-Gorman-Swaggart trilogy. Swaggart said more than once, "Victory over flesh does not come easily." But no child of the Freudian era would speak of victory over flesh as if Eros were the enemy of Psyche. Indeed Freud believed that trouble came when sexuality was in conflict with the spirit.

The Swaggart story is the essence of a larger melodrama, played before two American cultures. One that thinks the preacher has been led astray and another that thinks he's a neurotic mess. One thinks he can be saved and the other thinks he could use a good shrink. And it isn't just one congregation in Louisiana that speaks in tongues that sound strange to outsiders.

MARCH 1988

THE JOY OF THE BUSINESS
OF SEX

WHEN YOU GET right down to it, right down to page 41, Sydney Biddle Barrows wants to make sure you understand her modern entrepreneurial spirit.

"As I saw it, this was a sector of the economy that was crying out for the application of good management skills. . . . I had never really thought of going into business for myself, but here was a chance to do something nobody had ever done before."

Never mind what the tabloids screamed about the "Mayflower Madam," put aside your prurient interest in the call-girl business. The story told by Sydney Biddle Barrows, thirty-four years old, descendant of Elder William Brewster of Plymouth Rock, is not about sex, it's not even about money. It's about the joy of running your own business. The Story of B.

Barrows spent much of 1984 on page one. She was arrested when the police shut down her "escort service." She was tried, fined, released and wildly over-reported. She has now firmly reappeared at No. 3 on the best-seller list, telling her own story. Why give it away when you can sell it?

Before reading *Mayflower Madam,* I thought the current cult of business had been greatly exaggerated. Until recently, the only way to sell a book about a business magnate was with a sex angle. But today it appears that you can best market a book about a sex magnate with a business angle. The one passion that fills these pages is "A Passion for Excellence."

Barrows talks about selling women the way others talk about selling pork bellies or BMWs. There is a management team and a marketing strategy (upscale, of course), an agency, clients and even motivation. "I was sure," she writes, "we could provide a dramatic alternative to what was available and I was motivated by the challenge of doing something better than everyone else."

Blame her co-author, William Novak, if you want. Novak also wrote Lee Iacocca's book. Lee and Syd have in common a fervent self-image as merchandisers. Guess which one wrote this: "No matter what business you're in, you've got to know your customer and what kind of merchandise that he or she will like. . . ."

It was Syd, the same CEO who also prides herself on being an enlightened employer with part-time, flex-time policies, not to mention her company's comprehensive health policy. I kept waiting to read about her on-site day care. Who says that a corporation can't be profitable without losing its humanity?

There isn't an X-rated moment in this entire business-school case study. She is more concerned with explaining how her "young ladies" dressed for success at Saks Fifth Avenue, always wore stockings, and carried a basic briefcase to get past the hotel security.

The real heavy breathing begins with the revelation that her young ladies carried portable charge machines for credit cards in their evening bags and had a beeper when they were "on call." We're talking business techniques.

What did I gain from all this? Not sympathy for Barrows's business struggles. She is not the first CEO who had to finance a new office by liquidating "my personal cash-management account at Paine Webber. . . ." But she did convince me that in fact she belongs in a peer group of dedicated modern managers—who don't care what they are managing.

"I'm not ashamed, because sex is a commodity just like everything else," she said in one interview. "I looked at my job as a marketing job. I was good at it."

This is the modern management cult at its lowest common denominator. Read through the course catalog of an average business school. Sit through the local success seminar. You hear a whole lot more about process than about product.

With all the fascination on how to manage, there is little said about what to manage. And what not to manage. One of the concerns of American business is that the current class of mobile managers regard one company as interchangeable with another. It's more worrisome when we regard one goal as interchangeable with another.

The bottom line, if you will forgive the expression, is Sydney Biddle Barrows, a success in the commodities market, proudly peddling flesh and properly describing herself as a self-made woman. Keep an eye out for her. Pretty soon she'll be running management seminars on the Playboy Channel. After all, hustling is hustling.

OCTOBER 1986

OF FRIENDSHIP AND
COMPETITION

THEY ARE WAITING for acceptance. Or for rejection. Somewhere in an unfamiliar room in a distant town, a committee of strangers is passing judgment on these high-school seniors. It is a ceremony of spring rather like the Cherry Blossom festival, or more accurately, the Boston Marathon.

Next week, the last batch of college admission letters will be in the mail and so will the answers. Yes or no. In or out. Acceptable. Unacceptable.

The seniors have gone through this jittery process the way their parents' generation went through it. It is a gauntlet they run together and separately. At 17 and 18, they are classmates . . . and competitors.

"Getting into College," bears all the markings of a tribal rite of passage. There are the required number of tests, ritual markings, grueling tasks for the young to perform. They must go through the interviews and applications, the SATs and achievement tests, the endless questions from adults: Where do you want to go? At the end, they will leave their parents and childhood for the campuses of young adulthood.

But a friend insists that the pattern is not quite as universal as that. There are differences for the members of our modern American tribe.

In a so-called primitive culture, he says, the point of any rite of passage is to make sure that every child makes it. The whole society roots for their success. In that so-called primitive culture, the rite of passage seals a life-long bond between the young people as they become the adults.

In our tribe, though, success is not a sure thing. We don't let everybody in. Our tribe doesn't just welcome the young; we also weed them out. One of the tests of "success" in America may be the ability to beat out others.

I find this an uncomfortable notion, not the stuff of high-school memories. But there is truth in it. Every culture devises the admissions tests into adulthood that most fit its adult values. So, for many young people, "Getting into College," especially the colleges labeled competitive, may be a fitting initiation.

The adult world is, after all, built on the shifting grounds of friendship and competition. The double message of this society and economy are to get along and get ahead. We want our children to fit in and to stand out. We rarely address the conflict between these goals.

It is common in everyday life to work with our competitors and to compete with coworkers. Even ball players are, at the same time, team players and free agents.

Some of the most awkward encounters of adult life come when a success gap opens between friends. It is a rare person who has neither apologized for nor bragged about his own achievement. It is an equally rare person who hasn't felt a distance grow when a friend was promoted out of the coffee klatch or the neighborhood. Only the sainted among us have never taken out their rulers and measured their lives against their friends, even their best friends.

This tension between friendship and competition, between team play and the star slot, runs all the way through our tribe. Every child's life includes a host of admissions committees in which we are judged against peers, friends. The teachers who grade us on a sliding scale, the coaches who pick us out of the pack, the boy or girl who chooses us over another for love.

These acceptances that come next week by mail are not some final, or even critical, judgment. Those of us who have been through other seasons know that. But they come at a vulnerable moment, at the edge of adulthood, when the young are just about to become full-fledged owners of their own lives. The letters come, delivering tickets that lead in a hundred different directions.

For the very first time, inseparable friends opening those envelopes may feel the chill of distance. For the first time, a class of mates may really understand how our world tries to subdivide their future. So this spring rite of passage also tests friendship against competition in the raw form of the adult world. It's one way we come of age, a hard way, in this modern tribe.

APRIL 1986

BYE-BYE, BUNNY

IT ENDED in a garish room in a hotel at a highway intersection in Lansing, Michigan. On Saturday night, the very last Bunny in America encased herself in the very last bunny costume, did the very last bunny dip and closed the very last Playboy Club in the United States.

Meanwhile, out on the coast, in a Tudor mansion in Holmby Hills, California, "the world's most ineligible bachelor," the Premier Playboy of the Western World of America, was betrothed to the very last of his personal series of Playmates.

So it goes. The Bunny is extinct. Hugh Hefner is getting married. Do I hear the sound of an era passing?

A mere thirty-five years ago, Hugh was just another minister's son in a failing fifties marriage. He rounded up some old nudies of Marilyn Monroe and printed them for an eager audience. After a lot of heavy breathing, the sort normally found in Lamaze classes, a new magazine was born.

Seven years later, on a Chicago winter evening, men lined up to get a key to his kingdom. Playboy Clubs, the designated hutches of Hef's fantasy, sprang up in big cities across the country. They were full of Bunnies ruled by bunny mothers according to a bunny manual that warned: "Your proudest possession is your bunny tail. You must always make sure it is white and fluffy."

The sexual revolution bloomed. Centerfolds came and went, bunnies hopped in and out. There was an endless procession of nymphets-next-door. Baby-boom Bambis in the buff.

But in the midst of this, the real centerpiece was always Hefner himself: "What does it feel like being a living legend? Well, it feels great!" He added, "One of the curious things about the phenomenon of my life is that so very much of it has been lived out in a public way that it is related to people's views of sexuality and social conscience."

Hefner described himself as a "Rorschach test." Some people saw the play in the boy, a life in mansions full of toys, animate and inanimate. Barbi, Sondra, Shannon, Carrie—surely there was a Dawn in there somewhere—and now Kimberley.

Others saw the boy in the play. An eternal romantic who ate Wonder Bread, fell in love like a teenager, and never had to get out of his pajamas or get tied down. "Variety, vitality and adventure of experience are more meaningful to me than the security of marriage."

But either way, Hef and his hutch took us from the era when Nice Girls Didn't to the era when Everybody Had To and on to the era when Everybody's Scared To. From secrecy to swinging to safe sex. Somewhere along the way, his idea of liberation became the women's movement's idea of exploitation. Somewhere along the way, his daughter took over the company and a bunny at the Lansing club had a second job as a security guard. Somewhere along the way what was titillating became tacky.

It's no surprise what happened to the Playboy Clubs. They were done in by the three Rs of the eighties; raunchiness, righteousness and raised consciousness. The upscale crowd didn't do bunnies except on *Saturday Night Live.*

As for Hef, it wasn't the times but time that changed things. For years the primary constant in life was the age of the woman on his arm: roughly twenty-five. The second constant was his marital status: single. And the third was his philosophy: marriage kills romance. But after a stroke, a $35 million palimony suit and a sixty-second birthday, even playboys get the blues.

Hugh Hefner discovered mortality and Kimberley Conrad at about the same time. Mortality was a somewhat older concept. Kim is twenty-five, about ten years younger than daughter Christie Hefner and thirty-seven years younger than Hugh. Does Kim notice the age gap? "I don't even think about it."

As for Hef, "I'm at the point in my life where I've sown my wild oats. . . . I always had the feeling before that there was something else, some further personal adventure waiting over the hill." Or in the next edition. Now he's sixty-two, notably the worse for wear and finally ready for a commitment. Some things take longer than others. At least he's giving Kimberley a stepdaughter she can look up to.

If the bride-to-be is indeed a "homebody," the groom can spend his waning years teaching her about the old days. The days when the living legend taught his generation that marriage was a trap. The days when every fantasy female had a fluffy white tail. The days when he hung a Latin saying over his threshold: "If you don't swing, don't ring."

Today, the only swinging at the Playboy Mansion West is a door quietly closing on the past.

AUGUST 1988

PART TWO

PEOPLE

Americans have upped the ante on what makes a good person and a good life. We are now supposed to save the world and be home for supper.

BARBARA BUSH: THE

SILVER FOX

AT ONE MOMENT during the first weekend of the Bush administration, a woman turned from the television set to her friend and beamed, "I think we've got a hit on our hands." The hit was Barbara Bush.

Within days, the new first lady had turned the glamour thermostat down from a Reagan Red to a Bush Blue. With a series of knowing one-liners, Barbara Bush had established her own image: "Please notice—hairdo, makeup, designer dress. . . . Look at me good this week. You may never see it again."

The first impression of a nation was based, as these things often are, on appearances. And Barbara Bush's "hit" was in no small measure a by-product of the appearance of a woman on the center stage who dared to look her age.

The official trend-watchers called it "refreshing," "striking," even, heaven help us, a true fashion statement. Words like *matron* and *grandmother,* banned from the vocabulary of East Wing reporters, suddenly began creeping back into the papers.

Time magazine, gracing the cover with the first gray-haired woman since Golda Meir, gave the story her family nickname, "The Silver Fox." And in a comment that summed up the entire transition, a Los Angeles Republican fund-raiser, Annette Rolf Singer, told a Texas newspaper: "You know, she's really quite darling. My plastic surgeon will die if he hears I've said that, but she really looks darling."

What is going on here? "My mail tells me that a lot of fat, white-haired, wrinkled ladies are tickled pink," Mrs. Bush said in one of a string of comments that sounded sometimes like the kid in a playground who jokes about himself before he can get teased by the others. When asked by her husband whether she was going to eat dessert, she said, "I have to eat it for my fans."

It does seem that a national Barbara Bush fan club has been launched by all the women who ever failed to find a bathing suit they could wear. The delight in the new first lady is a spontaneous sigh of relief from women who were tired of scaling down their dress size and sick of worrying about their roots. I do not mean the genealogical kind.

This may say less about the first lady than about the country. It is ironic that Barbara Bush has spent a lifetime fighting for literacy only to be judged visually. But after two decades, during which the women's movement cracked the thirty barrier and then the forty, women are still looking for models of how to be sixty and satisfied. Especially with what they see in the mirror.

Simone de Beauvoir once wrote gloomily, "I have never come across one single woman, either in life or in books, who has looked upon her own old age cheerfully." In America, we have whole industries based on the notion that women are not good enough to come as we are. Especially if what we are is older.

Those of us who thought that work would change this have been sorely disappointed. Women who work have merely taken on the double burden of the double standard. They are expected to look young in two places.

Ours is an aging nation, but the pictures in our minds and magazines show the American upper crust as powerful men and their second wives, or wives who look as if they're the second. The public world resembles a local TV anchor team: a gray-haired man and a blonde. We have yet to see a white-haired female Cabinet member or Supreme Court justice and when we finally get a hefty talk-show host, Oprah, she reappears in size ten Calvins, wheeling seventy pounds of animal fat behind her.

It isn't just older women who get depressed checking out the before and after portraits of women who injected collagen into their laugh lines. The baby-boom generation of women, raised on youth and fitness, has turned forty, facing a future of Optifast, aerobics and sunblock.

It is no wonder that they feel hopeful when the spotlight shifts to a woman who has dealt with age armed only with three strands of fake pearls and a full calendar.

This attention to Barbara Bush's appearance will fade, as all first impressions do. She would rather be known for graciousness than gray hair, for wit rather than weight. We will shift our gaze from her hairdo to her deeds.

But in this first week of intensive training, it was clear how much American women want from their elders. We are eager to find a model who echoes in life the words May Sarton once wrote at seventy: "Now I wear the inside person outside and am more comfortable with myself." Barbara Bush sounds a lot like that person.

JANUARY 1989

JFK AND OUR NEED FOR

IDEALISM

I WAS TOO YOUNG to vote for Jack Kennedy. He was my generation's older generation. But when I think of him on this anniversary, November 22, I still think of youth. His, mine, America's.

I spent the Kennedy years in college and I can attest to the fact that not every young person during that time asked what he or she could do for his or her country. But it is true that Kennedy called us and we heard that call.

He made us understand that he and the country had expectations and even needs for our public service. As young people, we were wanted. And that was no small thing.

Now I am older than Jack Kennedy was when he was killed. The younger generation today, we are told, is not much interested in service, except the kind you find in the modern marketplace: self-service.

I spent an afternoon this month at UCLA with Alexander Astin, who runs the annual college freshman surveys. The major trend culled from his computer, he says with much regret, has been a "very strong materialistic tendency among students. They are more preoccupied with money, power, status and less concerned with serving society."

His data fits the stereotype of youth on a fast track to materialism, a generation that only gets worked up about aerobics. It is in sync with a cartoon from last commencement season that showed two college students crossing a campus. One is saying to the other, "This is incredible. Do you know that I, too, want as much as I can get as fast as I can get it."

But if there is a difference in the degree of engagement in public life and public issues among today's young—and I think there is—it's not that some spiritual flaw, some epidemic of narcissism, some warped sense of values has infested this generation. Nor has idealism and the urge to create a better community atrophied.

If the young are preoccupied with "money, power, status," it may be because they haven't been offered any better set of goals. By us. It may be because nobody in the current older generation, no leader, president, hero, has really called them to serve. Not the way Kennedy did.

This has been the decade of feel-good patriotism. All we had to do for our country was to get goose bumps when we heard the Star-Spangled Banner playing. The best and the brightest have been told by inference that the private sector is where the action is. The young in turn listen to any call to public service with a more sophisticated, even cynical, ear than we had. At least before we had experienced the death of the first Kennedy, then King, then the second Kennedy, then Vietnam and Watergate.

They have, among other things, much less certainty about the good of doing good, especially on a large scale. Wipe out a disease and you may face the problems of overpopulation. Clear a jungle and you may endanger a species or a culture.

The young, bombarded with ambiguities, seem to prefer a sure thing. Those who want to help are more likely to choose the soup kitchen and the shelter, places where there is little moral risk of going wrong.

At the same time these in-between years have been marked by greater attention to private life. We judge each other, we judge ourselves—and even this fallen President—by how we behave at home as well as in the community. We have become wary of people who dedicate themselves to public service while neglecting their private circle.

Americans have upped the ante on what makes a good person and a good life. We are now supposed to save the world and be home for supper. As personal lives have become much more complex and challenging, they, too, siphon some of the energy from public service.

But I believe the impulse to belong to something larger is very much alive among the young. Indeed, they seem melancholy at the absence of a public life. I have heard many search for something more engaging than a good job or a VCR. What is missing, if the word were not so open to ridicule, may be idealism.

I wish I knew what Jack Kennedy would have made of all this, how he would have crafted his call in the eighties, because he would have called and he was a fine craftsman. But it's left to those of us who were his younger generation, his sometimes disillusioned human legacy, to figure out a way to pass on that vision to a very different generation, at a very different moment in our country's history.

NOVEMBER 1988

JESSICA HAHN: SELLING
HERSELF

TOWARD THE END of the interview, after Jessica Hahn had told her story, after she'd said what still hurt—"I will never in my life know what it's like to make love for the first time with a man I love"—the men from *Playboy* offered her an out.

Maybe they were moved by sympathy or by a growing respect for their subject. Maybe they had the grace to feel uneasy exposing her once again. They told her: "We can do this without the pictures."

Somewhere in the *Playboy* offices, a circulation manager's heart must have stopped. Would the November sales have to hang on Danny Ortega's thoughts about Nicaragua? Hahn reassured them all, "Relax, guys. I know what I'm doing."

This is why the November issue of *Playboy* has a show as well as a tell. They have Jessica, topless.

Before the magazine arrived on my desk, I had worked up a list of one-liners for its promotion, a list that would rival those of the tabloids: BIBLE BELLE BARES ALL. BORN AGAIN IN THE BUFF. The pictures, after all, make it easy to think of Hahn as a phony, a sellout. How does anyone pose as an innocent when they are posing naked? How can she be seen as a victim with a reported $1 million check from *Playboy* in the bank?

But her story, read page after page, is much too sad for such glib dismissal. It's as dismal and pathetic an account of sexual abuse as can be read this side of a police blotter. "They did things that people are in jail fifteen and twenty years for—at least."

Call it a tale of date rape if you will, though there was no real date with either of the men she accuses, TV ministers Jim Bakker and John Fletcher. Call it acquaintance rape, if you prefer, since that is how we try to distinguish between back-alley attacks with knives and those that occur in hotel rooms with "respectable" men. Or perhaps you could call it a tale of incest since, in Jessica Hahn's description, PTL was family and these men were patriarchs.

By her account, there were years of aftershocks to one afternoon's violence, years when she repressed it, internalized it, blamed herself: "Don't forget these were two men I looked up to. . . . They could do no wrong. So if they could do no wrong, I thought maybe either I did wrong or I didn't understand. . . ." There were also years during which, in her own words, "I fought . . . to start feeling good about myself and my body again."

Her *Playboy* interviewers are not lawyers; the magazine is not a court of law. I have no way of being sure her version is honest. But a vein of truth runs through the story, in all its minute, telling detail: "So, he [Bakker] got off, brushed his hair with my hairbrush, and left."

How, then, can the text be reconciled with the pictures? Seven years after her encounter with the ministers, Hahn now strips for any male within reach of a magazine and calls it part of the healing process: "This is therapy." Months after watching her privacy invaded in the PTL scandal, she defiantly takes off the last veils that protected her from the public eye and tells *Playboy:* "You want to look? I'll *show* you." When even the *Playboy* editors offer her a retreat, she says, "I know what I am doing." What kind of psychological sense does this make?

I am struck with the belief that these new exposures are simply the latest aftershock of that long-ago afternoon. Here is a woman who found no way out of being a victim; so she became the manager of her own victimization. She is damaged enough to believe that being in charge of her exploitation is the same as being free of it.

"I tried to keep this private," she told *Playboy,* "but everyone, every story, tried to sell off a new piece of me. So I'm dealing with it publicly. Head-on. Only I'm at the controls."

What a dismaying illustration for this tragic biblical text. A centerfold of cynicism. If Hahn is honest—and I found her story utterly believable—she was once a trusting member of the church family. But in the final aftermath of abuse, she is left only with a hardened and solitary bravado.

During one telling moment in the interview, Hahn says, "I've just realized, just now, that that day seven years ago was a day when two men stole my life." The old Jessica Hahn was robbed of her self-respect. The new Jessica Hahn has learned to sell it herself.

FRED ASTAIRE: HE MADE IT LOOK EASY

Looking at the photos, those endlessly elegant portraits of top hat and tails, that ran beside his obituaries, I couldn't help wondering how the man would have fared in films today. There was no angst in Astaire. Nor any violence. Nor any heavy breathing.

If Fred Astaire was in a bedroom, he was dressed in silk pajamas. If Fred Astaire took a woman in his arms, it was to face the music and dance. If Fred Astaire and his costars made it together it was cheek to cheek.

Every one of the stories about his death at eighty-eight included the terse notes from his first screen test: "Can't act, balding, can't sing, dances a little." Every one of them included the telling remark of his old colleague, Ronald Reagan: "He was the ultimate dancer—the dancer who made it all look so easy."

Easily, Fred Astaire danced down staircases, on balconies and rooftops, in a living room, a ballroom, a garden. Easily, he danced on a wedding cake, on roller skates and on the ceiling. He kept his sweat offscreen.

It isn't like that anymore. Our Hollywood fantasies are pressed into "realism," even feigned realism. They do close-ups of the sweat these days. They add the sweat in.

What seemed so effortless in the Astaire movies was not just his own movement, but the way he danced in tandem. Fred Astaire almost always had partners, but not the way we think of partners now. In those days, they merged, they had the same rhythms.

When Astaire danced with Ginger Rogers or Cyd Charisse or Leslie Caron, the man and the woman flowed together. Astaire coupled in a way that seemed visually idyllic. Dancing with Rogers was indistinguishable from dancing with his own shadow. Two could move as easily—that word again—as one.

It was this idyll that attracted so many, the apparently seamless coupling of a man and a woman. The ability to choreograph a perfect love merger. Even with a hat rack.

Of course, we know at some level what Astaire himself said in an interview: "Dancing is a sweat job. . . . You may go days getting nothing but exhaustion. This search for what you want is like tracking something that doesn't want to be tracked." A man who, all his life, was addicted to soap operas knew something about the struggles of mating as well.

But we see only the finished product, the flawless pas de deux. In his musical unions, the image of two people moving in perfect sync is powerful.

It's no surprise that the Astaire genre didn't make it into the sixties. There were fewer leading men in the sixties. Fewer following women. The fantasy that if only one could lead and the other follow all would be well began to break apart.

Gradually *Top Hat* became *Hair*. Ballroom dancing turned to rock. Couples were now individuals lightly connected to each other. By the seventies, the struggle to keep their steps in any sort of sequence began to show.

And now? In the romantic movies of the late eighties, the sweat really shows. If there is a theme, it is of the desire and difficulty of finding your way back to connection, taking a single, sure step together.

In the "bratpack" films such as *St. Elmo's Fire* or *About Last Night,* the men and women leap into bed quickly but sidestep commitment. They don't glide, but lurch warily toward each other.

In films like *Nothing in Common,* solos are what come naturally to the yuppie set. They have to take lessons, work hard to learn the basics of togetherness. The desire for coupling contends unrhythmically with the desire for independence.

Our current movie models, ourselves perhaps, portray some barrier between man and woman—something as obvious as the Cyrano de Bergerac nose that Steve Martin wears in *Roxanne.*

As for Astaire? "The thing I hate most is nostalgia," said this dancer. Three generations now pay him the compliment of their late-night attention. Maybe it is nostalgia alone that draws us to this graceful, flawless star, and that makes his passing page-one news. But I don't think so.

Fred Astaire did something that seems truly remarkable in our modern eyes. He made dancing—together—look so easy.

JUNE 1987

OLIVER NORTH: THE GOOD,
THE BAD AND THE BOFFO

FOR PURE ENTERTAINMENT, you couldn't beat the guy. His daytime ratings outdid the soaps. He was producer, director and star all wrapped up in one. He even titled his own show: *The Good, the Bad and the Ugly*. And if you ever wondered who was going to play him in the movie, he left only one conceivable choice: Oliver North.

This Marine more than lived up to his billing. In full military regalia, he was a one-man repertory company. He alternately played patriot, patriarch, charismatic leader, dutiful follower and forgetful dad, the "old buffoon."

Here was a man for all seasons. A guy who would go one-on-one with terrorist Abu Nidal and still buy leotards for the kids. A man who hated communism and never "hanky-panked" with his secretary despite her "God-given beauty." A man who packed a poison pill on his mission to Iran and worried about a security fence to protect his "best friend" Betsy and the kids.

Oliver North's squared-off shoulders and take-charge glare (he blinked so rarely that if he had contact lenses, they would have dried out) began by mesmerizing the committee members and the country. North presented not just a masterful self-defense but, more importantly, a fascinating dramatic profile.

Americans more comfortable judging performance than substance, conditioned by television debates to watch for quivers and the sweaty upper lips, had to give him three stars. The most frequently heard question about North was not: "What did he do?" It was, rather: "How did he do?" And the answer, in the best *Variety* tradition, was: "Boffo."

Tom Brokaw put it this way: "You can almost hear his supporters around the country chanting, 'Ol-lie, Ol-lie, Ol-lie.' " We were the audience; he was the virtuoso performer. That's entertainment.

The most fascinating part of the Oliver North show was the way it reversed the "character" issue. All this political season, we have been asked whether a man's private conduct can affect his public purposes. Can he be disqualified because of it? The answer has been a qualified yes. A flawed character may make a risky policymaker.

In the case of the lieutenant colonel, we seem to be taking the opposite view. North defended his character—or saved his honor, if you prefer. He didn't, he says, take a penny. He never committed adultery. He was proud of his work. His ability to present himself as a man who erred only out of concern for his family or ardor for his country was allowed to whitewash his actions. The risk is that, in this case, private morality may cover or color a far deeper public immorality.

Consider just two excerpts from North's endless and elegant monologues. First there was his passionate description of the death of 11-year-old Natasha Simpson at the hands of terrorists in Rome: "Gentlemen, I have an 11-year-old daughter not, perhaps, a whole lot different than Natasha Simpson."

Next there was his emotional defense of the contras: "The Nicaraguan freedom fighters are people—living, breathing, young men and women who have had to suffer a desperate struggle for liberty."

A splendid show of emotion, a fine example of the Marine's character, stiff but with just the right amount of feeling. It was hard, sitting in the audience, judging this polished performance, to remember that this man thought it was a "neat idea" to sell arms to Iran and to crank up the war in Nicaragua against the knowledge and will of the American people.

More than a few 11-year-olds, "not perhaps a whole lot different than Natasha Simpson" or the North girl, have surely been killed by our weapons in the Middle East. More than a thousand civilians, "living, breathing young men and women"—including 210 under 12—have been killed by the war we created in Nicaragua. North helped make these things happen. So did his lies to Congress. Yet it took a demonstrator at the hearings just to introduce these faceless victims of war into the hearing room.

These hearings are not just about the Boland Amendment or even the Constitution. These hearings are not just about whether Ollie North is a great character actor, a swell husband, a loving dad and all-around honorable fellow by his own code. They're about illegally trading those arms, weapons of murder. What counts in this drama is the public morality. The plot. The good, the bad and the very, very ugly.

JULY 1987

CORY AQUINO: A WIDOW'S WALK

IN DECEMBER, a soft-spoken woman named Corazon Aquino said to an American reporter, "What on earth do I know about being president?" Two months later, the same woman was president.

The weeks in between were remarkable ones that filled the pages of our political album with powerful images. A crowd of Filipinos forming a human barrier against tanks. A still life of an uneaten bowl of caviar left on the dining-room table by a fleeing ruler. A wide-angle shot of Americans expressing relief that for once we were on the side of the good guys. But most remarkable was the portrait, seen in time-lapse photographs, of the woman in the yellow dress becoming a leader.

In the weeks ahead, some may trace a line from her childhood to her presidency. A teacher in Philadelphia points to the good omens in her good grades. College friends in New York read prophecies into the yearbook captions. But the reality is that Cory Aquino's path to power was a widow's walk, not entirely unlike the one that other women have taken.

Until the death of her husband, Cory Aquino's highest political post had been that of courier to her husband's prison cell and hostess to his inner circle of allies. If she had aspired to office at all, it was to the office of first lady.

It was only when the man she had stood behind was murdered that she was forced into the spotlight. She inherited the family business.

This most reluctant candidate—"I am not a politician"—took on Ferdinand Marcos in order to carry on her husband's work. Inevitably, she made that work her own. At the beginning of the campaign she was a symbol of her husband's martyrdom. At the end she was a symbol of her own bravery. She began as Mrs. Benigno Aquino and ended as "Cor-y! Cor-y!"

I don't pretend to know whether Cory Aquino will be as successful in office as she was in the pursuit of it. If it is one leap from symbol to leader, it is another from leader to ruler. But I do not find myself as dubious of her chances as many others.

Cory Aquino was hardly installed in office and Ferdinand Marcos had hardly landed in Hawaii before the first doubters began. It was one thing to be popular, they said, quite another to be strong. The questions asked in Washington corridors and on television talk shows came in elaborate and familiar code words. Is she tough enough? Can she handle it? Can a former housewife rule fifty million people?

Home economics may not be the preferred background for a political education. But listening to these doubters I thought of a time, not that long ago, when a simple man named Lech Walesa became a leader of his people. When people wondered about his potential, did anyone say, "But he's just an electrician?"

More recently, when Indira Gandhi was killed, her son Rajiv, a candidate as apolitical, as inexperienced, as reluctant as Cory Aquino was catapulted into her place. How often did the correspondents ask Rajiv whether an airline pilot could be a prime minister? Is a pilot or an electrician better qualified for leadership than a homemaker and a mother of five?

Maybe I have seen too many women who have taken that widow's walk into a whole other life. Maybe I have seen something familiar in Cory Aquino's transition, the way hard-earned self-confidence can replace self-doubt.

At some point in this short and intense initiation, Cory Aquino stopped comparing her qualifications to those of some mythical "president" and started comparing them to the competition. (What on earth did she know about being president? What did Marcos know?) At some point, she started to feel the strength that comes from building one small win into another and larger victory.

The Aquino government is in its infancy and the jostling for power has just begun. But I don't believe that Cory Aquino will end up as a figurehead in a yellow dress brought out for state occasions.

What are the odds against her success as president? In December, some of the oddsmakers bet that Cory Aquino wouldn't even live through the election. In January, they bet she'd lose handily. In February, they bet that Marcos would successfully steal the election. Yet this "widow" steered her people on a safe course between defeat and civil war. This "housewife" beat Ferdinand Marcos. The odds are evening up.

MARCH 1986

BISHOP TUTU: AN AFRICAN AND THE AMERICAN APATHY

IT IS LIKE THIS at every campus along his way. Students sitting. Students standing. Students sprawled on the floor of some auditorium to hear the small gray-haired man in a crimson clerical shirt talk in his lilting accent about "that vicious, ee-vill, immoral system," apartheid.

On a recent night at Harvard, these students overfilled the forum of the Kennedy School of Government. They were crammed in and around the VIPs and the press, legs dangling from the ledge of the balconies that step-stoned around the platform, listening to Bishop Desmond Tutu.

Students who have been labeled "apathetic" had come to witness a 54-year-old Nobel Prize winner who cannot vote in his own country. Young people wear-dated as "the uninvolved generation" had come to listen to stories told by an Anglican bishop who must go home every night to black Soweto.

When he spoke, the bishop saw something distinctive in his campus supporters. An earlier generation, organized against the Vietnam War, had self-interest among their motives, he noted. Many students were draft age. "The extraordinary phenomenon of anti-apartheid movement on campuses," he said, "is that in many ways you needn't be involved. But you are."

Tutu didn't ask why, but it is a fair question. Why, in a desert of college political activism, is there this South African foliage? Why, during commencements, when another class marches straight ahead into the work force, are there mortarboard protests over apartheid?

There are some who believe that apartheid has become a campus target largely because it's a hemisphere away. It's easier to be engaged at arm's length, easier to judge another government's misdeeds. You can hang up on a long-distance cause if it gets too expensive.

But the young I know are less concerned with distance than with certainty. Apartheid offers the luxury of moral certainty. There is no other side to this story; no good news about this political system. The students who oppose apartheid today do not believe that they will grimace over their naiveté at some tenth reunion. And that's important to this generation.

Today's freshman class was for the most part born in 1967, after John F. Kennedy's death, after the major civil-rights victories. They grew up against a backdrop of idealism debunked, leaders defrocked, Nixon's expletives, Kennedy's women.

By eighteen, they are a television audience that equates politics with products, campaigns with commercials, issues with slogans. By twenty, they are wary consumers who, above all else, don't want to be suckers.

In many of the college students I know, the desire to make a commitment fights with this fear of being wrong, being suckered. It's true in the classroom. It's true in their personal relationships—this generation of children that has lived through more divorces than any other. It's true in political causes.

South Africa is an exception to this so-called "apathy." So, too, is the other major involvement of students, their increased interest in what we once called charity. In the jargon of political scientists, apartheid is a "macro" issue; charitable work a "micro" issue. But they are both morally compelling and foolproof, or should I say suckerproof. There is also no way to make a political mistake by working in a soup kitchen. There is no harm that comes years later from helping an elderly woman do her grocery shopping.

Of course, even in these "safe" issues there is some irony. Inevitably, apartheid and charitable work are backdoors, sidedoors or corridors from opposite directions into politics. South Africa comes down to the campus in the form of divestiture and home to Washington in foreign-policy decisions. The soup-kitchen work expands into concern about causes of and cures for lines of people waiting for food.

Gradually this reluctant generation will be drawn into the mainstream of American politics. They will make political commitments, make decisions between imperfect options, take risks, make mistakes. It is happening already.

But for the moment, it is enough to watch Desmond Tutu, a man from another hemisphere, engage this wary generation of Americans with his compelling and seductive moral questions: "Are you or are you not on the side of justice? Are you or are you not on the side of right?"

JANUARY 1986

WALLY SIMPSON: "THE
PERFECT WOMAN"

S HE WAS BORN Bessie Wallis Warfield in 1896, and she died last week the Duchess of Windsor. In between she was Mrs. Spencer and Mrs. Simpson, but she played only one big role, one part for the history books, and the newspapers. She was the costar of "The Love Story of the Century."

The most memorable lines in the greatest romantic hit of the 1930s were not those delivered by or even to this American woman. They were the words spoken to the British empire by the man who loved her.

On December 11, 1936, the man who could not be both king and Mrs. Simpson's third husband said this to his people: "You must believe me when I tell you that I have found it impossible to carry the heavy burden of responsibility and to discharge my duties as king as I would wish to do without the help and support of the woman I love." Edward VIII's monologue sent goose bumps through an entire generation.

From that moment on, Wally Simpson would have to be a wife worth more than the crown of England and Edward VIII would have to find more fulfillment as husband than as ruler of the British Empire. Love had to be worth the price.

If the former king had second thoughts during their thirty-five years of marriage, he never expressed them. "She is the perfect woman," he said again and again. "We were made for one another—even if it meant giving up my throne."

But the woman on the receiving end of this exchange never quite could explain it. "Nobody ever called me beautiful or even pretty. I was thin in an era when a certain plumpness was a girl's ideal. My jaw was clearly too big and too pointed to be classic. And no one has ever accused me of being intellectual," she wrote. "Perhaps I was one of the first to penetrate his inner loneliness."

I don't know how this love story played out in its offstage hours. There are some who say it turned sour, the duchess a shrew and the duke a wimp, their three and a half decades spent at dinner parties and travels with pug dogs and visits to the couturier. Others say they were devoted; when he died, she kept his clothes pressed and shoes lined up in his closet.

But I do know something about how our love-story scripts have been rewritten. In the thirties, tales of romance were steeped in such sacrifice. The King of England, David as he was called, was the shining star of this period piece, but the cast of the times measured love through more plebian sacrifice.

It was routine for women in that era to give up titles—though far less glittering—for love. It was love that made some guy trade in his independence to support a doll.

Today we are not so sure. Today we talk about love as something meant to enhance an individual life. Love, we say, is a relationship between two people who are each stronger and better for it. Love, we declare, makes me a better person, makes my life fuller. The dialogue of our modern romance is less about merger and submerger than about individual gain.

If David and Wallis were to act out their pivotal scene now in the eighties, what would it look like? If David offered to give up the crown, would Wallis say, "I don't know if I can handle that, David." Would David's therapist encourage him to "become a whole person" first: "You cannot look to another person to complete your own life."

In a half century, we have become much more reluctant to ask or even accept everything of the people we love. We are far more skittish about carrying the burden of someone else's self-sacrifice. Nor do we sacrifice the way we once did. For every man or woman who would give up a crown for love now there are a thousand who are not sure that they would give up a transfer to Silicon Valley.

"I have had to live in the knowledge that . . . my every action," wrote this woman who died at eighty-nine years old, "is inevitably judged against the fact of my being married to a former king." This footnote to "The Love Story of the Century" carries more of a shudder than a goose bump into our modern consciousness.

We have learned the costs of sacrifice. We don't want to lose our own lives in partnership. The tenuous quality of today's love stories encourages us to withhold, keep some part separate just in case. But this same withholding may make love more tenuous.

The Duchess referred to the Duke as "My Prince Charming." Have you noticed how few lovers believe in fairy tales anymore?

APRIL 1986

Hedda Nussbaum: The
Woman with the
Punching-bag Face

NOW THE ATTENTION is focused on Hedda Nussbaum, this woman whose punching-bag face and battered psyche have been reconstructed into some semblance of normalcy. It's Hedda Nussbaum now on the cover of *Newsweek*. Hedda Nussbaum, whose halting, searing testimony tops the charts in Manhattan's TV ratings, wiping out even Oprah and Phil.

Her lover—a bizarre misuse of that term—is the one on trial for the murder of their adopted daughter, Lisa. But public attitudes toward Joel Steinberg have become as uncomplicated as the judgment uttered by Mayor Koch: "I'd like to dip him in oil many, many times." It is Nussbaum who has become the morbid target of public fascination.

Why didn't she just leave? This is the question asked by any woman chilled at this testimony. The question asked of everyone who has worked with battered women. Why didn't Hedda Nussbaum leave the first time he hit her? The second time? The twenty-fifth time? The time she had her nose broken, her ear cauliflowered, her spleen damaged so badly it had to be removed.

How did this woman descend to the point where she was unable to defend herself and then—even more terrifying—where she was unable to defend her child? In the days before Lisa's death, Hedda Nussbaum testified that Steinberg threw the girl down repeatedly. "What did you do?" the assistant district attorney asked. "Nothing," she said. "Why not?" he asked. "I'm not really sure," she said.

For a year this case has been the country's most infamous tale of family violence, and not only because of the gory details of Lisa's death. Her parents couldn't be filed away under some suitable heading. One had been a children's book editor, the other was a lawyer. They were middle-class, white, educated, Jewish, inhabitants of Greenwich Village. No matter how many researchers of family abuse report that it happens everywhere, they were not the "sort of people" we persist in associating with violence.

In the attempt to distance ourselves from violence, to seek out a safe emotional suburb far from the inner city, we have long tagged family abuse by race and class and place. But when that doesn't work, we hunt to find another difference between us and them, a line that promises to keep danger remote.

In the case of Hedda Nussbaum, our protection rests now on the notion that she was crazed, must have been crazed because she never left him. That diagnosis is spoken in the street talk of New York. The words are precise: He must have been nuts to do that. And she must have been sick to stay with him.

But the portrait that emerges of Hedda Nussbaum isn't even that comforting. This is a woman who oh-so-gradually lost control of her life, until she no longer had the free will to dial 911 while her daughter was dying in her arms. She was subtly and overtly, emotionally and physically, isolated, and then destroyed by a man who, in the words of one who knew him, "could manipulate a banana out of a gorilla's hands and make the gorilla think he'd gotten a prize."

"Those of us outside the relationship can say that the sane thing to do is to leave," says Susan Schechter, the author of *Women and Male Violence*. But in interviews with battered women, Schechter has seen them "trying to make choices when the outcomes all looked negative, and trying to make choices while being assaulted." Indeed, Nussbaum tried several times to get away, making it to the airport once before her will gave out.

Abuse is not only physical assault. It's what Schechter calls a pattern of coercive control, from outright assault to the monitoring of phone calls and work patterns.

We know a handful of certain things about this violence. That some get away and some don't. That most of these women are terrified and most have no place to go. That shelters help victims. That law enforcement—the arrest of the abuser—is also a powerful aid. And that there are too few shelters and too little law enforcement.

Under these circumstances "leaving can also be a very dangerous act," says Schechter. You don't have to be crazy to be terrified or for that matter to be victimized.

If Nussbaum is to be believed, Joel Steinberg isolated his "lover" and cowed her into obedience. No, she isn't Everywoman. Everywoman does not think her abuser is a "healer." Nor is she the woman next door. The woman next door doesn't believe she is controlled by a cult with hypnotic powers.

But there is very little protection in an analysis that marks her as one of "them" because "we" would have the strength to leave. Or dismisses her as nuts. The safety is in seeing that women like this most famous victim have a place to go and someone to protect them. Hedda Nussbaum has that now. Her daughter Lisa never got the chance.

DECEMBER 1988

FAWN HALL: THE FANTASY SECRETARY

I T WILL BE ironic if Fawn Hall, the secretary who "can type," goes down in history for a $10-million typo. It will be equally ironic if the leading female role in the Iran–contra scandal is cut to a bit part: one night of shredding bliss and a transposed number on a Swiss bank account.

Hall's two days in the limelight turned out to be more than a photo opportunity. Articulate and poised, she embarrassed those who had lumped her in the bimbo brigade. Young, pretty and crucial, she unsettled the men who interrogated her.

For two days, contradictions and psychologically mixed messages flew around the hearing room. "I believe in Colonel North and what he was doing. I had no right to question him," she insisted. If she was told to alter documents, "It was not my policy to ask questions." If she was told to shred papers, "I was purely just doing my job."

And yet Hall also described herself, felt herself, as "part of the team." As a member of the team she worked twelve hours a day, five days a week, without complaint. As team player, she snuck documents out of the office past the FBI, hidden in her shirt and her boots.

None of the men questioning Hall seemed to light on the contradiction. A team player and unquestioning subservient? What kind of a game is that?

They accepted as normal the fact that Hall stood simultaneously beside and behind her man. That she had both protected and obeyed him. Perhaps they were even envious. By the end of the testimony, I had the sense that this young woman was testifying under a second sort of immunity: secretarial immunity.

The men in that room—lawyers and legislators—had one thing in common: a secretary. Fawn Hall may have entered the hearing room as a sexual fantasy. But she left it as a secretarial fantasy.

How often was Hall dubbed the ideal secretary? How many goose bumps did she raise on the arms of male bosses with her own job description: "For the nearly four years that I worked for Lieutenant Colonel North, my hours were long and arduous but I found my job to be most fulfilling." How many of them dreamed of having someone like that "facilitate the smooth operation of the office"?

Loyal and smart, loyal and skilled, loyal and articulate, loyal and beautiful, loyal and loyal and loyal. Hall was no oppressed typist waiting for five o'clock, no mother anxious about her child care, no ambitious woman waiting for the next opening.

She took, in more ways than one, dictation. She shared the ideology of her boss without expecting the details. She considered herself a team player without having to be brought into the decision-making huddle.

Remarkably, Oliver North didn't hesitate before he asked her to alter documents. She was his secretary, after all, his good right arm. For her part, even when she felt "uneasy," she says: "I believed in Colonel North and there was a very solid and very valid reason that he must have been doing this."

Isn't this Everyman's fantasy secretary? Everyman's fantasy wife? The fantasy secretary is hardworking out of devotion, not ambition. The fantasy secretary doesn't see the flaws, even the idiosyncracies, of her man. It isn't her policy to ask questions. The fantasy secretary believes.

For every interrogator who criticized Hall's disloyalty to the law there was another who breathed heavily over her loyalty to the man.

Fawn Hall was twenty-three when she came to the National Security Council and twenty-seven when she left, stuffing documents into her clothes. It's heady stuff to be that close to power, to action, to the colonels and generals of the world. Heady to type words that may change history.

But eventually this particular secretary was doused with reality. The boss with the ideals was also, it appears, the boss with the bogus traveler's checks. The patriot may have also been a profiteer. The boss who walked her protectively to her car late at night involved her in a shredding party.

All good fantasies die hard, even the fantasy secretary. In the hearing room, Fawn Hall also said: "I am a grown-up, an adult and . . . I can form my own opinions and morals." In the end, the woman who awed so many with her loyalty proved that she could do more than type. She told.

PART THREE

BIO AND OTHER ETHICS

If a mother can legally turn over the rights to her womb, then the ethic of the marketplace has won. Pregnancy becomes a service industry and babies are a product for sale.

IS IT RIGHT TO HELP A
SUICIDE?

IT IS CERTAIN that Peter Rosier wouldn't be on trial today if he hadn't been on television two years ago. If he hadn't told all of Fort Myers, Florida, that, "I administered something to terminate her life."

His wife Patricia, after all, a woman whose lung cancer had spread to her other organs, had told everyone that she intended to commit suicide. Indeed she planned her death as a final elaborate production.

Perhaps it was a dramatic attempt to control, or shape, or choose the terms of her death. Perhaps it was an attempt to win some perverse victory over her cancer. Either way, Patricia Rosier, forty-three, picked the date, the time, even the wine for her last meal. She picked out the pills and she swallowed them.

Death, however, didn't play the accommodating role that had been scripted for it. While the Rosier children slept in the next room, the deep coma induced by twenty Seconal pills began to lighten. Her husband Peter, a pathologist, went desperately searching for morphine. And then, as he said a year later, he "administered something."

The irony is that if Dr. Rosier told the truth on television it was not the whole truth. The morphine he administered wasn't the immediate cause of his wife's death. Patricia's stepfather would testify to that after being granted immunity. At the scene of this botched attempt, Vincent Delman feared that she would become, in his words, "a vegetable," and he put his hand over his stepdaughter's mouth and nose.

So it was that Patricia Rosier began by attempting suicide and her stepfather finished the job. But it is, nevertheless, her husband who is on trial for murder, for attempted murder, for conspiracy to commit murder.

In its simplest terms, the case asks whether Dr. Rosier is guilty of these crimes. But in more complicated terms, the case asks us to think about the moral difference between assisting suicide and committing murder.

The one thing everyone agrees upon is that Patricia Rosier was determined to end her own life ahead of the horrors she read into her cancer prognosis. The law today allows—if that is the right word—people to commit suicide. But what happens when someone who is terminally ill and utterly rational needs help to carry out the wish to die?

That is not an idle question. All over this country, husbands and wives, AIDS victims and lovers, friends and parents and children have made pacts to help each other "along the way." But if we provide the pills—or for that matter the bullets or the morphine shot—they request, are we just the errand-runner, the legs for these wishes? Or are we the active accomplices in their deaths?

Our refusal to help means, for example, that only those people healthy enough to get a prescription themselves can choose their own death. Our inability to help means that many will die alone. But our agreement to put pills on a nightstand or in a mouth could mean that complicity in death is justified because someone asks for it.

The Rosier case is a particularly strange one. When Patricia Rosier's suicide attempt began to fail, her panicky husband had already been drawn into the drama. Caught up in the power of her last wishes, he felt compelled to fulfill them. Her stepfather, standing over the woman in a coma, said to himself, "Enough is enough."

Was Dr. Rosier morally right when he administered the morphine? Would it have been morally right to allow his wife, who had chosen suicide, to end up in a coma? I am not at all sure.

Is he, on the other hand, a murderer, even an attempted murderer in the way we understand that term? That I can answer with certainty: no. No, because he didn't begin this death. No, because he didn't complete it.

The saddest part of this story is that Patricia Rosier decided to commit suicide in the first place, to secure a gentle death. "It is," worries Dan Callahan, an ethicist at the Hastings Center, "an increasing terror of medical progress" that lurks behind many such a choice among the ill. "People feel the only way they can regain self-control is to have available the possibility of suicide."

The fear of unnecessary pain and the fear of losing control to a technological death have changed the nature of many last wishes. So, the most telling part of the Patricia Rosier story is not the one played out on television or in the courtroom. It's the tale of a woman who finally believed that suicide was more merciful than medicine.

COURTROOM MEDICINE

AT THE OUTSET, the court coolly offers a rasher of sympathy. "Condolences," they begin, "are extended to those who lost the mother and child."

I don't know how I would take those words if I were the parents or husband of the 27-year-old Washington woman who lost her rights before she lost her life. How would I respond to the condolences of a court who justifies the decision to treat a sick woman as if she were already dead?

The woman I know only as A.C. was a fighter. She had to be. A.C. had bone cancer at thirteen, spent much of her life in and out of hospitals, in and out of surgeries that left her with one leg.

At twenty-seven, married and believing she was free of cancer, she became pregnant. Then, on June 11, the doctors told her that the back pain and shortness of breath were due to a large tumor in her lung. She went from being an expectant mother to a terminally ill patient with perhaps only days to live.

If A.C. had not been pregnant, she might have died as she chose. After all, we have become sensitive to the wishes of the dying. We don't override their desire to control or refuse intervention. Indeed we require the informed consent of any conscious adult.

But A.C. was carrying a 26-week-fetus. So, unknown to her, the administration of the George Washington University Hospital called the hospital attorney to ask if they were required to perform a forced cesarean section.

The lawyer in turn requested an emergency ruling from the District of Columbia court. In less than six hours, through a series of bizarre and rushed hearings, the D.C. appeals court gave its final ruling while she was being prepped for surgery: The hospital had to try and "save the child."

Despite the objections of a woman, who was well enough to communicate clearly—"I don't want it done"—despite the objections of her family, despite the objections of her physicians, a cesarean section was performed.

The baby, by no means "viable," died immediately. A.C. died two days later. On her death certificate, it lists the surgery as a contributing factor.

Now, months later, the court that issues its "condolences" also upholds the view that A.C. properly forfeited her rights because she was about to die. As the attorney for the fetus had said, "All we are arguing is the state's obligation to rescue a potential life from a dying mother."

Is this to be a new standard then? Is this how we are to think about other dying people? Would we allow the state to harvest organs or bone marrow or blood from a dying member of society against his will to give it to a "viable," existing adult? Do you lose rights as you lose your health? Or is it only if you are a pregnant woman?

Increasingly, pregnancy is the exception to the rule. In several states that have a "living will" statute, everyone has the right to refuse extraordinary treatment except for pregnant women. We have seen several cases where a brain-dead woman has been kept on respirators so that the fetus might survive.

More controversially, we now see pregnant women who are not brain dead, not even terminally ill, being threatened or forced into medical treatment. Last year, Pamela Rae Stewart was arrested in California on the charge of fetal neglect for having disobeyed her obstetrician's orders. The case was thrown out of court, but the pattern exists.

There are some twenty-four women who have been ordered to have cesareans. In the case most commonly cited by courts a Georgia woman in her thirty-ninth week was ordered to have surgery because, the doctors said, there was a 99 percent chance the fetus could not survive delivery. The courts fail to add that before the surgery could be performed, the baby arrived on its own, healthy.

Lynn Paltrow of the American Civil Liberties Union, which is petitioning for rehearing, believes "we are treating fetuses with rights above and beyond any existing person." In this case, she adds grimly, "The question is no longer whether the fetus is viable, but whether the mother is."

The court argues that A.C. lost only a few hours or at most days of life. But those hours and days are not the state's to decide.

The court treated A.C. as if she were dead. They shortened and brutalized her life in a wholly misguided fantasy of playing savior. All they offer is a pious condolence. Justice would be a more appropriate memorial.

DOES THIS PATIENT HAVE
AIDS?

THESE DAYS, Dr. Lorraine Day goes into her operating room in full protective gear. Two pairs of gloves, goggles, a face mask, double sleeves, double shoe covers, boots up to her knees. The chief of orthopedics at San Francisco General Hospital is trying to practice safe surgery. But she is scared anyway and not a little angry.

"Yesterday, I did five operations," says Dr. Day. "Thirty percent of my patients are at high risk for AIDS. One of my patients recently needed 250 units of blood. It was pouring into him and all over us. They tell us to be careful. But as a surgeon you cut yourself many times. Would you tell a carpenter, don't cut yourself for the rest of your life?"

How frightened is this experienced surgeon about getting AIDS from a patient? "Honestly?" she asks, and answers, "I have to decide whether I want to continue in medicine."

What angers Dr. Day and many of her quieter colleagues is that she has no right to know which of her patients carry the deadly virus. What bothers her further is that she has no right to refuse to operate, even minor elective surgery, on a patient with the virus.

It is not surprising that these concerns—like the virus itself—have hit first and hardest in San Francisco. But they are spreading as widely as the disease. Are doctors, nurses, expected to place themselves at risk every day without information? Are they legally or morally obligated to give AIDS patients the exact same treatment they would give others?

So far, it is believed that only a dozen health workers—including a technician here at San Francisco General—have been infected on the job. Statistically, Hepatitis B, which killed 100 health workers last year, seems a much greater risk. But risks are not spread equally through the medical population. Nor are the feelings of risk. Dr. Day believes fervently, "It's only a matter of 'when,' not a matter of 'if'."

In another corner of this hospital, Dr. Molly Cooke, an internist, is familiar with this anxiety. The mother of three small children and wife of Dr. Paul Volberding, who cares for AIDS patients, went through "absolutely excruciating anxiety, almost intolerable" when she realized the nature of the disease to which she and her family had been exposed. But as an internist she tends to think of the reassuring statistics, while the surgeons tend to think case by bloody case.

Still Dr. Cooke, like virtually every other doctor I spoke with here, is uncomfortable not knowing which of her patients carry the virus. Even Dr. Mervyn Silverman, president of the American Foundation for AIDS Research, says, "In the best of all possible worlds, physicians should know." He opposes mandatory testing for hospital patients because "this knowledge has side effects that are disastrous." Among those side effects may be the refusal of medical treatment.

Should medical people be allowed to withhold care? The easy answer is a blanket "no." It is unethical for a doctor to turn away someone who is sick. "When you get your medical degree," says Dr. Silverman, "it doesn't come with a limited warranty, only good for non-risky situations."

But there are times when the benefit to an infected patient may not warrant the risk to a physician. Should a doctor have to operate on a broken ankle rather than set it in a cast?, asks the orthopedic surgeon. Should you have to perform a bunionectomy rather than prescribe a therapeutic shoe?

"If we lost a doctor for each AIDS patient," says internist Dr. Cooke, "society might decide this is not how we want to spend our doctors. But the risk is lower. At some point we accept the loss of doctors to take care of hundreds of thousands of sick." But at what point and for what goals?

This horrific epidemic is still relatively young. Our statistics are raw. We are just beginning to deal with the real medical and ethical dilemmas.

If we are going to trust the health-care profession to treat the sick, part of that trust is to give them privileged information, the tools of their job. In an emergency, there is no time for an AIDS test. But when possible, a doctor should know whether a patient is infected. Some may abuse that information, some may indeed refuse care. We'll have to depend on their professional ethics and pressure to minimize such breaches.

We must also reframe the arguments about treatment. It can't be cast simply as the patient's right to all care versus the doctor's right to any refusal. We need to assess more fully the benefit to a patient against the risk to health-care workers.

We are in this AIDS epidemic for the long haul. Those in the hospitals are taking risks; we expect them to. Tomorrow, Dr. Lorraine Day will operate on five more patients. If we want her and her colleagues to go on, we have to devise strategies that offer the profession what they offer patients: better care and better protection.

FEBRUARY 1988

BABY M I: MOTHERS IN
THE MARKETPLACE

HER PARENTS cannot agree on anything these days, not even on her name. Her biological mother, Mary Beth Whitehead, calls the five-month-old girl Sara. Her biological father, William Stern, calls her Melissa. The court in Bergen County, New Jersey, just calls her Baby M.

The case that will come up on September 10 is no ordinary custody fight between estranged partners. These two parents never had a relationship; they had a deal. The intimacy was not one of man and woman but of sperm and ovum. Mary Beth Whitehead was hired to be a surrogate mother.

When Stern, a biochemist, and his wife Elizabeth, a pediatrician, decided it was dangerous to have children together, they went to an infertility clinic. There, they met Whitehead, a 29-year-old mother of two, the wife of a sanitation worker. And there, they drew up a contract.

Whitehead agreed to be artificially inseminated with Stern's sperm, to conceive and carry a baby for the couple in return for $10,000. She signed on the dotted line, a promise that she would not "form or attempt to form a parent-child relationship" with the baby she carried.

But when the baby was born, Whitehead welched on the deal.

After turning Baby M over to the Sterns, refusing their money, she "borrowed" her back. When the Sterns tried to reclaim the baby, the Whiteheads ran off with her. Finally on July 31, Baby M was tracked down in Florida and returned to the Sterns and New Jersey.

"People treat it like we're fighting over a car," says Mrs. Whitehead now. "But she's not a possession, she's a part of me." She is also a part of William Stern.

What is notable about this custody wrangle is its utter predictability. This was, everyone in the field will agree, a case waiting to happen.

When the first stories written about surrogate motherhood made their way into the media, it sounded as if the biological mother suffered nothing more damaging than stretch marks. It sounded as if surrogate mothers were just an easy helpmate for the infertile. But there was always that question hovering in the air: "What if she changed her mind?"

Could the biological mother be held forcibly to a contract for the sale of her egg and use of her womb? If she reneged, could the biological father demand back his money or his genes? If she changed her mind, what would happen to the baby?

The sad human part of this drama is that neither the Whiteheads nor the Sterns predicted her emotions. "I was completely devastated having the child taken from my arms," Mary Beth wrote after the fact. "I felt like I was used for one purpose and was no longer needed or wanted."

This was exactly what she had promised: to be no longer needed or wanted. But is it something a person can promise?

I don't know how the courts will deal with this question. There is very little law governing surrogacy so far. The technology of parenthood has run far ahead of the courts.

It is possible, assuming blood tests confirm Mr. Stern's fatherhood, that they deal with it as a contract case, testing whether it is legal to make such a deal and illegal to break it. They may deal with it as a straight custody dispute.

I do not believe that anyone should be able to sign away parental rights before they have even borne the child. A baby is not a piece of goods and human emotions do not make for neat contracts. But at the very least, a mother should have a matter of days after delivery to change her mind. If she does, she should have an equal right to custody.

Does that muddy any agreement for surrogate motherhood? Does that increase the risks for the couples who want a child this way? Absolutely. A biological father could end up without even visitation rights.

But the opposite scenario is more unsettling. If a mother can legally turn over the rights to her womb, then the ethic of the marketplace has won. Pregnancy becomes a service industry and babies are a product for sale.

I do not know what the end of this story will be for Baby M. I suspect that the *M* stands for Messy. The Sterns, the Whiteheads, the baby have formed an emotional triangle. But they have also become the stars of a cautionary tale about the surrogate motherhood industry itself. Be wary of people with contracts in their hands who promise a real easy deal on a brand-new baby.

BABY M II: M FOR MONEY

IT IS THE ONE unmentionable word. The lawyers don't talk about it directly. The parents behave as if it has no bearing. The media refers to it only obliquely. But in the Baby M trial, *M* stands for money.

As this test case on surrogate mothering shifts focus from contracts to custody, from the conflicting rights of the parents to the best interests of the child, there is barely even a veiled message about the role money may play in its outcome. People are testifying and behaving as if class—a dirty word in the American language—or socio-economic background, if you prefer, is irrelevant.

The lawyers do not bring in economists to describe the difference between the Whiteheads and the Sterns. That would be too crass. They bring in psychologists.

Nobody suggests in court that the wife of a garbage collector and the husband of a pediatrician are not equal under the law. Nobody states overtly their ability as providers. But it is money that determined Baby M's birth and money that may well decide her custody.

In the beginning, both the Whiteheads and the Sterns chose to believe that Mary Beth wanted to carry this child for altruistic reasons. I don't dispute that belief. But in real life the wealthy don't become surrogates and the poor do not buy surrogates and the hired matchmakers do not work for love.

Psychologist Lee Salk may have been too crude in his testimony when he said that Mary Beth signed on to be a "surrogate uterus," not a surrogate mother. But the financial arrangement is telling: She would be fully paid by the customer only if she delivered his product, finished the job.

What now of the custody struggle between those who have more and those who have less? THREE EXPERTS SAY BABY M'S MOTHER IS UNSTABLE read the headlines. We hear about her death threats and her hysteria, her "mixed personality disorder," her "immature personality structure." One psychiatrist says: "Her need for having possession of the baby is so overwhelming that it seems to impair her judgment in properly caring for Sara/Melissa."

Those "experts" are more confident than this reader in judging Mary Beth's behavior. "Her need for possession of the baby"? What if this mother was driven to "craziness" by the loss of a child and then lost again because she sounded crazy?

But we are talking about money. The court record also shows that Mary Beth worked briefly as a go-go dancer, that she was on welfare, borrowed money for her house and faced a foreclosure. The facts subliminally add up to the portrait of unstable family. Or is it, rather, just the portrait of a family on the financial margin?

What should a high-school dropout who married at sixteen and had her first child at seventeen do for a living when she is separated from her husband? Brain surgery? Add another $20,000 a year to the Whitehead bank account and would the family suddenly become more stable? Stable enough? A stronger contender for Baby M?

I write this because quite frankly, as a custody judge between two equal claimants, I would award Baby M to the Sterns. In the best interest of the child, I would go with the odds, keep her in the home which appears to offer her a better chance. I would entrust her to the parents who had the better education, whose lives were more predictable and less volatile, who seemed more able to attend to her emotional and personal needs.

But having said that, I am aware of how class and money factor into this equation. How many other mothers in more conventional situations have lost custody of their child to a father who can provide it with a house, a better neighborhood, dancing lessons or summer camp?

In the end, the Baby M trial may be resolved as a contract case or a custody case. But either way, the whole sorry business of surrogate motherhood is riddled with economic bias. It's rife with messages about buying and selling children, about who can "afford" to have them.

If this woman indeed has a "personality disorder"—immature, impulsive, narcissistic, possessive—then she was exploited by the clinic and by the Sterns: her genes sold, her uterus rented.

If not, she is an equal contender, and one of the reasons she may lose the baby is because of this unmentionable: money. In a courtroom that's inundated with lawyers and judges, M.D.s and Ph.D.s, the Whiteheads are simply outclassed.

FEBRUARY 1987

BABY M III: THE RIGHT TO GIVE AWAY YOUR RIGHTS

IN THE FINAL moments of the Baby M case, the lawyer for the Sterns made what sounded like the feminist case for his clients. He told the judge that ruling the contract invalid would limit the right of future women to choose, to decide what they would do with their own bodies.

If, he said, "you prevent women from becoming surrogate mothers and deny them the freedom to decide ... you are saying that they do not have the ability to make their own decisions, but you do. It's being unfairly paternalistic and it's an insult to the female population of this nation."

Gary Skoloff's point was that any bona fide adult, over eighteen, able to read the fine print, is grown-up enough to take responsibility for his or her own action. Signing up for maternity was like registering for the Marines. Anybody who said that such a contract should be prohibited was a relic from an era when women were prohibited from all sorts of economic activities.

Maybe I have a rather tough hide but, somehow or other, I won't be insulted if the court limits the business arrangements women can make with their genes and their wombs.

There are two parts to this impossible, no-win case that will be decided on March 30. One part has to do with the contract that produced Baby M. The other is about the custody of Baby M.

In the contract debate, the Sterns' lawyer wants to prove that Mary Beth Whitehead was competent, cool, strong enough to make a rational decision. In the custody debate, he wants to prove that she is too emotional, unstable and unfit to be the better parent of the child.

Much of the recent attention has been focused on the custody fight, which is as irrational as similar cases between divorcing couples. Indeed the publicity has served to reveal the terrifying absurdity of expert witnesses called to judge parents according to their ability to play "patty-cake" and choose the right toys.

But while the judge is reading his Solomon chapter on custody disputes, it's worth a look back at the actual contract under dispute. Just what freedom of choice did Mary Beth Whitehead execute, when she signed the document?

We all know that she agreed to artificial insemination, to bear and deliver a child in return for $10,000. We have read that she agreed to the absurd idea that "in the best interests of the child, she will not form or attempt to form a parent-child relationship" with the fetus. But there are a few other wrinkles, or clauses, to this contract.

The Whiteheads agreed to assume all risks, "including the risk of [Mary Beth's] death." They agreed that if she miscarried before the fourth month there would be no payment. If she miscarried after the fourth, even if the baby was stillborn, she would only be paid $1,000. She wasn't to be paid for her services, but rather for the product.

More intrusively, the contract states that Mary Beth promised not to abort the fetus unless the doctor said it was necessary for her physical health. Conversely, she also agreed to amniocentesis and promised if the "test reveals that the fetus is genetically or congenitally abnormal . . . to abort the fetus upon demand of William Stern." If she refused, his contractual obligations were over.

As a final touch, the contract compelled Whitehead to follow all the medical instructions of her physician and "not to smoke cigarettes, drink alcoholic beverages . . . or . . . take medications without written consent from her physician." It said nothing about childbirth, but presumably those decisions were also up to the doctor and father. In short, she sold her body, put her womb in the hands of others.

Now the lawyer for the Sterns pleads that the judge uphold every woman's right to enter into such a contract. He would secure the freedom of a woman to give up her freedom. To control her body by choosing to give up control of her body. And to give up the right to a child not even born. Is this what we want?

When it's released, the custody decision will inevitably be messy. I don't think the mother has a stronger claim to their baby than does the father. But the contract is an easier call.

Perhaps there are women who want to be biological entrepreneurs. Perhaps there are some who want to market their genes, to hire their wombs to an absentee owner. But the one right we don't need is the right to sign away our rights.

MARCH 1987

SPLEEN FOR SALE

JOHN MOORE never planned to make his fortune out of his spleen. The 43-year-old Seattle sales manager had already hit one jackpot. In 1976, he'd been treated for leukemia and recovered. Nevertheless, Moore may go into the annals of medical history as the Three-Billion-Dollar Man.

As part of the treatment to cure his cancer, doctors at UCLA in Los Angeles removed his spleen. He probably gave it no more thought than you might give a tonsil or an appendix left on the cutting-room floor. But it turns out that John Moore's spleen wasn't like yours and mine. It was unique.

Two researchers, Drs. David Golde and Shirley Quan, took his tissue and, using genetic-engineering techniques, split it, recombined it and developed a cell-line that could be enormously helpful to cancer victims. And enormously profitable as well.

The doctors neglected to tell Moore what they were doing with his tissue. For seven years, he came from Seattle for checkups. Each time they took a bit more blood, blood serum or skin. They never asked him for permission to use any of this for commercial purposes.

Once it has left the body, a person's spleen or blood or even urine is the trash that you don't want washing up on the beach. But these researchers took out a patent on Moore's trash. They entered into contracts with a bioengineering firm and a pharmaceutical company that were worth close to $500 million. These companies figure that the products made from Moore could be parlayed into that $3 billion by 1990.

Now Mr. Moore wants a piece of the action that comes from the pieces of his body. And last week, a California court ruled for the first time that he or anyone else has the right to his bodily parts, even when they're outside his body. Blood and bodily substances, those waste products, are his "tangible personal property." So Moore has the right to sue for some of the money.

Admittedly John Moore's spleen wouldn't have been worth a chicken's liver without the doctors' brains. The researchers maintain that they were actually paid for their hi-biotech services, not for his very raw material. But it was his unique material.

In the biotech revolution, it is the human body, not iron or steel or plastic, that's at the source. Are the biocapitalists going to be allowed to dig without consent into our genetic codes, then market them?

Arthur Caplan, a bioethicist from the University of Minnesota, thinks of John Moore like a farmer with oil on his land. "He can't do anything with it. He doesn't have a drill or a pump. Only the oil company knows how to turn his resource into something valuable. Nevertheless, like the farmer, he says, 'It doesn't matter if fate put this on my land. If you want it you have to pay for it.'"

But until now, few people thought their bodily waste products—most of which will not be named in this family newspaper—still belonged to them. "With gene-splicing techniques, the sudden question," says Caplan, "is what right do I have to control what happens to my spleen or uterus or even urine? If someone draws my blood to test it, is it still mine?"

The court's answer? "A patient must have the ultimate power to control what becomes of his or her tissues. To hold otherwise would open the door to a massive invasion of human privacy and dignity in the name of medical progress." If anything is truly personal, uniquely ours, it's our genetic code.

This case has riveted the attention of the exploding biotechnology industry. The biocapitalists don't want to bargain for every cell with its owner. The researchers don't want to share the rewards from their labor. And every hospital worker can envision a new avalanche of paperwork—consent forms—to be filled out before anyone allows the use of their "waste" products for research.

None of this paints a very attractive picture. There may be people who market their tissue as if it were pork bellies or wheat futures. If we discover the cure for AIDS in one person's blood, he or she can offer blood up for auction. The whole thing lacks something called altruism. But when scientists go into big business, why should the patient be the only altruist?

John Moore has every reason to try and reclaim some of the take on his tissue. He is unlikely to set off a rush of people who go digging in their biological backyards. Three-Billion-Dollar Men are even rarer than dirt farmers who strike oil.

JULY 1988

A Custody Fight for an Egg

THIS IS HOW it happens in ethics class. The teacher begins the morning with a carefully constructed and rather farfetched hypothetical case. Today, it's a doozy.

Imagine, just imagine, says the teacher, that a couple comes to divorce court to split up their property. They are not wrangling over a house or a boat or car. What they each demand is custody of their seven pre-embryos, the creations of his sperm and her eggs that lie frozen at the in vitro fertilization clinic.

The class lets out a collective groan. Come on. Too farfetched. That would never happen. Give us a break.

Well, students, the ultimate hypothetical has now happened in Maryville, Tennessee. The main players in this true story are Mary Sue and Junior Lewis Davis. The outcome is up for grabs.

During their ten years of marriage, Mary Sue had five tubal pregnancies that finally led the couple to an IVF clinic. There the doctors fertilized eggs in a petri dish and tried unsuccessfully twice to implant them in Mary Sue's uterus. When the marriage disintegrated, the remaining seven pre-embryos became its most dramatic leftovers.

Now a Blount County judge has wisely restrained access to these fertilized eggs. But when the husband and wife formally split, the court must decide the fate of what they joined together.

This is more than a bioethics freak case. There have been well over 4,000 children born from IVF. Only this once have pre-embryos been part of a property claim in a divorce settlement. But the questions it raises are at the center, not the periphery, of this still new technology.

Is an embryo really property? This is one that our ethics class could debate for days. Junior Davis listed these fertilized eggs under joint property. Mary Sue says, "I consider them life." The head of the IVF clinic, Dr. Ray King, believes "they should be treated like children." Junior Davis's lawyer, Charles Clifford, says: "In the law, if they are not human beings they are property."

If embryos are property under the law, how does the court decide whose property? It cannot, after all, rule for joint custody, one week in his freezer, one week in hers. It could, I suppose, divide these fertilized eggs the way California divides assets, right down the middle: three for Junior, three for Mary Sue and one up for grabs. That hardly solves the puzzle.

Alternatively, the court could decide "ownership" on the basis of what sociologist Barbara Katz Rothman describes reluctantly as "sweat equity." Mary Sue's participation—hormonal treatment, ova extraction, unsuccessful implants—was greater than that of her husband as sperm donor. The court could also calculate the dollar equity. Whoever paid for the clinic might own the "product." Taking the most logical steps can lead down the most bizarre trails.

The other ways to determine possession do not promise to be easier. Perhaps the pre-embryo should go to the one most in need or most eager to "use" it. Mary Sue, who can only have children through IVF, has said she wants to be a mother, although she is not sure she has the emotional or financial resources to try again. Junior has not said what he would do with the embryos.

There is also the sticky matter of rights. Junior says he doesn't want to father children now. Does he have a greater right to determine the pre-embryos than a man who fertilized an egg in, shall we say, the more traditional way? Mary wants to mother a child. Does she have a greater right to bear her ex-husband's child than another divorced woman? After all, Mary Sue could use these eggs after their divorce. Junior could end up responsible for the child. Whose rights are right?

Lest this ethics class get way out of hand, one other set of possibilities. If the court awards the pre-embryos to one or the other, what is to stop either from donating them to other infertile couples? Or using them in second marriages?

Hard cases make bad law and dilemmas make bad ethics. The Davis story teaches both those maxims. Not even an advanced seminar could work out a perfect resolution.

But there is a way to prevent such a hypothetical from becoming a reality again. Six years ago, another couple, Mario and Elsa Rios, died in a plane crash, leaving no instructions for the fate of the fertilized eggs which are still stored in a clinic in Australia.

In the aftermath, many clinics drew up agreements, asking couples what they wanted done with the fertilized eggs if they could no longer use them. They could add what I would call pre-conceptual clauses to these agreements. Husband and wife would decide in advance which would control the fate of their biological merger if they uncouple.

The new technology allows us to imitate the act of creation in a laboratory petri dish. But it has devised no biogenetic way to resolve everyday human conflicts. We are left to sweep up after the new technology. This ethics class will meet again.

MARCH 1989

MIXED INFORMATION ON
AIDS

ARE YOU a member of a high-risk group for exposure to mixed or misinformation? Have you had visual or audial contact with a self-proclaimed AIDS expert? Casual? Intimate? Repeated?

If so, by now you may be exhibiting all the symptoms of AIDS-information whipsaw. High anxiety. Confusion. Cynicism. A desire to put a bag over your head until it all goes away.

The fear of the AIDS epidemic has spread so much faster than our knowledge of the disease that it's spawning whole cottage industries of "experts," with varying credentials and agendas, all advising the public on their sexual behavior. Some have been manufacturing alarms and others have been peddling reassurance. The results are bewilderment and a building consumer resistance to any information.

In the past month, we had Dr. Robert Gould, a psychiatrist, telling That Cosmo Girl in her favorite magazine that there was virtually nothing to worry about from normal heterosexual relationships, beyond a broken heart. There wasn't evidence that the fatal disease was "breaking out."

Now we have the physiologists of the sexual revolution, Dr. William Masters and Virginia Johnson, along with Dr. Robert Kolodny, insisting in a book called *Crisis* that AIDS is "now running rampant in the heterosexual community."

Masters, Johnson and Kolodny studied 800 heterosexuals between ages twenty-one and forty from four cities. Half of them were monogamous and half of them had more than six partners in the past year. Of those with multiple partners, 7 percent of the women and 5 percent of the men tested positive for AIDS—a number far higher than any other study.

Armed with these numbers, they accuse the scientific community of "benevolent deception." The Centers for Disease Control estimates 1.5 million Americans are infected. This trio doubles that estimate. They also say that 200,000 non-drug-using heterosexuals are probably infected, a number seven times higher than the one given by the CDC.

Are you developing an immunity to AIDS statistics? "The public has had an excess of assurance followed by an excess of alarm from so-called experts on both sides," says Dr. Harvey Fineberg, dean of Harvard's School of Public Health and one of those trying to maintain some sort of balance.

We get tossed between such scientific extremes in part because we don't have satisfying data, but we do have a lot of fear. Anybody can play with probabilities until they match their own anxieties. It's been estimated, for example, that the risk of transmitting the virus through one act of unprotected vaginal intercourse is one in a thousand. Is that a lot or a little? Over an evening, a year or a lifetime?

The trio who wrote Crisis estimates that the risk for a woman is one in 400 sexual encounters. Does this signify a disease running "rampant"? When asked why he called it that, Masters said, "I simply believe it."

This is the sort of thing that drives the cautious health community to distraction. They have to light a match under Gould one day and put out the Masters and Johnson fire the next.

Crisis even raises the flame on "casual" contact, saying that it's theoretically possible to get infected in a touch football game or from a toilet seat. As Fineberg says, "It's theoretically possible that a meteorite could hit the World Trade Center."

If epidemiologists were forced to choose between the alarmists and soothing-sayers, they would reluctantly choose alarms. "But my fear," says Dean Fineberg, "is that the public will say nobody knows anything; it feeds into the anti-expert mood. They won't want to hear any more."

There are many reasons for the dueling experts. They range from honest scientific differences to hustles. But the public is interested in one thing: How scared should I be? How careful should I be? And there is a certain constancy underlying all but the most irresponsibly rosy scenarios about how to behave sexually in this epidemic.

Crisis offers the chilling notion that only 10 percent of their sample with numerous sex partners thought they were at risk. None of them were regular condom users.

In the face of all this, the prescription is the same one we heard last month, last year, the year before. Abstinence or a monogamous relationship with an uninfected person is the best protection. The use of a condom and spermicide every time is second best.

And while you're at it, be wary of unprotected relationships with untested "experts." Misinformation is highly infectious.

FETAL NEGLECT?

THESE DAYS the turf around the courthouse in El Cajon, California, looks a lot less like solid legal ground and a lot more like a slippery slope.

This is where Pamela Rae Stewart was arrested, charged and jailed for neglect of a fetus. The authorities claim that the 27-year-old mother didn't follow the doctor's orders.

Stewart was charged with using amphetamines during her pregnancy, but that is not the primary offense. According to Harry Elias, the deputy district attorney, the woman had a condition called abruptio placenta, a tendency for the placenta to separate from the uterine wall. "She was advised," says Elias, "that if she began to hemorrhage she should go to the hospital right away. Instead she waited twelve hours and by the time she got there, the baby was in fetal distress."

Last November 23, Stewart's baby was born with massive brain damage, and on January 1 the baby died. Someone in the hospital notified the child protective services and someone there notified the police, who in turn notified the D.A.'s office.

The charge against her is a misdemeanor: withholding medical care. Under California law, no parent can "willfully omit to provide food, clothing, shelter, medical attendance or other remedial care" to a child, and the word *child* specifically includes the fetus. The clause was written in 1925, largely to force fathers into paying support to pregnant women. But in El Cajon, it is being used in a way that fits these times all too well.

In recent years, science has fixed its focus on the fetus. We have learned fascinating details about the complex biology of pregnancy. We know a good deal about genetics and even more about the womb's environment. Today our society allows a woman to choose abortion, but at the same time we hold her more responsible for the fetus she chooses to carry. There is a shared belief that a pregnant woman has an obligation to do what she can to ensure a healthy baby. It is common now to disapprove of a pregnant chain-smoker, common to feel outraged at the agony of a newborn addict.

Now doctors, and the law, are siding with that fetus against the mother. Pregnant women have been committed against their will to mental hospitals because they were drug addicts. In Georgia and Colorado, two women were forced to have cesarean sections "for the sake of the child." In Chicago, a judge gave a hospital lawyer temporary custody of a fetus when the woman refused to consent to surgery.

It's one thing to argue that a woman has a moral obligation, it's quite another thing to turn it into a legal obligation. This is where the slope gets slippery.

Stewart's lawyer, Richard Boesen, said melodramatically: "There ought to be a caveat put out to all the prospective mothers of the world: Watch out. If you don't follow your physician's advice and you have some problem in delivery or give birth to a disabled child, you might be open to prosecution."

Modern pregnancy is plastered with warnings. We know that cigarettes and alcohol contribute to a lower birthweight. We put labels on cigarette packages and require notices in some bars and liquor stores. How far is it from a warning to a warrant?

"I have never heard of a vaguer crime than 'fetal neglect,'" says George Annas, Boston University medical ethicist. "It gives you a license to do whatever you want to a woman."

Under this rubric, the doctor has the authority to make decisions for the woman and the law enforces them. "If the doctor says, 'I think the fetus is endangered by this woman,' are they going to lock her in a hospital?" asks Annas. And what if a doctor can detect a problem in utero that might be corrected by fetal surgery? Would it be fetal neglect to refuse?

There are people, including the D.A.'s office in La Cajon, who argue that there's no difference between withholding medical treatment from a thirty-five-week-old fetus or from a one-day-old baby. But there is one crucial difference: to get to the fetus, the law has to reach literally into a woman's body.

Many of us recoil from this intrusion into a woman's autonomy, and yet also share the desire that babies be born as healthy as possible. It is, in real life, rare that these two conflict. Women who choose to have their babies are more likely the advocates than the enemies of these offspring. They are more in need of help than handcuffs.

Pamela Rae Stewart, having lost her child, was arrested for disobeying her doctor's orders. If this is a landmark case, then the land is easy to assay. At the bottom of this slope is a country where pregnant women must live by medical rules in the custody of the law.

In George Annas's fantasy, this place would look "like a giant country club for pregnant women. It would be pleasant, everyone would be required to jog every day and eat healthy food and do things that were good for the fetus." And after a while, they might not even notice the fence that runs all around them.

OCTOBER 1986

PART FOUR

KEEPING IN TOUCH

Without even knowing it, we are assaulted by a high note of urgency all the time. We end up pacing ourselves to the city rhythm whether or not it's our own. We even grow hard of hearing to the rest of the world.

A CARAVAN TO COLLEGE

IT IS A LATE summer day when we migrate south. The two of us, mother and daughter, join that long caravan of families in borrowed station wagons and rented vans, moving the contents of a million bedrooms to a million dorm rooms.

The cars in our sixty-mile-an-hour lane are packed to the hilt with student "basics." Stereos and stuffed animals pop up into my rearview mirror in Connecticut. Guitars and quilts are strapped onto rooftop boxes in New York.

When we take a fast-food break on the New Jersey Turnpike, the wagon trains going south mix with those traveling north. One car carries Washington license plates and a University of Vermont sticker. Another has Maine origins and a Virginia destination.

As a driver on this journey, I have the sudden impression that we are part of a gigantic national swap fest. Western parents delivering their children East to school, Eastern parents delivering their children West. Northerners and Southerners taking their young to teachers in other cities, the way their ancestors once apprenticed children to distant masters.

The symbolism of our trek doesn't escape either of us. Loading the car, driving it and finally unloading its contents into her new room, we are both companions and accomplices to her leave-taking from home. We are in this separation together.

Like the other parents in this ritual, I have offered more than my permission for this transition. I have proffered my approval, pride, pleasure, confidence. The young woman is taking off and I am giving away her hand in independence.

What will I go home to? The room my daughter left behind is remarkably, unrecognizably neat. When we finished packing, it looked just like a guest room. Or—I will say it—an empty nest.

A long time ago, I thought that mothers who also had work that engaged their time and energy might avoid the cliché of an empty-nest syndrome. A child's departure once meant a mother's forced retirement from her only job. Many of us assumed that work would help protect us from that void. Now I doubt it.

Those of us who have worked two shifts, lived two roles, have no less investment in our identity as parents, no less connection to our children. No less love. And no less sense of loss.

Tomorrow, for the first time in eighteen years, the part of my brain that is always calculating time—school time, work time, dinner time—can let go of its stopwatch. The part of me that is as attuned to a child's schedule and needs as it is to a baby's cry in the night will be no longer operative. I don't know how easy it will be to unplug.

What do you do with all the antennae of motherhood when they become obsolete? What do you do with the loose wires that dangle after eighteen years of intimate connection to your own child? What use is there for the expertise of motherhood that took so long to acquire?

I will go home to a new demographic column: households without children. Are these families? I will enter the longest and least-heralded phase, that of parent and adult child.

I am not altogether unprepared. This summer, my husband and I laughed about our impending freedom. We imagined the luxuries of life without the deadlines imposed by children: working late when we need to; falling asleep without waiting to hear a car pull into the driveway; making last-minute plans.

When the absolute priority of children sloughs off, emotional space will open our lives. But will that space also have the empty look of a guest room?

My friends who have taken this trip many times before tell me wryly that Thanksgiving comes soon. One friend has calculated his own ironic formula: The higher the school tuition, the shorter the school year. Another tallies up her long-distance phone bill.

But today it is only my traveling companion who makes me feel at ease with this journey. "This is *exactly* what I want to be doing now," she says excitedly as we graze through the local salad bar for our last lunch. Hours later, on a street corner in a strange city, I hug this tall young woman and tell her, "Go fly." It is time.

THE RISE OF THE COUCH
POTATO

ONE OF THE great pleasures in life is watching a lowly, disparaged and oppressed group of Americans come into their own. I am speaking of those maligned people known as couch potatoes. Or if you prefer, sofa spuds.

For the past decade, Jane Fonda, Richard Simmons and the entire medical establishment have led the rest of us down the aerobic path of life. We have spent our weekends and paychecks on leotards and lessons. We have bought bicycles to nowhere and suits to sweat in. Neither rain nor snow nor sleet has stopped us from speed walking.

But all this time, there existed among us a large number of low-profile Americans who showed true grit, strength of character and staying power. They sat out the jogging craze. They sat out the aerobic craze. High impact *and* low impact. They sat out racquetball. Indeed, they sat and sat.

While all around them, people were on the move, they remained rooted in front of the tube, exercising only their eyeballs. For this consistency, for their ability to not march to the beat of a distant drummer, they were vilified.

Couch potato was not a term of endearment. Indeed, many of us looked down upon these people, and not just because they were sitting. But all that is in the past. The couch-potato movement (if that isn't a contradiction of terms) is showing its newfound pride. The sofa spuds are flexing their muscles. Such as they are.

The year 1987 has become the year of the couch potato. They have at last risen up—without getting up, of course. They have begun to boast of the advantages, the life-style, of the easy chair.

After all, not one couch potato has ever come down with tennis elbow. Not one has ever had a shin splint. Maybe one or two got stiff fingers from pressing the TV remote, but they haven't suffered a single major injury. Except, of course, to their pride.

New York magazine, the herald of trends, was the first of the mainstream to put forth a cover story on couch potatoing as a new in-group activity this fall. We have now seen the growth of Potato Power. The Christmas marketplace boasts couch-potato dolls, a couch-potato quilt, couch-potato T-shirts.

I even received a trademarked Couch Potato Game: "the outrageous game that's played while you are watching TV." And I am told of a newsletter for those who network entitled "The Tuber's Voice."

In January, a couch-potato convention will be held in Chicago. It features, or so I read, a soap-opera seminar, a TV buffet dinner and a TV star lookalike.

Is it possible that we may live to see an Olympic event in marathon television watching? Or is this too American an event to go international? A founding father, Robert Armstrong, explains the potato philosophy this way: "We feel that watching TV is an indigenous American form of meditation." He calls it Transcendental Vegetation.

All this notoriety is wonderful news for those who spent years feeling down on themselves, not to mention their sofas. At last, they are getting their due.

But quite frankly, I have begun to worry. Will success spoil the spuds? Will all this attention—indeed, all this activity—encourage the great American couch potatoes to leave their posts and go out into the marketplace?

There is danger in the merchandising and exploitation of inaction. Will they ruin everything by developing some get-up-and-go? Can a true member of the species play a board game and attend a convention without losing contact with his roots?

To find out the future of the couch potato, stay tuned to this station. And don't move a muscle.

DECEMBER 1987

THE LITE POWER LUNCH

THIS TIME I think they've got it. This time it looks like the top-of-the-line lunch is going the way of all flesh.

To my surprise, one of the less controversial items in the new tax-reform plan is one that would cap (or rather, decapitate) the business lunch. Under the plan, the deduction for any meal over about $25 would be cut in half.

Predictably, the restaurant owners have been poor-mouthing. But very few corporate types seem eager to join them in another food fight. We may be about to see the demise of the demon called the "three-martini lunch."

In the future, social historians will figure out just when and why the business lunch began to lose its political weight. But we know even now that it's become the $7,500 coffeepot of the business world. It's the symbol of public-funded gluttony where the expense-account rich sit and eat at the public trough.

The irony is that this image of corporate gourmands is way out of focus. It's left over from the era when the J. P. Morgans of the world ate a bushel of oysters for their appetizer. In those days, the words *capitalist pig* were redundant.

Today's business lunch is not all that indulgent. Indeed, the more outrageous the bill and the more luxurious the surroundings, the more utterly Spartan the menu.

Just ask the people who routinely fight over who will pick up and write off the check. Or just look at them. They are all lean and hungry. The current class of executives all have exercise charts as complicated as their spread sheets. They run six miles every day before entering the rat race. They have as much heavy lifting at the health club as at the office. They do not do "carbohydrate loading" at lunch.

No self-respecting yuppie eats cow in public at midday. Only the downwardly mobile order their first baked potato before the sun goes over the yardarm. There are no credit cards flashed at all-you-can-eat buffets. Indeed, eating (as in chowing down) has become absolutely déclassé, an admission that you might be uncertain of the whereabouts of your next meal.

In New York City, where all the trends meet their makers, the power lunch has now become the willpower lunch. Across elegant tables set with the finest china, publishers and agents share their spa menus, trying to get one up by undereating. Any author who reaches for the rolls is relegated forever to paperbacks.

In the other major cities, with the exception of Chicago, the chefs in greatest demand are graduates of the culinary school of minimalism. If a modern American can never be too rich or too thin, a modern American restaurant can never be too expensive or too spare. Portions are called discreet. The plates arrive looking like the raisin faces we used to make on our oatmeal, only without the oatmeal.

It was not easy for restaurants to make the transition to the willpower lunch. The ultimate challenge these past years was to figure out how to keep raising the prices while lowering the calorie count.

Enormous amounts of imagination and planning, not to mention raspberry vinegar, go into menu planning. The meals involve first-class flights of fancy: asparagus from Australia, mussels from New Zealand, yellow peppers from Holland, salmon flown from one coast to the other.

By now, there are half a dozen restaurants—three of them in San Francisco alone—where it's possible to eat at the rate of 75 cents a calorie. You open with Perrier (with or without lime) and close with cantaloupe sorbet, a choice of brewed decaffeinated coffees, and a bill that equals your first monthly mortgage payment.

Anyone who calls this "tax-supported hedonism" should try grazing through a salad of radicchio, arugula and watercress. It isn't fun. It's work, ergo, business.

Just to keep the historic record straight, midday restaurants have become a meeting place where corporate Americans go in order not to eat, together. And maybe, just maybe, that's why the moguls have given up fighting for their right to deduct the entire rent of a table. Maybe they aren't tired, just hungry.

Besides, have you ever tried to talk high finance with watercress between your teeth?

BEAT THE CLOCK

I HAVE TAKEN time off. Literally. The watch that straps my workaday wrist to its demands sits on the kitchen shelf.

I have shed its manufactured time, its minute hand, hour hand, just the way I shed my city wardrobe, makeup, panty hose, skirt. Gradually, I have even begun to lose track of time. First the minute and then the hour, finally the day. My watch and I have wound down.

I reckon my real vacation from the moment I forget whether it is Thursday or Friday. And the moment I realize that it doesn't make any difference. At last, I tell myself, I have slipped out of one time frame and sunk into another one. I have left a world divided by nothing more than numbers, sixty minutes, twenty-four hours, seven days a week. I have entered a world of seasons: blueberry, raspberry, blackberry season; lobsters that shed old shells and then harden new ones.

My daily life here is more connected to the tide than the time. At low tide I can harvest the mussels that lie under great heaps of seaweed clinging to rocks by their umbilical beards. At high tide the mackerel may swim in hot pursuit, into the cove. The cove is not a store with hours set by its owner.

Like most people in the Western world, I have grown up in the artificial environment of modern society. It's a place dominated by external timekeepers, calendars, schedules, clocks. Our lives are subdivided into fiscal years, academic years, weekdays, weekends, deadlines. We are taught that there is a time to get up, a time to go to work, a time to eat. We set the clock by a single standard.

Time orders our lives and, inevitably, orders us around. We are so removed from natural rhythms that we are rarely confront how "unnatural" this is. How unnatural to strap time on.

We didn't always live with this artificial timing. In *Time Wars,* Jeremy Rifkin explains how recently people have been alienated from natural rhythms to those of the schedule, the clock, and now the computer with its nanosecond culture.

The schedule—that control on our lives—was the invention of the Benedictine monks whose early passion for organizing and filling every minute of the day grew from St. Benedict's warning that "Idleness is the enemy of the soul." His followers reintroduced the roman hour and invented the mechanical clock.

Not until the fifteenth century did clocks, those icons of temporal time, begin to rival churches in the city squares. Not until the seventeenth century did clocks have a minute hand. "Medieval time," writes Rifkin, "was still sporadic, leisurely, unpredictable and above all tied to experiences rather than abstract numbers." It was the merchants and factory owners who eventually, and with great difficulty, trained workers—those who had previously lived in accord with the seasons—to become as regular as clockwork.

Today, writes Rifkin, "the high achievers see time as an obstacle to overcome, an enemy to defeat. They equate faster and faster learning with victory over time; to win is to beat the clock."

Is it any wonder that many of us choose vacations that stretch uninterrupted from sunrise to sunset, choose to reenter the natural cycle, days of idleness, that friend of the soul? Is it any wonder that we seek, for just a while, not to think of time as a commodity to be spent, saved, wasted, used, but to live from tide to tide?

My own escape is hardly complete. A creature of habit more than habitat, I have yet to spend a day without once looking at a clock or asking the hour. My vacation itself is circumscribed. I have only a certain amount of time allotted to timelessness. It will end at a predetermined moment. I will go home according to the boat schedule, write on deadline.

But on this day, the ghostly white impression left by the watch on my arm has finally browned. I can barely see its imprint on my life.

AUGUST 1987

A MINISKIRT ATTACK

JUST WHEN we thought it was safe to wade back into high fashion along comes this news from trend spotters on the shore: *The mini is back!* Yes, yes, *the* mini, the very same skirt that brought goose bumps to the arms of men and chilblains to the thighs of women in the late 1960s. The mini is back and it is after *you.*

There were, of course, scattered sightings of this menace over the past year or two. Teenagers—a generation once carried in the wombs of women dressed misguidedly in maternity minis—were spied innocently baring their knees. But who among us ever imagined the mini would reappear in such a big wave, threatening to swamp our hopes for a graceful midlife?

Didn't designers promise us that this was the era of choice, that hemlines were a matter of personal preference? Hadn't they insisted that no modern women could ever again be driven into a fashion pool, or forced to travel upstream to where the thigh meets the hip?

But while most women of a certain age spent this spring gaping at resurrected crinolines, giggling at the reappearance of hoops, and wondering why anyone would want to return to the ghastly yesteryears of the 1950s, these same perfidious designers were sharing their 1960s scrapbooks and scissors.

The reports out of Paris and New York predict that next fall will be mini and skini. Skirts are going up—as is their price per inch—and the fashion writers are predicting with a breathlessness I haven't heard in years that anyone who doesn't want to look dumpy better dump a few inches. The only good news is that these are vertical inches.

According to Goodman's Rule, anything you wore the first time around, you are too old to wear the second time. This is applied, by and large, to Dr. Dentons, Mickey Mouse hats and pedal pushers. But it also works for miniskirts. I have therefore taken a personal exemption. Still, I cannot figure out why designers think the time for the mini has come back.

In the 1960s, this shortest skirt was regarded by some as an artifact of the youth cult. In *The Language of Clothes,* Alison Lurie lumped it with babydoll pajamas, as evidence of the era when grown women wore their clothes at the same distance from the waist as two-year-olds.

Others thought it was part and parcel of the sixties sex cult. Exactly twenty years ago, the Vatican weekly condemned the fashion, saying: "Some brainless women, professing a pseudo non-conformism, end up resembling monkeys in adopting the most capricious excess of fashion."

There was clearly a touch of rebellion in 1960s fashion: Baring your knees was thumbing your nose. In Greece, the Minister of Health ordered all female workers to keep their knees covered. In Morocco, schoolchildren were asked to pray for the salvation of women in miniskirts. In Zambia, miniskirted women were attacked on the street. In America, there were mini and non-mini jobs and restaurants.

But the eighties are supposedly the sober era of AIDS and aerobics, entrepreneurship and values curriculum in the schools. A fashion that seemed liberating to women in the sixties can be utterly inhibiting in the eighties. Any veteran can remember the restrictions of real life in a miniskirt. You cannot bend over, sit down, get out of a car or run . . . for Congress.

The only thing that's truly "eighties" about the mini-surge is the attempted coup by a traditional junta to get the hierarchy back in order. They make, we buy.

The original mini was probably brought down, literally, by three things: December, January and February. Now the same designers want to see if women will once again prove their allegiance with a badge of frostbite.

What to do when you find yourself surrounded by racks of miniskirts? When you catch yourself hoisting your own skirts in the mirror just to see how they look? When you try to remember how to do the hemstitch? In the event of a miniskirt attack, remember my favorite relic from the 1960s:

In 1969 a bulletin from the federal government warned: "The legs of young women respond quite rapidly to exposure of cold temperatures. The bodily response is a quick buildup of successive layers of fatty molecules under the skin areas of the thighs, knees, calves and ankles of female legs." There you go. Fat knees or covered knees: It mini-mizes the issue.

SNAPSHOTS

THE PHOTO ALBUM, covered in worn green velvet and held together with ornate brass hinges, lay in a jumble of lace and candlesticks on an old table. It was, like everything else in the hall, a piece of used goods, the refuse of previous owners. Or, if you prefer, an antique.

I opened the album the way someone in the market for a new home might read the real-estate listings. Was this property something that would suit my family? I thought no more of the former owners than I might have thought of the family who planted the tree in the backyard or added the dormers to the roof of a house for sale.

But it turned out that this place was still inhabited. There were people living in this picture book, their story frozen, like their images, in time.

The story began with a pair of wedding portraits, husband and wife in profiles carefully marked 1898. The photos that followed showed one christening after another and then another, followed by the images of these children growing up.

There were pictures of school and graduations, portraits of one rowing team, and another lacrosse team. Two sons were shown grinning in their full military uniforms and then at home again, and finally married with their own children.

Standing in the middle of this antique show, I felt like a voyeur. It was as if I had happened upon a diary while touring a house and, just out of curiosity, read it.

I put the album back on the table. To have placed my own family in that book, I would have had to evict theirs. I wasn't ready to dislodge them from existence.

I couldn't help wondering how this family—kept and groomed so carefully for posterity—had ended up in the hands of strangers. Had the family come to an end, like Abraham Lincoln's, with the death of his great-grandchild last month? Had the album's line of inheritance been disrupted by geographic or emotional distance? Or had someone simply discarded history on the way to a smaller place or a new life?

I cared because I am also a haphazard keeper of family lore, a sometime recorder of family images. Each holiday season, I add a photographic entry, a set of slides or prints to the visual diary. I keep these pictures for pleasure and for some notion of history.

At the same time I am the curator of an older collection. Through death, divorce, remarriage, relocation, I have inherited the snapshots of earlier generations, the portraits of their weddings, the albums cleared from larger houses.

It is this family collection that has grown less familiar over time. I cannot name all the brothers and sisters lined up beside my girlish grandmother. My daughter doesn't know all the cousins on the beach with me. There are strangers among the snapshots. Like distant relatives at a family reunion, I need name tags to know how we are connected.

My predicament as both collector and curator is not unusual. Once it was just royalty who had their histories recorded, just the rich who had their images reproduced. Now it is the rare American without some record of his or her family life.

The camera has made the past democratic. Everyone can keep it. The tape recorder, the movie camera, the video camera are all tools of a middle-class memorabilia. We have the conceit that those who share our genes will want to share our lives.

Yet handling that green velvet album, I realized how easily one generation's memories may become the next generation's clutter. Instead of cherishing mementos, families may be flooded with them. Eventually, our grandchildren or great-grandchildren won't be able to hold all the images of all their ancestors any more than they could store all their furniture.

The antiques for sale in this hall were heirlooms without heirs or old things that didn't fit into new lives. They were the leftovers of broken homes. So, too, were these photographs.

Pictures are far more personal but far less valuable than necklaces or chairs. One person's priceless snapshot may be worthless to another. The family story in the green velvet album was created by someone trying to pluck one family from time and from the multitude. It was created by someone writing a personal history out of snapshots. But fifty years later, there was nobody left who cared. How sad to see such a family estate fall into the hands of strangers.

FROM THE RANKS OF

SUPERWOMAN

EVERY FEW MONTHS, there is another public announcement of retirement from the ranks of superwoman. The notice may be posted in a newspaper or in a magazine, the woman may be a disillusioned lawyer or a disillusioned MBA, but she is sure to be a high-powered professional who decided to go home.

The articles invariably contain a paragraph or two explaining how "the feminists" convinced her that she should do it all: work, wife, mother. Anything less was, well, less. But there came a moment, or a second child, when she felt something had to give and so she gave up the office. Family came first.

The responses to these announcements are almost as familiar by now as the notices. In letters to the editor, one woman will surely (and perhaps angrily) remind the author that not every mother has an economic choice. Another will resent the fact that the author blames feminism for the stress. A third will bristle at the implication that the children of employed mothers suffer.

And then, in a little while, the argument that has no final answer, that remains as emotional as any in our public private life, fades out of print only to recycle over and over again.

This time it has been written large onto the cover of a new book, *A Mother's Work*. The author flags the dilemma this way: "Like many women I was educated to feel that my career and my family should both come first. One day I had to make a choice."

The "I" is Deborah Fallows, a woman who wrote an early-retirement notice that ran some years ago in the capital city of work obsession, Washington, D.C. It got notice and notoriety. Now in a more subtle mood, Fallows struggles to defend her decision to go home, without attacking mothers who are employed. Her desire to be fair, to employed mothers and even to day care, is palpable. But in an odd way, the very delicacy, the very carefulness of her book, reminded me of how difficult it is for one woman to make claims on the turf of motherhood without raising the defenses of other women.

The qualified bottom line for Fallows is this: "Whenever possible, parents should care for children themselves. . . . Other conditions being equal, children are more likely to thrive when they spend most of their day with a parent. . . ."

There is nothing intrinsically hostile about such statements. Yet it is as hard for an employed mother to read those declarations neutrally as it is for a mother at home to react impersonally when an employed friend exclaims: "All things considered, the woman who stays at home has less impact on the world. . . . On the whole, the woman in the work place feels much better about her life."

The reality is that women take these statements personally—because they are personal. The social argument that has filled two decades is not about the behavior of rats in mazes, but about how women should live their lives and treat the people they love.

We are in a particularly uneasy state of balance now. There are almost equal numbers of mothers of young children in and out of the work force. It is one thing for these women in "mixed company" to join hands and mouth support for each other's right to choose. It is quite another to believe it. Mothers may feel judged, challenged, by nothing more than another's decision.

Every time a woman in an office leaves for home, every time a woman in a neighborhood leaves for work, there is a ripple effect. The waves of ambivalence can swamp self-confidence and even friendships. In such an atmosphere, employed mothers share their anxieties most easily with each other; mothers at home circle their own wagons. Each group may still, more than occasionally, feel the other attacking.

This social argument goes on and on because in fact, there is no certainty, no right way to live. Even Fallows' bottom line that children do best when they are in the day care of their own parents is a belief, not a fact. In the business of creating our own lives, or caring for our children, we are all experts and amateurs, opinionated and uncertain, wildly subjective.

We have only one sample of children and a limited number of years and no guaranteed rewards for our behavior. Parents—mostly mothers—who have choices must make them. Not in a vacuum but in a space inundated with worries about our psyches and pocketbooks, our children and selves, the present and future. We do make these choices but our confidence may be fragile and our skin thin. The shifting winds of the social argument, blowing pros and cons at us, all too easily raise the hackles of our own anxieties.

SEPTEMBER 1985

DICK AND JANE PLAY
TENNIS

DICK AND JANE play middle-aged tennis.
See the brace Dick puts on his right arm to protect his tennis elbow.
See the high-top shoes he ties to support the foot which he broke
playing middle-aged squash.
See the double socks he wears to shield the bone spur on the other foot.
See Jane's orthopedic lifts, specially made for her tennis shoes.
See the elastic support on her right knee.
See the X rays of her back.
This is how Dick and Jane prepare to play middle-aged tennis this morning.
Dick stretches his hamstrings.
Jane stretches her back.
Dick takes aspirin.
Jane takes calcium.
Dick drives to the tennis court to save wear and tear on his bone spur.
Jane walks to the tennis court to warm up her spine.
Dick and Jane take out their middle-aged, mid-sized racquets, their sun block,
their yellow balls, and play.
Look at Jane lunge.
See how she winces.
Look at Dick hitting a backhand.
See how he twitches.
Dick and Jane are playing middle-aged tennis to stay in shape. The shape of
a pretzel.

Dick and Jane have two friends. They are Jack and Jill. These two do not play tennis. Nor do they run. Nor do they ache.

But Dick and Jane worry about their friends' health. "What will become of Jack?" frowns Dick at times. He sends Jack articles about exercise and blood pressure. "What will become of Jill?" frets Jane. She sends Jill research about aerobics and heart disease.

Right before Dick's fortieth birthday, he and Jane began to read about health. They read that exercise was an antidepressant. They read that exercise promoted a longer life. They read that exercise helped the cardiovascular system.

Right before Jane's fortieth birthday, they began to notice wear and tear among their athletic friends. They saw their casts and crutches. They saw their X rays and membership cards at sports medicine clinics.

Dick and Jane decided that there were two choices for middle age. They could be depressed or broken. They could strain their hearts or their backs. They could choose between cardiologists or orthopedists. They could live a shorter life of leisure or a longer life of injury. They could be Jack and Jill or Dick and Jane. They decided to play for the long run.

See Dick and Jane now as they finish their game of middle-aged tennis.

Off goes his elbow brace.

Off goes her knee support.

Dick stretches out his hamstrings.

Jane stretches out her back.

Dick drives home to save wear and tear on his foot.

Jane walks home to cool down her vertebrae.

Listen to Dick as puts the flexible cold pack on his toe: "I feel great!"

Listen to Jane as she puts the flexible cold pack on her sacroiliac: "Fit as a fiddle!"

Dick and Jane are willing to sacrifice every bone in their body in order to stay healthy.

AUGUST 1986

CASUAL PHONING AND THE
COLLEGE STUDENT

MY GRANDFATHER had a six-pack of sisters who lived on the other side of the continent. When he got a telephone call from San Francisco, he never once said "Hello," or "How are you?" He picked up the receiver with one stock greeting: "What's wrong?"

Long distance was for disasters. Good news could wait for the mail; bad news came by phone. Maybe a Hollywood mogul made a long-distance call to cement a deal or check up on his tootsie, but toll calls were as foreign to my family as tootsies.

Throughout my childhood, it was clear that these lines were not for conversation but for announcements. We were as likely to reach out and touch someone by telephone as we were to communicate by using a cattle prod. Casual phoning was as rare as casual sex.

Today, however, I do not answer the phone saying, "What's wrong?" I answer it saying, "Yes, I will accept the charges."

As a parent I have learned that the marketing miracle of the age—the century's greatest scam—is the success of the telephone company in selling something as ephemeral as conversation. They have convinced a generation of young Americans to casually—nay, whimsically—use the phone.

It isn't only an extraterrestrial creature who yearns to "phone home." Our own little earthbound kiddies learn their telephone numbers before they learn to count change. In the best *Sesame Street* style, they have their priorities straight: digits before dollars. And long distance is just three little digits.

The business plot comes into its profitable peak when our young move to another area code and join that expensive subspecies known as college students. Having spent high school attached umbilically to the extension cord, they move into a dorm where they are immediately entrusted with the one thing we withheld: their own touch-tone.

What they do with it can only be explained through a series of anecdotes that lurk in the telephone bills gathered for the Annals of Collegiate Communication: (1) a long-distance call in pursuit of someone else's long-distance number; (2) a call from a panicky young cook who needs to be talked through a crème anglaise; (3) a call from an operator checking if the child in city *A* could call the friend in city *B* and charge it to the parent in home *G*. *G* as in Goodman.

The building of a truly impressive phone bill, one that rivals the cost of tuition, is not all the fault of the telephone company and its diabolical direct dialing. The university colludes in this. It brings together students who do not ordinarily live anywhere near each other. Inevitably they become friends. Friends by the modern definition are people who must be called regularly during vacations.

Love also rears its expensive head. Researchers have determined that it is biologically impossible for a college student to fall for someone who both summers and studies in the same area code. Accountants calculate that a relationship with the girl next door would save the average college family $89.56 each quarter. There are two such families in existence.

As a concept, casual phoning was sold with the premise that a brief call is quite cheap. If this were a drug clinic they would call the marketing strategy "giving out samples." The student can explain just how cheap a call is as easily as they can explain why, according to Wittgenstein, your life is built on an entirely wrong philosophical foundation.

If you begin to win such a discussion, this student has a backup position. She will promise that the next time she calls Bruce et al, she will just talk for three minutes. This will happen only if Bruce isn't home and she gets his baby sister on the line.

Then there is the final line of student defense. You've heard the one that goes: "The check is in the mail." The undergraduate being cross-examined about the need for another transcontinental chat has a better one: "I'll pay for the call." This is delivered with great moral righteousness and absolute safety, because parents know the only way she can pay for it is with food money.

But in any family, the time comes for a serious conversation about casual phoning. No problem. You will find them absolutely cooperative, even happy to discuss the matter at great length—which is to say, at long distance.

And if you finally get hysterical, the bewildered telephone abuser will innocently echo his ancestor's anxious cry: "What's wrong?" Where, oh, where is Grandpa when you need him?

FEBRUARY 1989

COUNTRY MUSIC

"IS IT QUIET up there?" My friend asks this question wistfully. She has called long distance, from her city to my countryside, from her desk to my cottage.

"Yes," I answer her. There is no urban clatter here. No jarring cosmopolitan Muzak of subway and construction, rock and rush-hour voices. We are protected. The water that surrounds this island absorbs the din of the other world. Yes, it is quiet up here.

But when I return to my listening post at the hammock, I know that I hear more sounds than silence. The motors of passing lobster boats, the foghorn across the bay, the language of a dozen different birds.

Slowly, I sift through the hundred sounds that form this rural chorus. A honeybee shopping the rose hips in front of the porch, a vole rustling through the bushes, a hawk piping its song above me. If I concentrate, I imagine that I can even make out different voices of the wind moving through alder, bayberry or birch.

When I walk the island roads, I hear my own footsteps on the dirt. When I read, I hear the pages of my book turn. With time, I may even be able to distinguish the separate sounds the incoming tide makes lapping at seaweed or rock or mussel bed.

It has taken me a week to tune into these low decibels. To really hear the quiet. I do not live my urban life at such a frequency. Like most city people, I have been trained to listen each day only to the squeakiest wheel, the most insistent, hardest-rock level of audio demands.

The sounds of my urban life are manufactured to compete with one another. The honk of a horn, the ring of a telephone, the alarm of a clock, the siren of an ambulance. For the most part, they issue orders: Pay Attention to Me! They are all deliberately loud and louder, programmed to jar us into some reaction. Move into traffic, pick up the phone, wake up, get out of the way.

Without even knowing it, we are assaulted by a high note of urgency all the time. We end up pacing ourselves to the city rhythm whether or not it's our own. In time we even grow hard of hearing to the rest of the world. Like a violinist stuck next to the timpani, we may lose the ability to hear our own instrument.

Some of my friends by now have senses so damaged by the urban cacophony that they squirm when they are left alone with crickets. They cannot adjust to country music. And yet it seems to me that it is only when we leave behind the alarms and bells and buzzes and sirens, all these external demands, that the quietest sound of all comes into range: our inner voice.

George Eliot once wrote, "If we had keen vision and feeling of all ordinary human life, it would be like hearing the grass grow and the squirrel's heart beat and we should die of that roar which lies on the other side of silence." I think of that sometimes. How overwhelming to literally hear the life story of everyone we meet. But I think more often of the roar that keeps us from silence, the roar of daily life that makes it "impossible to hear myself think."

Up here, anyway, it is quiet. Quiet enough to hear a pen scratching across the page. Quiet enough to hear someone breathing or thinking. But soon the patterns of my own life will lead back into the city. I'll follow the highway like a stream of sound to its source.

I will take a lot of things home with me. A handful of yellow periwinkles, a bunch of sea lavender, even some raspberry preserves. But how do you put up a batch of country quiet for the long urban winter?

AUGUST 1986

TAKING UP FIDGETING

HAVE YOU TRIED jogging only to learn failing? Have you started aerobics and ended up in orthopedics? Do you own running shoes, tennis shoes, racquetball shoes and wear only slippers? Did you begin lifting weights only to return to lifting forks?

Now at last there is a sport for the sportsorexic, an activity that everyone can do, a magic way to lose weight without pulling your hamstrings or getting your hair wet. It's called fidgeting.

You remember fidgeting. It's what your poor misguided grammar-school teacher told you to stop doing. Indeed it may be those teachers who are to blame for enlarging American hips in the attempt to enlarge American minds.

But in today's leaner, meaner America, a new crop of scientists has inadvertently begun a revival of this much maligned habit. A National Institutes of Health research team has discovered that the subspecies of Americans who squirm, shake their legs, and tap their fingers actually wiggle away hundreds of calories every day. Hosanna!

In the study they designed, 177 volunteers spent twenty-four hours apiece in a room having their "spontaneous physical activity" measured. Their movement was limited to "(a) strolling around within the chamber and (b) movements of the limbs with little displacement of the body's center of gravity." In other words, fidgeting.

Some of the people burned up a mere 100 calories. But others burned up 800 in the persistence of their assorted nervous habits, without even donning a sweatsuit. What we're talking about here is a real scientific breakthrough. So what if an athlete can burn 360 calories an hour bicycling, 480 calories an hour skiing. Fidgeting is a sport you can do any time and any place: during an office meeting, on a blind date, trapped on the subway.

The researchers say that the level of "spontaneous physical activity" in any individual is inherited. There may be a fidgety gene. Indeed, the study was done to help explain why some people can naturally eat more and weigh less than others.

But anatomy has never yet stopped an American from the pursuit of a lean destiny. Anything can be learned for the sake of bodily self-improvement, even an overhead serve and a taste for bean curd. If only those people who were genetically fit took aerobics, where would the tights industry be today?

If fidgeting burns calories, then Americans will learn how to fidget. We may even open a new chapter in the history of the diet industry of the United States.

Welcome to the world of the Fidget Diet. By February, *Woman's Day* will feature a cover story: 25 Ways to Fidget to a New You! *Glamour* will follow that up with a real-life story, accompanied by before and after photos, of one editor who fidgeted fifteen pounds in five weeks.

In the spring we will see a best-selling diet book entitled *Fat or Fidget*. The book will set up a goal of three hours of seat squirming a day.

Meanwhile, the health clubs who found their clientele drifting away to this solitary squirm will organize group lessons to take place in drained swimming pools and converted racquetball courts. In Beginning Fidgeting, people will learn to twist their hair, wiggle in their chair and jiggle their feet. In Intermediate, they will do all of the above at the same time, not to mention the crunch: two hundred repetitions of crossing and uncrossing legs. There will be a special class offered, Fidgeting the Amniotic Fluid, for pregnant women who want to be able to give their children the proper prenatal environment.

Needless to say, the most committed will demand a wardrobe to go with their activity. Color-coordinated hair shirts and Harris tweed underpants will be a useful aid to constant motion. They will be worn even at home to accompany the best-selling videotape of Jane Fonda urging, "Squirm, squirm, squirm."

But all this will be of little avail until we take our newfound knowledge of weight-control-through-perpetual-motion and reach children in their bodily formative years. Are there preschoolers in your house who sit quietly through the dinner hour? Do your children spend long hours in the car looking peacefully out the window? Don't wait another minute. For the sake of their future waistlines, look these creatures in the eye sternly and utter the cry of the times: "Start fidgeting!"

PART FIVE

WOMEN

Women who want it all have typically had to do it all. An offer to ride on the mommy track may look like a sensible compromise or it may look like capitulation.

WORKING GIRLS

AS THE CREDITS rolled into *Working Girl*, the opening shot revealed a yellow Staten Island ferry as it chugged its weary way to Manhattan. Where had I seen this boat before? Didn't this ferry make the same cameo appearance in the opening shot of *Wall Street*?

As the working girl (Melanie Griffith) started pretending to be a boss, it was déjà vu all over again. Wasn't that the act that mailroom boy Michael J. Fox did in *The Secret of My Success?*

In the last year or more, there have been enough movies about how people succeed in business—sneakily—to make any self-respecting CEO reach for the antacid. For the most part, they have featured young, hungry, frustrated outsiders from Kansas, Queens or Staten Island who are closed out of the action in the Big Apple because they didn't come from the right families, the right towns or the right colleges.

These movies are new variations on the class-conscious themes of the 1930s, when the working-class kid was competing with some high-society snob for true love. Back then, the outsiders were always trying to get the girl or the guy. Now they're trying to get the company. In the thirties, they wanted to make a marriage. In the eighties, they want to make a deal.

But what is different about *Working Girl* and what got it a certain attention and boffo reviews is that it features women playing the games that mother never taught them. Both the villain *and* the heroine, boss *and* secretary, insider *and* outsider, are females, sisters under the silk.

In a sense, *Working Girl* begins where *Nine to Five*—a movie written straight out of the sisterhood-is-powerful manual of the 1970s—left off. Melanie Griffith, as Tess McGill, is desperately trying to get out of the secretarial pool. But all that the men offer her is, uh, lateral movement.

Hope springs when Tess is assigned to work for Sigourney Weaver, who plays Katharine with her good bones, breeding and business-school background. Katharine says, "Consider us a team" and Tess believes "it's like she wants to be my mentor."

The plot then thickens into a post-feminist or maybe a disillusioned-feminist flick. It becomes a story of the era when just enough women have moved up the ladder to shatter the dream of sexual solidarity.

Tess soon discovers that women can also oppress their secretaries and steal their business ideas. And the movie settles down to take a good hard look at the disappointed expectations of the eighties. The expectation that somehow or other when women got power they would be better than "that," better than men.

Nine to Five predicted that after the revolution it would be all day-care centers and solidarity. The premise of *Working Girl* is that, during the evolution, the daughters and sisters of the establishment look a lot like their fathers and brothers.

This subtle and disappointed idealism can be seen on or off the screen. It infuses a strain between women who manage and the women they manage—whether it's doctors and nurses, account managers and typists, management trainees and clerical workers.

For every woman who prefers working for a female there is another who feels she's gained nothing by the advancement of women except another layer of human beings over her head. The woman in management is often judged by the (male) standards of her peers and the (female) standards of her workers.

The woman who has gotten ahead is expected—often expects herself—to be more sensitive to the women who work for her and tougher than the men who work beside her. To be twice as good in every way.

Katharine, the boss as bitch, certainly fails that test. She made it into the entering class of women by being as cutthroat as any man. She's hardly a sympathetic figure. But when you get down to it, she is punished by the screenwriters, and punished brutally—stripped of her job and her man—for not being better than men. That's a sentence that seems familiar.

Finally, what makes this a truly post-feminist flick is that not even the heroine really expects that women can change the system anymore. Tess just wants a chance to get in it. Indeed, she turns herself into Katharine, taking everything from her accent to her wardrobe to her boyfriend.

In the last scene of the movie, our heroine wins the symbol of success: The secretary gets a secretary. But the only progress she promises is that, as a boss, she'll get her own coffee. Solidarity forever. Hold the cream.

JANUARY 1989

HANDS-OFF HARASSMENT

ELIZABETH REESE doesn't fit the public profile of a victim of sexual harassment. She isn't a secretary or a mine worker. She wasn't backed into a corner of her office or chased around the desk. She wasn't propositioned or threatened with the loss of her job. Nobody laid a glove on her.

Nevertheless, this 33-year-old Washingtonian has in her bank account a freshly minted check for $250,000 in damages for sexual harassment. In a District of Columbia courtroom last fall, she beat the odds and beat the indifference of a firm that refused to pay attention to a pattern of verbal abuse.

Three years ago, an attractive, self-possessed young professional woman who had never encountered sex discrimination was greeted by her superior with these words: "Elizabeth, do you f— for the firm?" From then on, as she said in court, this man persistently told her that she should prostitute herself for business, and then told others that she had. His incessant, lewd inquiries into her sex life and his insinuations tracked and finally stalled her career in marketing at the Washington branch of the architectural-design firm, Swanke, Hayden & Connell.

"I had all the usual thoughts," says this woman. "Am I being too sensitive? Am I bringing this on myself? Am I doing something to intimidate this man? This kind of thing destroys your self-esteem. It gets you wondering about your capabilities and your objectives."

Beth Reese tried everything she could imagine to deal with the situation herself. She tried making jokes. She tried confrontation. She tried, one after another, going to the partners in the firm. "Nobody took it seriously." The same firm that restored the Statue of Liberty let the woman in the office be smeared.

Because she liked the work, because she was good at it, because the harassment came from one manager, "I took it and I took it." The very last straw, the very last day, was when Reese saw this man approach a colleague, seven months pregnant, with a bent coat hanger in his hand. Looking directly at her womb he said, "I guess I am too late for this." Beth Reese then and there decided to quit and to sue.

"This man took my job away from me. I couldn't perform my work. This man reduced me to a wreck. This man put a screeching halt on my career," says Reese, who still struggles to maintain her composure when she talks about her year at Swanke.

"When she came into the office, she looked like a rape victim without the bruises," says one of her lawyers, Susan Brackshaw, with just an edge of melodrama. "She was shaky, self-questioning. Every woman who comes in on this kind of case says, 'I just know you aren't going to believe me.' Each one feels like an isolated being."

The issue wasn't whether this man was a sleaze. Or whether the firm was guilty of bad management and wild insensitivity. Sleaziness and bad management aren't illegal. The question was whether verbal attacks—with the knowledge of the company—would be accepted by the jury as harassment.

There are two sorts of sexual harassment that fit the definitions of sex discrimination. One is called quid pro quo, when an employee is required to engage in sex to maintain her job. The other is when an employer creates a hostile or offensive work environment. As one court put it: "A requirement that a man or woman run a gauntlet of sexual abuse in return for the privilege of . . . work . . . can be as demeaning . . . as the largest of racial epithets."

The lawyers who took this case to court worried that a jury might say, "This is the modern world, this is the way people talk and behave in the business big leagues." Victories in these cases were spotty enough to give them pause. "My lawyers asked me what my goals were in filing the suit," remembers Reese. "I wanted someone to make this man stop. Even if I took it to court and lost, I would have made someone wake up."

But the jury of seven women brought in a verdict that would wake up even a $29-million-a-year corporation such as Swanke. When the lawyers' fees are added to the judgment, the bill is close to $750,000. Her tormentor, by the way, is no longer there.

As for Reese? "I feel as if I've been circling National Airport for two years. It's changed everything in my life. I don't know that I'll be as naive and trusting; I'm afraid I'll be hard and cynical."

But such a case as this has a ripple effect, encouraging other women and warning other companies. A judgment against hands-off sex harassment is still rare. Reese is just beginning to understand that hers is more than a personal victory.

MARCH 1987

HOW TO CLOSE A CLINIC

IN MY TOWN, there is a women's health clinic. To go there, whether you need a pap smear or pregnancy counseling, you have to run a gauntlet of anti-abortion picketers.

I have something in common with that crew. I would also like to close down the abortion business of that clinic, send their vacuum aspirators and surgical tools to some museum of medical history.

In my fantasy, the abortions would be phased out because every pregnancy was a welcome one. But in the real world of imperfect and sometimes desperate human experience, I put my hopes on a new pill to replace the surgery. The pill called RU-486.

These are two distinct ways to close an abortion clinic. Make it illegal or make it unnecessary. And right now they are in a conflict that is generating extraordinary heat.

In the course of one dramatic day last week, the pill RU-486 was abruptly taken off the world market by its European drug maker. Roussel-Uclaf did this under intense pressure from anti-abortion groups. The very next day, it was ordered back on the market by the French government. The official called it the moral property of the women of France. On the day after that, in the United States, pro-lifers by the hundreds targeted clinics all over the country in a planned protest against abortion.

If the international conflict over the pill was explosive, if the sidewalk demonstrations in America were especially intense, it is no wonder. The abortion debate is now in a new and climactic phase of conflict, revolving around technology and law. Can a law stop the technology from spreading? Can the technology make an end run around any law?

RU-486 and its look-alike drugs make abortion as private as a prescription pad, as personal as swallowing a pill. For this reason, Faye Wattleton, the president of Planned Parenthood, says: "The right-to-lifers are fighting the last gasp. If these drugs get to the market it is really all over."

Chemically, this pill prevents the cells in the lining of the uterus from getting progesterone. Without progesterone the wall of the uterus breaks down just the way it does for menstruation. RU-486 can prevent a fertilized egg from ever implanting in the uterus, or it can ensure that an implanted egg sloughs off. And it can do this in the earliest days and weeks of pregnancy, before a surgical abortion is possible, before a fetus is even formed.

In short, the drug makes abortion easier, safer, less traumatic, less expensive. To some, there is good and bad news buried in that simplicity: RU-486 could also increase the number of women using abortion as birth control. But the doctors who created a storm of protest over the brief banning of RU-486 reminded the world that 200,000 women die every year from botched abortions in countries where doctors are few and facilities are far between. In addition, this pill may be used in treating breast cancer and ectopic pregnancies.

But today, RU-486 is unavailable in the United States. The large American drug companies that aren't intimidated by "controversy" are terrified by liability suits. Anything to do with reproduction sends them skittering. Inevitably, though, a small drug company will ask to market this drug. When that happens, we will see the last major battle over reproductive rights.

This fall, almost against the candidates' will, abortion became a campaign issue. In the aftermath of the first debate, we learned the Bush way to close an abortion clinic: by making criminals out of doctors, though not their female "victims."

What would be the effect of the new technology on this old argument? Once the abortion pill is available in the black market, could we still call the woman who buys and takes these pills a "victim" or would she be a criminal? What of the mother who smuggles a pill in to that 12-year-old? What of the 12-year-old?

The right-to-lifers know that the abortion pill is their most potent enemy. That is the reason behind the pressure on the drug companies. Once there are no clinics to protest, no fetuses to photograph, no clinic staffs to blame, abortion is most obviously, most completely, a private matter. The right-to-lifers don't want abortion to be easy, or painless, or a choice.

But even if this opposition manages a legal ban, the abortion pill will become available. These pills are what they call in the trade "bathtub" drugs; they are easy to make. You can get such pills over a drug counter in Thailand today. Anyone who believes we could control their import hasn't checked the cocaine business recently.

RU-486 and its copycats are nevertheless powerful drugs that can be dangerous if they aren't carefully made and prescribed and monitored. So in this final debate about abortion, we come down to the same familiar argument. Not abortion versus birth. Not abortion versus adoption. Rather, legal versus illegal abortion.

Faye Wattleton, an old hand in this field, says of the abortion pill: "It's coming. The question is whether it will come unsupervised and unsafe or supervised and safe." And that's what the debate has been about all along.

NOVEMBER 1988

THE NEIGHBORHOOD
MOTHER

I
T WAS THE fourth no-school day of the year. The Neighborhood
Mother had just heard from two of those she refers to privately as her
"clients."

One of these clients was the mother of Jason. The other was the mother
of Andrew. The boys were friends of her own six-year-old son, Matthew, and
the mothers all knew each other through that chain that connects the parents
of classmates by a Xeroxed telephone list. The Neighborhood Mother was
familiar with that school list because she had typed it.

The first of her clients was a single working mother, the second was half of
a two-working-parent family. Both these work lives were inflexible enough that
the very first flake threatened them with disaster. But because there is no Red
Cross for working parents faced with a no-school day, they called the Neighborhood Mother.

So it was that by 9 A.M., the N.M. had the boots, snowsuits and energy level
of five children, including Jason's brother, under her roof for the entire day. At
times like this the woman, who had not worked outside her home since her
second child was born, nostalgically remembered mornings when she took a cup
of coffee to her desk and worried about the sales campaign for a line of natural
shampoos.

The N.M. didn't mind taking on her small extras. She understood the lives
of her neighbor-clients. She knew that some longed for her option. Certainly
she knew the alternative for her young visitors was to spend the day alone.

Yet there was something bothering her when we talked. Maybe it was the way Jason's mother had anxiously said "since you're home, anyway." Maybe it was the way a man at the last PTA meeting had asked her the classic question, "Are you working?" Or was it because even her clients regarded her as a volunteer?

It occurred to the N.M. that as fewer women could or did make the choice to stay at home with their own children, more and more was expected of them. In the past year, she had been room mother, PTA representative, had gone on three school trips as bus monitor, and brought cookies and juice for as many birthdays. Because she was home. Anyway.

The N.M.'s name was listed under "In Case of Emergency" for no less than half a dozen kids, including her own nieces, who had spent two sick days on her daybed. Two or three times, when the baby-sitter hadn't shown up at a friend's, she had done after-school care for two or three more.

It wasn't just child care, mind you. In the weeks before Christmas, the United Parcel delivery man had been at her door often enough to start a rumor, if there had been any neighbors around to gossip. He left a streetful of packages for pickup by their owners. She also held keys to the houses next door, and at one time or another had let in a repairer or deliverer to each of them.

The woman was not oppressed by this. She could and did say no. But she wondered sometimes whether anyone knew about her multi-service center. Knew how many depended on how few women who were home. Anyway.

The N.M. thought about all this especially hard because next year she would in all probability be closing down her center and reentering the work world. This endangered species would lose another member due to the environmental pressures on a single paycheck. How would she replace herself?

Was it possible, she wondered, to create a semi-professional network of Neighborhood Mothers and Fathers each on a retainer for school trips and no-school days, with a fee schedule that might include sick days? Was that too mercenary?

What about swapping then, or compensatory time off, as they say in the business world? For every car pool and after-school project, every sick or snow day, each client could return the favor with equal hours of child care or maybe even—this is her fantasy—an occasional housecleaning. And what about a workplace that factors in snow, not to mention children?

Her point is that we are running the 1980s world along the 1950s model. Once almost every family had its wife and mother. Now there is, at most, one per neighborhood. Yet the same rules, the same expectations, the same needs exist. There has been no real replacement.

So, she says, as the five snowed-in children play in the background, that next year she will be part of the problem and cannot figure out a proper solution. All she knows for sure is one thing. If she calls for help, she swears, she will never, ever, say to another N.M., "since you are home, anyway."

JANUARY 1987

MRS. DOLE'S EARLY
TAKEOFF

ELIZABETH DOLE is taking off ahead of schedule. This itself is a unique event in the annals of modern transportation. The woman is leaving Washington in order to become—heaven help her—a frequent flier in the presidential campaign of her husband, Robert.

But the Secretary of Transportation is taking more than the usual amount of carry-on baggage for this trip. She is bearing some ambivalence in her trip from secretary to spouse. And in the way of the world, she's also bearing some heavy symbolism. Elizabeth Dole is being seen as one case study of a near collision between two soaring careers. She took a dive just in the nick of time.

On the night of her announcement, Peter Jennings led the ABC evening news with the line, "One of the most important women in government has given up her job for a man." It was a warning calculated to send tremors of anxiety throughout the entire dual-career passenger list. If Liddy can't do it, we'd all better buckle up for a bumpy ride.

Even a GOP loyalist like Mary Louise Smith, former head of the Republican National Committee, had to say wistfully: "I guess that's the downside. She's going from a very visible, powerful position to being a helper." A Democratic strategist, Ann Lewis, puts it more directly: "It gets back to the idea that the job a woman holds is just a little more expendable. How do you put it on your résumé? 'Left job for husband's sake'? It's something a number of women have had to face."

Just weeks ago, under pressure to choose, Dole asked out loud why a spouse was expected to give up her job to campaign when a candidate wasn't: "It does begin to sound to me as if there's something different if you're a spouse." She carefully said the word *spouse,* but she meant the word *wife.*

Lest we get carried away with this, Secretary Dole is not a model of Every Workingwoman whose husband has just gotten a job opportunity 1,500 miles away. If she isn't exactly copiloting this campaign, she has her eyes fixed on the same destination: the White House. Dole is one woman who would turn the first lady from a role into a job. Her résumé is hardly at risk.

The double standard here is of a somewhat different order. An updated order.

For the past five years, the Doles have been the quintessential Washington power couple. The secretary and the senator have appeared together on everything from placards to *People* magazine as a daring modern duo. They joke that they are the only lawyers in Washington who talk to each other.

Elizabeth has never been the sort of wife who laid her husband's shirts and socks out at night. They have been a team, a fact her husband happily acknowledges: "She is probably the greatest resource in my campaign." Together at any event, Dole and Dole are a fund-raising dream. When she's on her own, the senator refers to his North Carolina–born wife as his "Southern strategy."

Indeed, much of Elizabeth Dole's value to her husband is tied to her success. Much of the reason aides wanted her as a full-time campaign asset is perversely tied to their image as real partners. As Ed Rogers, a senior aide in the Bush campaign, has said, "She's a great asset, an excellent role model, and her independent success is very appealing to people these days."

It is Elizabeth Dole who makes many moderate Republicans, especially women, say things like, "How conservative could Bob Dole be with a wife like that?" When his image tips too far to the right wing, she pulls in the flaps. In the language of the image makers, she softens the senator's reputation, both politically and personally. Bob has a reputation for acidity, Elizabeth neutralizes it.

How ironic then that the senator wins credits for being half of a modern partnership marriage, while also winning the benefits of a full-service political wife. Even if he doesn't win the race, he has won the secret envy of many a modern man. He has all the perks of having a successful wife with none of the problems, all the assets and none of the debits.

Elizabeth Dole had good reasons for making her choice, but Bob Dole had the better choices. Did she give it all up for a man? Not exactly. Did he get it all? You betcha.

SEPTEMBER 1987

A Mother's Place in the Workplace

WE DON'T generally get lessons in new math from writers. Writers work with words; even the ones who get paid by the line have a bit of trouble with their multiplication tables.

But last week at the PEN International Writer's Congress in New York, women writers including Betty Friedan, Gail Sheehy, Grace Paley and Margaret Atwood added up the panelists for the meeting and then divided the total by two: two sexes. There were one hundred and twenty men speaking to the group and only twenty women.

When Friedan went to deliver the imbalance sheet to PEN President Norman Mailer, he reportedly laughed and said, "Oh, who's counting?"

Numbers, numbers, numbers. What a bore. The PEN conference was concerned with such lofty ideas as imagination, the writer and the state. Here was a group of small-minded accountants, literary inchworms measuring the marigold.

Who's counting? It was, of course, the minority who were counting. It always is.

Most of the women I know today would dearly like to use their fingers and toes for some activity more enthralling than counting. They have been counting for so long. But the peculiar problem of the new math is that every time we stop adding, somebody starts subtracting. At the very least (the advanced students will understand this) the rate of increase slows.

When the Reagan administration stops counting female Cabinet members, the number goes down from three to one. When those in charge stop making a conscious effort to add women to a board of directors or a faculty or a firm, they unconsciously stop adding. The minority members of any group or profession have two answers: They can keep score or they can lose.

The woman in the boardroom or on the committee—two if they are lucky— is left holding the calculator. She can risk being labeled petty and tiresome or she can stand by while other women get eliminated from the equation.

There is a new philosophy that comes with the new math. The mid-eighties have been cheerfully designated the "post-civil-rights era." Some in the establishment have declared "victory" over discrimination, the way others once urged us to declare victory over Vietnam so we could leave the field of combat.

They say that women and blacks can now rise on merit. We won't insult them anymore, we won't injure their mental health and self-esteem by considering them in percentages instead of unique digits. But by some mysterious calculation, the same men who invited women in because they "needed one" now find it remarkably difficult to identify women who "merit" inclusion. To wit, Mr. Mailer: "More men are intellectuals first, so there was a certain natural tendency to pick more men than women."

Forgive me if I step gingerly from the turf of Mailer to that of Ed Meese. A more deadly version of new math is now on the White House blackboard. Today if employers with federal contracts ask "Who's counting?" they are told that it's the government. Under affirmative-action orders, 125,000 employers have to meet "goals and timetables" for hiring women and minorities.

The government is an easy grader. In 1983, the Labor Department found that companies were only reaching 10 percent of their goals. But only fifteen companies have been barred from government work in the past decade.

Not surprisingly, the best hiring records were held by companies that were getting their records checked. Now the attorney general, among others, says the government should lay down its arms, or rather its fingers and toes.

According to his new math, goals equal quotas; affirmative action equals discrimination. It's enough to make you math-phobic.

If we lived in a post-civil-rights era, I would turn over my Arabic numbers and Roman numerals to Meese. I know no woman, no minority, who doesn't want to be accepted as an individual rather than as a class action. But in large measure, women and minorities still have only two choices: affirmative action or reaction. The sums can come up positive or negative, plus or minus.

Numbers may not be as eloquent as literary or political ideas. Goalkeepers and timetable makers may not always be welcome. But from PEN to Pennsylvania Avenue, somebody has to keep counting.

MOMMY TRACK OR

TROUGH?

THIS WINTER Felice Schwartz gave the business world a few facts of life. Using the *Harvard Business Review* as a forum, the longtime supporter of working women told the collectively powerful that, because their attitudes and policies were too inflexible, they were losing many of their best and brightest women. She gave them bottom-line reasons for changing.

But in the middle of this measured advice, there was a red flag waving. Schwartz suggested that businesses identify two sorts of women: those who put their careers first and those who are more interested in balancing career and family. The first should be encouraged on the fast track. The second should be valued at a less-than-overdrive work pace.

At the time, I expressed unease with distinctions that aren't nearly as distinct in real life. I worried that this tracking might justify a system that had fast-lane men and a few women above; most mommies and a few daddies below.

Well, Schwartz's piece bubbled underground for a while. It was passed around offices and management seminars. Then it erupted again, red flag flying, carrying the headline THE MOMMY TRACK.

Depending on your point of view, the Mommy Track is either: (1) a dream job that allows women the flexibility to do work they enjoy while still having time for school plays and deep breathing; (2) a ghettoized second-class job that fits what the employment pages call Mother's Hours.

The conflict between these two points of view has sparked a current and intense argument that is in many ways an updated version of the "Can We Have It All?" debate, circa 1975.

Then the question was whether women could work and mother. Now women who work and mother are asking whether they can head for the top without losing a rich family life. They have ratcheted up their ambitions.

They also ratcheted up their ambivalence. Those who have chosen to work some stretch of slower track wonder whether they are missing the express. Those who go full speed ahead wonder if they are missing the landscape.

They may both wonder whether the conflicts between work and family, late-eighties style, are personal or institutional. Are we really wrangling over the immutable constraints of time: how to divide up twenty-four hours a day? Is this a struggle between two sets of wants: wanting to be at the Little League and at the sales meeting? Or are we faced with these choices because of the sluggish pace of change in society, the workplace and marriage?

Women who want it all have typically had to do it all. An offer to ride on the mommy track may look like a sensible compromise or it may look like a capitulation. If a company gives mommies a special ticket to work part-time, flex-time and all that, does it create a separate class that leaves the whole structure unchanged?

At the moment, it is often women doctors who staff the HMOs for their office hours, women managers who job-share, women lawyers who work "limited" forty-hour weeks. These options may give them the best of both worlds, or they could be the route on which women bear the double burden indefinitely. It may be a new way to undermine the goal of shared work and parenting. A new way to keep the room at the top an enclave for workaholics. A new way to exclude men who want the same choices.

Felice Schwartz—who has gotten something of a bad rap in this debate; she never once used the words *mommy track*—is an advocate for flexibility and all the goodies that come with it from child care to respect. But as someone who works with corporations, she spoke in their language, suggesting concrete ways to manage flexibility, to plan for it, to program it. But can you manage flexibility? Is that a contradiction in terms?

Businesses want plans and controls. The new workers want options and individual treatment. Indeed, this may be the ultimate challenge that women initiate in the workplace.

Any business that supports a range of options for men and women short of the rat race is a welcome model. Life is long and complicated. Parenthood is as different as nursing and filling out college applications. Our interests and goals change. We want the workplace to change with them.

But what fuels this debate is a concern that a cry for flexibility could be translated into a new kind of rigidity. We don't want the desire for personal treatment to fall into a single-sex track that looks a lot like a trough. A mommy trough.

WAS THE WOMAN REALLY
LESS QUALIFIED?

BY NOW I am not surprised at any reaction to affirmative action. The issue has been hanging around so long that attitudes have hardened into reflexes.

Indeed, last week when the Supreme Court made a definitive—at last, at last—decision upholding a voluntary plan in Santa Clara County, California, that takes gender into account in hiring and promoting, the comments sounded as if they were all pre-scripted.

The winner, Diane Joyce, cried out: "A giant victory for womanhood." The loser, Paul Johnson, growled: "Putting it mildly, I think it stinks."

From the left, Judith Lichtman of the Women's Legal Defense Fund volleyed: "Ecstatic."

From the Reagan right, Clarence Thomas of the Equal Employment Opportunity Commission thundered: "Social engineering."

So it wasn't the predictable public noises that struck me this past week. It was, rather, the undertone. I heard the low and lingering rumble of those who believe that affirmative action is a pole used by inferior candidates to jump over their superiors.

In the wake of this decision, almost all of those opposed to affirmative action, and even some who support it, talk as if the court had simply chosen gender over merit. As if they were allowing employers to favor random women or minorities over qualified men and whites.

These are the same perverse or reverse rumblings heard in a thousand offices when someone "new" gets a post from which "their kind" was excluded. At least one disgruntled coworker is sure to suggest that "if Diane Joyce had been Don Joyce, she wouldn't have her promotion today." With this widespread sort of sentiment, it is possible to win the advantages of affirmative action in the courts and lose them in the public consciousness.

But if this case can clear up the fuzzy legal status of plans such as the Santa Clara County one, it can also be used to clarify the whole peculiar matter of "qualifications."

Consider the protagonists, Diane Joyce and Paul Johnson. When the job of road dispatcher came open in 1979, Diane, a 42-year-old widow and Paul, a 54-year-old, were among twelve applicants. Nine of the twelve were considered "qualified." They went before a board and got ranked. Paul tied for second with a 75 and Diane came in right behind with a 73. This is how Paul got the public title of "more qualified."

These very objective, even scientific-sounding numbers were assigned by a very subjective oral interviewing process. In the real world, there is little pure and perfect ranking of qualifications.

Paul and Diane were then given a second interview by three agency supervisors. Who were these arbiters of merit? The same men who had been selecting and promoting the candidates for skilled work at this agency throughout its recent history. Not a one of their 238 skilled workers was female.

Diane, who was also the first woman to be a road maintenance worker, had reportedly had some run-ins with two of the three men. Indeed one is said to have called her "a rabble-rousing, skirt-wearing person," whatever that might mean.

As you might have predicted from this history, the board unanimously chose Paul. So it is not shocking that the county, instead, gave Diane the job. Their affirmative-action plan was made for the Diane Joyces, excellent candidates for jobs in a carefully kept male preserve.

The scales of tradition were balanced against her; the affirmative-action plan did just what it was intended to do, added weight to her side, to open up the door for women.

As the Brennan opinion makes clear, the plan didn't discharge a white male, it didn't set up quotas, and most of all it didn't give preference to women whose only credential was in their chromosomes. It said, in essence, that a subjective two-point difference between Diane and Paul wasn't as important as a 238-job difference between men and women.

I think this distinction is important, because there is something insidious about the "qualification" issue. For most of history, the men in power determined that women were intrinsically disqualified for "men's jobs." Eventually we labeled that attitude discrimination. But when we implement plans to open up the work world, many carry along the closed mind.

Women, such as Diane Joyce, who were once barred on account of their sex are now told they were only chosen on account of their sex. Permit me a groan.

After this decision, Charles Murray, a conservative political scientist, commented that "affirmative action is just leaking a poison into the system." But the poison was already there. It's wearing the same old label: prejudice.

APRIL 1987

THE RETURN OF THE TEASE

EACH MARCH, I make a modest safari through the fashion magazines to see what new ways they have to decorate the species. My harbinger-of-spring tour through this designer world usually picks up a little news. This year the message is positively minimal: Less is more.

The skirt rose last autumn; the bodice is falling this spring. There are holes and cut-outs, ruffles and roses in all the wrong places. Women are busting out of what isn't barely stretched over. And the copywriters are also bursting—with enthusiasm for the new sexiness.

The new sexiness? If I had bought stock in fashion futures, I would have put my money on a very different costume. This has been touted as a more sexually conservative era. Women are not just being warned about the dangers of sex; in many ways, they're being asked again to take on the role of sexual controller.

The high fashionables, however, seem to be contrarians. Everybody's running for cover, so they sell exposure. The same women who are being told to buy condoms and caution on one page are being marketed décolletage in another.

Is something going on here? Just say no, but dress for yes? Are we witnessing a revival of a truly retro style: The Return of the Tease.

Those born after 1950 may have only dim memories of the stock female figure of the pre-(sexual)-revolution era. The tease was the girl who promised him anything, but gave him less. On the high-school scale of things, being called a tease was only a notch or two better than being called a slut or, for that matter, frigid. And it was the boys who gave out the labels.

The tease was the double messenger of the double standard of mid-century America. In the earlier Victorian era, women were presented as rather sexless creatures, meant to appeal to a fleshless virtue. By the 1950s however, a woman was supposed to negotiate a much trickier path. She was supposed to be sexually attractive without being sexually active.

Success demanded that you lure a man; safety that you keep him at bay. This was to be carefully managed. Sexual favors were to be dispensed in a timely fashion, coordinated with varsity sweaters and ID bracelets, fraternity pins and diamonds. Men were to press, women to resist. The path was to lead inexorably to the altar where, magically, wives were to be transformed into eager partners.

Not every young woman could maneuver this path so perfectly. Some promised too much or gave too little. And some of these women were labeled teases. "The tease" itself might have come from her angora sweater, her walk or her laugh. The label might have been dispensed by a male out of his frustration, his anger or his confusion.

Novels and movies, humorous and bitter, were written by fifties men who felt manipulated by women. But the tease was a product of an era when the consequences of unmarried sex—pregnancy—were disastrous.

Today, the one thing that has survived the sexual revolution, locked in deep storage, is this notion of woman as agent of sexual control. This is another era when the consequences of teenage sex—pregnancy—and "casual" sex—AIDS —are seen as disastrous.

The campaign to just say no is directed at girls. It is assumed that boys are pressuring them. The campaign among heterosexuals for condoms and caution has also been directed at women. But so is the notion that they must continue to appear sexy while behaving safely.

It isn't just fashions—to wear and bare—that are sold on sex. Every shampoo ad carries the message that you can wash that man right into your life. The sentiments abound. To fail to sexually attract a man is to be lonely. To succeed is to be endangered.

Women are urged back to their post as the traffic cops of sexuality. This time they're expected to push the red and green lights at the same time. What better setup for the return of the late and unlamented tease?

When you go looking for an outfit for the sexually conservative era, something special for the safer-sex ball, skip the high-fashion glossies. They haven't got a thing to wear.

MARCH 1988

SEQUEL TO THE *SILENT SCREAM*

EVERY HORROR MOVIE has its sequel, and this is no exception. Dr. Bernard Nathanson, the producer, is at it again. He has put together *Silent Scream II*, or what he has titled *Eclipse of Reason*.

Last time out, the right-to-lifers' favorite filmmaker purported to show a first trimester abortion. It was a box-office sensation, especially on the home tube. This time he has used two lenses, one inside and one outside the womb, to focus on a politically more vulnerable spot, the second-trimester abortion.

The film, far more graphic than its predecessor, was premiered in the Senate Office Building on Wednesday and released just in time for the annual Right to Life March today.

Dispensing with credits, it opens with a fiber-optic shot of an eighteen-week fetus and a warning: "During the next eight minutes, you will be witness to an ultimate act of violence. This child will be destroyed before your eyes." We are indeed shown a D and E (dilation and evacuation), complete with a series of bloody instant replays.

A good filmmaker, I am told, can make you suspend judgment. But I cannot watch Nathanson's work without wondering about its direction. Where does this doctor find the players for his films? Presumably, a patient had to permit her abortion to be filmed. Did this woman do so with informed consent about its use? Did her doctor perform the abortion for her or for Nathanson's audience? Did Nathanson pay for it?

These questions come to mind because the filmed abortion itself seems to violate proper medical procedures. The insertion of a fiber-optic camera, the apparent use of general anesthesia, the surgical techniques described as unskilled by other physicians all put the woman at greater risk, though they show a clear picture of the fetus.

This is symbolic of the Nathanson cinematic and political style. His lens looks straight through the woman, as if she were an invisible vessel. The pregnant patient is faceless, reduced to a bit role as villain or, to be more specific, murderess. We learn nothing about her, her life, her health, nor the reasons that she chose abortion. All we know is that she bleeds.

Nathanson plays to an audience that is uneasy about abortions that take place after the first trimester. Most of us are. At some point we are legally allowed to abort a fetus that can also be saved. The law, as Justice O'Connor wrote, is on a collision course with technology.

Today, 92 percent of abortions are done in the first trimester. Only 1 percent are done beyond twenty weeks. In practice, we are already restricting the outside limits of abortion.

But the dilemma ignored in this polemic is that those who choose abortion in the sixteenth week or the eighteenth week are most often teenagers who haven't been able to face their pregnancies or their parents. The rest of second-trimester abortions are chosen largely by women who have serious health problems or have found they're carrying abnormal fetuses.

At the risk of competing for most horrific story line, Dr. William Peterson, the head of obstetrics and gynecology at the Washington Hospital Center and someone who has performed a number of second-trimester abortions, says, "We've had women come in where the fetus has no head, or the kidneys aren't developed, or with serious neural-tube defects where the child may be a vegetable or have very marginal capabilities." The ethical questions are far more complex if you air the real stories.

Nathanson lumps all second- and third-term abortions into what he repeatedly calls "late abortions," implying that these are all viable fetuses. He implies also that third-trimester fetuses are being aborted by D and E and aborted as late as eight months. As Peterson points out, even to save the life of a mother, an eight-month fetus is not aborted, it's delivered.

At the end of this film, in his best medical voice, Nathanson intones, "Abortion, all abortion, is violence ... there is no rightful place for violence in a world of reason." Indeed there is a place for reason, for reasonable debate about midterm abortions. But it does not have room for the man who originally called this tract *Revelation and Nightmare*.

Nathanson does not reason, he manipulates. He doesn't make documentaries, he makes propaganda. The scary part of his horror films is that the central character—the woman—keeps disappearing from the cast.

JANUARY 1987

THE MOTHER AND THE
MALINGERER

THIS IS a tale of two lawyers, one a mother and the other a manager. It is also a tale of malingering and macha maternity, but that comes later.

The mother in question is Joan Bernott, straight arrow and Reagan Republican in the U.S. Department of Justice. There, her reputation as a trial lawyer is, in the word of one former colleague, "legendary." After ten years, Bernott is one of six women among the top twenty-five lawyers in the department.

Her loyalty would sound like a parody coming from a less sincere soul. She says: "It is an honor to represent the United States. I love my work. I deeply respect the Justice Department. It is a privilege to serve the citizens of this country."

Indeed, the only humor that this humiliated senior staffer sees in her current plight comes in the form of irony. "One of the first things that occurred to me is that it is a plot by one of my friends to turn me into a liberal." But on with the story.

Bernott's first pregnancy was right by the book, the guidebook for high-ranking professional women who are expected to arrange birth at a time convenient for the office. (This is an upscale version of dropping babies in the rice paddies.) Five years ago, right after the birth of twins, she went to work temporarily to prepare a case for trial. She returned permanently after three months.

The second pregnancy started out on the same schedule. She even drafted a Supreme Court brief the day she went into labor. But this time Bernott committed the professional woman's mistake: She couldn't rebound as quickly.

With her well-honed analytical skills she can tell you why: "I'm a 42-year-old woman who delivered two eight-pound twins and one ten-pound baby girl in five years." So after using up her sick leave and annual leave, Bernott asked for four additional months of leave without pay.

This is where the manager comes in. John Bolton is the new chief of the Justice Department's civil division. Between the troubles of Ed Meese and the chaos in Justice, one might assume that Bolton had enough to worry about. Representative Pat Schroeder asks: "Has war on maternity leave replaced the war on drugs?"

But Bolton targeted Bernott—whom he'd never met—for his shape-up-or-ship-out policy. First he denied her request for unpaid leave because she hadn't proved a profound medical disability to his satisfaction. Then, in a bizarre sequence of events, he accused Bernott of making a fraudulent medical claim, dragged her in for an interrogation, and gave her several "options," from a demotion to a heave-ho. He treated her more like a defendant than a respected colleague.

Lest you think ill of the star manager, Bolton explains: "My wife is also forty-two, and we just had a little girl fifteen months ago. I have some sensitivity to the difficulties of pregnancy and early child rearing." Bolton, who has no visible stretch marks, actually took a couple of days off himself after the birth.

This isn't a question of maternity, he insists, it's a case of proper management. There is work to be done. "You understand she is not entitled to this maternity leave as a matter of right," says Bolton. The "norm," he explains, is three or four months' leave. Bernott asked for three beyond that.

If you think he's a bit miserly, Bolton adds defensively: "Our maternity-leave policy is more generous than most private law firms." Here we get down to it. He may be right.

Many women have assumed that the higher up the ladder they climb, the more flexibility they get. But Bernott is not the only woman of status and experience who becomes suspect at childbirth.

The top of the ladder is more like a high-pressure pyramid. The higher you get, the narrower it gets. Executive mothers like Bernott may continually need to prove they're equal to the job, and up to the men, by returning to the office before they can return to their dress size. Many do and those who can't may be doubly faulted, left to proclaim, as did Joan Bernott: "I am not a malingerer."

Our astute manager insists that this mother's absence places a larger burden on the other employees. That's a real-life problem. But we're talking about three months. Is it worth losing a superb ten-year veteran in a quibble over a three-month leave? Or are we just talking tough guy?

As things stand now, the manager says that if she doesn't convince him of her profound medical disability, the mother can either return to her job by May 31 or be listed AWOL. The good news is that being AWOL from the Justice Department doesn't mean you get shot.

MAY 1988

AN AMERICAN SUCCESS
STORY

THE WOMAN beside me is, by any measure, a success story. The business she started three years ago already has shown more than a respectable profit. She has a dozen people working for her now.

She talks eagerly about the advantages of being her own boss, the excitement of running her own show. She tells me her plans for the future.

But when I ask why she left the corporation, some of the sheen of optimism dulls. It's hard to explain, she says. She had been there for years. They were pretty good to her.

Then she sighs uncomfortably, as if reluctant to complain or even to remember. For many years, she had been "the only woman" in one meeting after another.

"One day I was sitting there while the men were talking about the game Saturday. One of the guys made his usual crack about cheerleaders. Suddenly I was just so tired of it. I was tired of having to fit in, tired of being an outsider. I felt like I was wasting so much energy."

It was like trying to work, she said, in clown-sized wing-tipped shoes. They slowed her professional pace.

This entrepreneur from Tennessee doesn't know the businesswoman I met last spring in Michigan. But her success story had a similar subtext. Why did this Midwestern woman leave a major bank to set up her own business? After a decade, she was told that she would never become vice president unless she made some changes in her style. Not her management style, her personal style.

The powers that be thought her hair was too red, her car too flashy, her presence too, uh, feminine. She was also a kind of misfit.

The third "misfit" I met last month was in Florida. Her story was even more common. The corporation she left had no room for mothers. She had not been able to be manager and mother in the same schedule. There was no room in their business structure for change and so she went into partnership with another young mother. Their financial and family planning are now in a profitable sync.

These are not the only management "misfits" that I have met. Not by a long shot. But sooner or later, all three of these women will pop up in some puff piece, some personality profile praising the new wave of women entrepreneurs. And it is clear to me that their success is in many ways a corporate loss.

Women-owned small businesses are the fastest growing part of the economy. Something to brag about. Nearly four times as many women as men have gone into business for themselves in the past decade.

We don't keep records on how many of these women are refugees or deserters or escapees (choose one of the above) from larger corporations. We don't have data on how many of these women left because they got tired of adapting to the corporate style or life-style.

Indeed their former bosses and colleagues might be surprised, because these were not the kind of women to cry sexism at the meeting. Nor are they the kind to sign their letter of resignation, "Your former misfit." The best and the brightest are also, by my sample, the most likely to just pack up their energy and leave. But anyone who talks to these successes hears the same set of stories.

There are similar tales, I am sure, from male entrepreneurs. There are blue-jeaned men who feel trapped in three-piece corporations. There are men who feel they can't push through the ceiling, men who want to make their own rules and hours. They, too, choose to be on their own.

But women are still, almost by definition, aliens in most corporate cultures. Those who were once satisfied, even pleased just to be allowed in to this male world, are increasingly restless in the place.

The new breed are among the liveliest, most exciting businesspeople I meet. I don't want to read failure into their personal success. But few are starting the next IBM. Few will become the employers of hundreds and thousands.

And as they leave larger firms, those work places are diminished. They lose another agent for change. More to the point, as these entrepreneurs walk out the door, one by one, American corporations lose another source of ideas, of innovation, of energy.

And sometimes, after I have heard these success stories, I wonder how many of their old colleagues and bosses ever realize the gap left by another "misfit" who dropped a pair of old floppy wing tips beside the exit door.

PART SIX

HIGH-TECH LIVING

We are less accepting today of accidents, frailties, even "acts of God," because we depend less on nature and more on technology.

USER-HOSTILE

I AM mechanically illiterate. I cannot blame my mother for this one. I inherited the deep disability from both sides of my family.

To the best of my knowledge, my father never made a household repair, with the single exception of changing a fuse. This was a task he managed to cloak in such mystery that my sister and I would gaze in admiration when he descended the cellar stairs in darkness and returned in a halo of resurrected light.

As for the one machine he used, the car, my father had only the fuzziest notion what made it go forward or backward, let alone what made it break down. It is my impression that he regarded the stick shift as a kind of wand.

So I read with some bemusement the latest survey from the National Science Foundation. They proved to their dismay that large numbers of Americans do not know a double helix from a cross stitch. By our own admissions, only one in three Americans claims to know what a molecule is; one in six claims a clear understanding of DNA; one in three, of radiation.

The survey/quiz master, Jon Miller, noted that the people who knew the least about science were the most superstitious. Moreover the people who ranked lowest in science literacy felt they had "little control over their own fate" and that they had to depend on experts. I was not surprised by all this. There is so much more information about the scientific world than there was a generation ago that we have all increased our opportunities for ignorance. There are more things not to know.

What I now realize, though, is that it's equally true in our everyday domestic lives. The machinery that we deal with is so much more complex that it is possible to become dysfunctional at a much higher level of performance.

I, for example, have outdistanced my father's mechanical incompetence by technological leaps and bounds. This is an accomplishment like the old Woody Allen line: Success has helped him to get refused for dates by a better class of women.

But with all respect to the National Science Foundation, I believe it is not deep science but middle and high tech that infects our everyday lives with incompetence. Even those of us who can define *and* spell deoxyribonucleic acid often have "little control over their own fate" in electronic households.

Consider the number of machines that have entered my family since my father's triumphal processions to the fuse box. I have an oven which, in concept, can itself turn on, cook the food, then turn itself off while I am at the office. It's been four years now and I have yet to figure it out.

In the den, there is a VCR that can record twelve separate TV shows on twelve separate channels over time. After a private tutorial session with a man of saintly patience, I had this under control. When we got hooked up for cable TV, however, one system broke down and another never successfully emerged.

The latest answering machine I live with but cannot work promises to answer the phone *and* deliver messages from remote places. It even has a code for secrets. I regard that code as unbreakable. When the machine and its real owner leave for college, it may learn some tolerance for human beings.

I do not, blessedly, have one of those coffee makers you set at night, or a fancy stereo that comes with indecipherable buttons, or a washing machine with thirty-two options. But I feel put upon by the electronic demands of living in a modern home. There is nothing you simply turn on anymore. You have to program.

In truth, no "molecule," however misunderstood, would make me or many fellow illiterates feel this powerless. Molecules mind their own business. The real culprit is a user-hostile appliance.

I console myself with the myth that I have chosen to flunk mechanics. I can either learn how the U.S. Senate works or how to get my oven to roast a chicken while I'm at the office learning how the Senate works. But the National Science Foundation people are right: The less you know about something, the more superstitious you are. The more you believe in magic.

Take this word processor. All I can tell you is that for some mysterious reason it obeys my "commands." In a moment I will add a few mystical letters to the top of this column. I will then press a button, add an eye of newt, spittle of toad, and instantly it will travel four hundred miles south. How? Why? It's abracadabra to me.

JUNE 1986

TESTING THE FUTURE

A FRIEND of mine, prone to misplacing her keys and the names of colleagues, marks this weakness with some offhand remark about it being "a symptom of early Alzheimer's." She says this lightly, mind you, but she says it frequently. It isn't hard to hear in her words the accent of anxiety.

The woman has, in fact, seen this disease rob others in her circle of their memory, and then their ability to reason, and then their lives. If each of us focuses on some future dread, hers comes with a name.

Not surprisingly, it was this friend who pointed out the article. A biochemist, Miriam Schweber, has announced a new blood test that may diagnose Alzheimer's in its early stages, that may indeed be used in the future to identify healthy people who are at risk. Would you, she asks me, want to know? Would you want to see, clearly, the handwriting on the wall?

I don't answer her right away. It occurs to me that I have thought a great deal more about the right to know than about the desire to know.

Twenty years ago, doctors and families often conspired to keep the truth about terminal diseases from patients. Even today, in the glasnost Soviet Union, doctors regard openness about cancer prognoses as cruel. Yet it has always seemed clear to me that adults should know if they are sick, should have the name for their "long illness."

But what about people who are healthy now? What if we can make a prediction for a disease that will strike, not today, but in five or fifteen or twenty-five years? What if there is no cure for that disease? Would I want to know?

These are not arcane questions today, when medical futures are not seen through crystal balls but through microscopes. If a test for Alzheimer's is in the future, a test for Huntington's disease is available now and so, of course, is a test for AIDS. There are already thousands, perhaps millions, of people trying to decide whether and what they want to know.

Those who test positive for HIV infection may not get symptoms of AIDS for three or five or eight years or, perhaps, ever. It is my impression that people at low risk may express enormous desire—even an urgent need—to be tested while many at high risk express equally enormous reluctance.

The gay neighbor of a prominent California public-health official checks himself daily for symptoms but rejects entreaties that he be tested for infection. "I couldn't stand it," he has said. A well-known doctor who had a number of transfusions after his own surgery a few years ago tells me that he, too, has consciously decided not to be tested.

Playwright Larry Kramer speaks for many when he says, ". . . I don't want a sword of Damocles hanging over my head if I test positive." Yet others clearly want the verdict, even the worst, in order to plan. Some may choose the bleakest form of control (eight percent of those with Huntington's commit suicide), but they choose to know.

I do not mean to lump these diseases or decisions together. AIDS is clearly a special case. It is infectious (the men I mentioned take pains to say they are not endangering others), and there is some treatment, if not cure. Furthermore, society has motives for knowing about AIDS infection that go beyond those of the individual. There are different but real consequences for knowing a bleak medical future, in terms of employment, insurance, social ostracism.

But each of these tests may offer healthy people the same science-fiction possibility: the morbid ability to see into the future. Increasingly, scientific tools modify the unknown with statistics of chilling likelihoods. It may be possible to predict, not the day and street corner, but the likely end. And to decide whether we want a present shadowed by a future.

"Would you want to know?" my friend asked. I confess a prejudice toward information. I don't want to shut my eyes during the scary parts. But what a curious sort of knowledge this is. I can't think of it as an unmitigated blessing. In the most graphic and immediate way, it brings up all the questions about fate and free will, how to live with certainty and uncertainty.

There is an ironic thought written by playwright Tom Stoppard: "Life is a gamble at terrible odds. If it was a bet, you wouldn't take it." Now scientists are composing a tip sheet. I wonder how we will take that.

April 1987

BABY GIRL WHO

IN A FEW YEARS, you can bet on it, Baby Girl Who is going to turn to her parents and ask, "Where did I come from?" This question won't bring on the normal, scaled-down, blushing nursery lecture about sex. Oh, what a different tale these parents have to tell.

Baby Girl Who (as in "who" does this baby belong to?) was conceived last August. The egg and sperm of a couple from New York got together in a petri dish in Cleveland. What came from this union was an embryo. The embryo was implanted into the womb of a woman from Detroit.

The genes of the first woman and her husband were nourished and carried in the uterus of the second woman, who was paid $10,000 for fetus care. Then, on April 13, in Ann Arbor, Baby Who was delivered into the arms of the couple from New York.

This is a story complex enough to make the average parent long for the simple delivery system of the stork. In the origin of this member of the species, the birds and the bees had less to do with reproduction than doctors and lawyers. For the first time, the word *mother* was not defined in the delivery room, but in the courtroom.

Baby Who was the product of one woman's genes and another woman's womb. She had, in effect, a genetic mother and a gestational mother. These two women were not in conflict; indeed they were in cahoots. The genetic mother was fertile but had no uterus. The gestational mother had a womb for rent.

Nevertheless they all went to court to clear up the question of parenthood before delivery. There, a Detroit judge ruled that the genetic mother and father would be the real parents of the baby in the other mother's womb.

Is this beginning to sound like something out of Gilbert and Sullivan? *Brave New World?* Does it remind you of Margaret Atwood's *The Handmaid's Tale?*

Slowly, one step at a time, we have been separating reproduction from sexual intercourse. Artificial insemination, in vitro fertilization, surrogate motherhood. Now, in logical sequence, we have the surrogate motherhood of an in vitro fertilization. It requires a very tiny leap, more of a hop, to imagine a future embryo created from sperm donor and egg donor, implanted into a second woman, all for adoption by a third.

Who is the mother in that case? The one who provided the genes, the one who supplied the womb, or the one who set the whole project in motion in order to raise the child? We have never before had so many motherhood options. More to the point, we have never before said that a woman who just gave birth to a baby is not its mother.

I am uncomfortable enough with a technology that reduces the pregnant woman to the status of a commercial vessel carrying genes to term for her employer. I am more uncomfortable when the courts take the motherhood title away. If the egg donor is the "real" mother, then she might even win the right to protect her embryo if the "vessel" was smoking, or eating improperly, or resisting medical treatment.

The situation is even more unnerving from the point of view of the baby, who has come from the egg and out of the womb. For two or three days, Baby Girl Who was in a legal limbo while the physicians did tests to confirm that the baby was the offspring of the genetic parents. She was born a motherless child.

"It's intolerable to have a newborn baby and not know who its parents are," says medical-ethics lawyer George Annas of Boston University, "If the question is what's best for the child, I would argue for the gestational mother. You know who that is. There is never any question in anyone's mind."

The presumption that the woman who carried the baby is the mother is common law in most states. It should be everywhere. The genetic parents can always adopt the baby. It may sound odd to adopt your own genetic off-spring—what if the woman decided to keep Baby Who?—but it is the lesser risk.

All of these quandaries, like the babies themselves, are born as we attempt an end run around nature. We don't accept limits, even the limits of fertility. Men and women who cannot conceive or carry children expect science to figure out a way for them to have babies, even their "own" babies. Science is most obliging.

By now, we are so far removed from nature that we need a law to determine motherhood. How odd that we find ourselves arguing about the definition of the very first word in any baby's vocabulary: "Mama."

APRIL 1986

A, B, C TYPES

OVER THE PAST several years, I have learned about something called the Cancer Personality. According to my reading, there are certain kinds of people who are most likely to get this disease. The fault lies not in their cells but in their psyches.

The Big C types, say the theorists, are passive, emotionless, hopeless and helpless. They don't have the chemical grit, as it were, to get up there and fight the cancer before it spreads. They sort of roll over and play dead. This does not, of course, explain John Wayne's death, but you get the idea.

The Cancer Personality profile was drawn by an advanced corps of the mind/body connectors: These are the researchers who spend their days linking mental health to physical health. Some of their work shows that people who are happy at work and in their relationships are more likely to be healthy. On the other hand, people who are grief-stricken, isolated, or generally miserable are more likely to die young. This finding has undoubtedly cheered the grief-stricken, isolated and generally miserable right out of their old blue funk.

In all probability, the Big C personality type was a logical heir to the Type A executive. Type A, you may remember, charged full speed ahead into the cardiovascular unit. Together, Big C and Type A offer the average citizen a terrific set of options. We can choose between being a depressed cancer candidate or an anxious heart-attack prospect.

The cancer research, however, has gone a bit further. Today, when people talk about "shrinking" the cancer patient, we don't know if they're getting ready to call the radiologist or the psychiatrist. Some believers in mind over malignancy have gone so far as to promise cures to those who visualize good cells eating bad cells—the PacMan approach. Others have prescribed life-styles or laughter in place of Lourdes.

It's gotten to the point that anyone who gets a cancer diagnosis better feel terrific about it. If they don't have the power of positive thinking, they're writing their own negative prognosis.

But now at last there is some balance back at the tower of psycho–babble. The cancer profile hasn't been debunked exactly, but it's been downgraded. In the current *New England Journal of Medicine,* it is reported that a positive mental attitude, good social contacts and a happy life aren't enough to help advanced cancer patients survive longer or prevent relapses.

Mind you, I don't really regard this as good news. As someone with "a positive mental attitude, good social contacts, a happy life" and a perfectly dreadful family cancer history, I rather thought the psychological oddsmakers were on my team.

But the side effects of mental treatment for the physically ill were dreadful. The research managed to convince a number of patients that they were, somehow or other, responsible for their own cancer. Not by smoking, but by living alone or being depressed or not watching enough Marx Brothers movies. They wouldn't be sick if they hadn't lost their sense of humor. That sort of thing.

It even managed to convince a coterie of patients and families that the best treatment to their disease lay right between their own ears. They regarded a losing fight against cancer as a personal weakness.

I suppose it is easy to blame the victim when we cannot cure him. And maybe that is at the core of the personality research. At times, standard cancer treatment can be as sophisticated as Sherman's march to the sea. There is no penicillin, no Salk vaccine for the diseases we lump together under the heading "cancer."

Mystery lends itself to mythology. Myth rushes in to fill a scientific vacuum. It emerges as folklore: Be quiet or you'll get an ulcer; slow down or you'll have a heart attack; stop being unhappy or you'll get cancer. Myths explain the unknown: He was "cancer-prone"; she had a "cancer personality."

But it is amazing how quickly myths disappear when there are cures. I am sure there are many links between mind and body, between psyche and cells. But we know less about the way they work than about the way a cell metastasizes. A study like this one puts a check on glibness and maybe even on cruelty.

The next time someone offers to paint a cancer profile for you, tell them you are a perfect Type S. The S is for "skeptical."

WARNINGS AS EXCUSES

ANY DAY NOW, television will get a warning of its very own. I don't mean one of those stickers alerting us not to drop it into the bathtub. This is about programming, not electricity.

The warning comes from the American Academy of Pediatrics in the form of a zippy cartoon message for kids: Watch too much on the tube and you may turn into a couch potato. Children will be humorously admonished to "avoid this dread disease; be choosy in what you watch." They will also be told, "Don't just plop in front of the TV cause you've got nothing else to do."

At first glance, it is surprising that stations would agree to air video ditties urging that viewers tune out. It's rather like an ice-cream store putting up a sign warning customers to eat less ripple fudge to avoid cardiovascular disease.

But isn't that what's going around? A foreigner coming to this country would be astounded by the warnings put up like billboards along the consumer highways. Any number of goods are being marketed aggressively while being warned about artfully.

I suspect the warning binge began in its current form with cigarettes. In the 1970s, the obvious health risks of smoking clashed with the obvious political risks of banning tobacco. A compromise was devised. A public warning was attached to a private product. We let the consumer beware.

The irony in this approach is that the warning is often better protection for the producer than the consumer, whether it's the producer of cigarettes, movies or sweeteners. The cigarette labels didn't stop many from smoking, but they protect the companies from lawsuits. The ratings on movies equally mute the outrage of an audience.

Let a consumer complain and those in charge are sure to say righteously: Hadn't they seen the handwriting on the wall, the printing on the pack, the rating on the marquee?

Warning has become a high art form in the science and medical news. We are confronted daily with danger signs. We are expected to become informed about an extraordinary array of things, from the steroids fed to beef cattle to sodium levels in baby food.

In California, there is a law requiring a warning be posted on anything that poses a "significant risk" of causing cancer or genetic injury. In theory (although not yet in practice), people in the market will be faced with a full basket of information.

But even there, the onus is on the individual to make an unending series of health decisions and risk assessments, merely to get through the day. Where on the shopping list of worries should they place pesticides on the lettuce? Was this grapefruit sprayed with lead arsenate?

We often accept the notion that our health and safety is merely a matter of proper warning and personal choice.

The other day, a woman whose family lives downwind from the Hanford plutonium plant in Washington state was interviewed. Radiation had leaked unannounced and unadmitted from that plant for decades while her family had suffered from a host of thyroid symptoms. What did she tell a reporter? "They never told us so we could protect ourselves."

Is that all we expect now? A warning on the plant, prominently displayed, so we can choose to stay or leave? A warning about the holes in the ozone so we can apply sunscreen? A warning about polluted water so we can buy it bottled?

It's easy to lose the distinction between the dangers that are a matter of personal choice and the dangers that are a matter of public inquiry and control. We can check our own house for radon, cut back on eggs for breakfast and alcohol during pregnancy. But no person can make his or her choice about the air we breathe and the rain that brings acid down on us.

The television warning lies in the crowded overlapping arena of public and private decision making. Kids do have the power to turn the tube off. But the admonition that they be "choosy" viewers, picky visual consumers, is pure hype. A "public-service announcement" doesn't excuse the fact that television offers kids so little of value.

So this anti-TV commercial is more than a spoof. It's a kind of training film for kids. Soon they'll enter a world where they are treated more like individual consumers than like public citizens.

In this world, warnings are often used as an excuse. Maybe this announcement should carry a label of its own. Caution: Even warnings can be hazardous to our public health.

OCTOBER 1988

The Man Who Forgot

ALVIN C. FROST is my kind of guy. Computer-literate, thirty-eight years old, feisty . . . and conveniently absentminded.

Frost was working in the middle-level microchips of District of Columbia finances when he got into something of a snit not long ago. He wrote a letter of protest to the mayor and somebody broke into his queue and printed out copies of it.

Frost then took it into his head to change the password that allowed anyone access into the computer program that oversees the city's financial life. This action alone was enough to chill the soul of a supervisor. But it got worse. Frost let the password drift back out of his head. Frost "forgot."

When the boss and then the media came around asking him for the good word, he said, "I can't remember." Indeed, all he could recall was that the password had seven letters and was inspired by the Declaration of Independence. (Could the word have been *tyranny,* perhaps, or *perfidy?*)

His superiors then did what rulers do. They escalated. They called him names: "a nerd and an imbecile." They issued him a reprimand. They locked him out of his office. And finally, they got somebody else to break the code.

But none of that could change the pristine beauty of the moment. All by himself, Alvin C. Frost froze a chunk of the government of the capital of the free world. He did it with seven little letters inspired by Thomas Jefferson. (*Warfare,* perhaps, or *redress?*)

I can't prove that Frost was subversive instead of happily forgetful, but either way he pulled off a great computer coup. For that, I'm inclined to sign my John Hancock on his declaration of independence. I find a perverse pleasure in identifying with any guy who throws a monkey wrench into the machinery, especially when the machinery is on microchips. (Maybe the right word is *justice?*)

Like my friend Frost, you see, I work with computers—although I'm not really a worker anymore. I am a user. It says that in the instruction manual. For that matter, Frost and I and all of us are barely even citizens anymore. We are entries.

In an average week, without a single hostile encounter, I am now required to remember and to give up no less than two secret words just to perform my basic functions. At the office, where the computer knows me as USER GOODMA, I need one password to log on to what is called the System, a sinister hi-tech political term if I ever heard one.

At the computer wall where I go for money (I refuse to call it a bank), I need another. The wall will only give me cash if I give it my word. We make a deal. It's all very hush-hush.

At night I cannot even get in my door unless I give the house the password. If I forget, an alarm goes off and a computer sics the police on me as if I were an ordinary felon.

That is nothing compared to the number of numbers I am required to stand and deliver to other computers on demand. The Social Security Administration has given me one number, the telephone company another, Blue Cross a third, American Express a fourth, and that doesn't include my Frequent Flyers. *(Savages? Tyrants?)*

The fact is that I don't know anyone who isn't a system-user and/or system-used these days. King George III was a pussycat compared to the tireless electronic rule which in Mr. Jefferson's declaration now "evinces a design to reduce [us] under absolute despotism." (*Evinces* is a seven-letter word.)

So it is no wonder that Alvin Frost has become something of a Modern Times hero. Basking in the celebrity of his selective amnesia, Frost boasts that he programmed yet more glitches into the city's computer. Furthermore, the man now says that he is considering running for mayor.

Well, I say hang on to your floppy disk. We may have the first candidate who ever hacked his way into history. Allow me one cheer or at least a chortle for Alvin Frost, the populist for the eighties, a "nerd," an "imbecile" who has found the software underbelly of America. *(America?)*

FEBRUARY 1986

NANCY'S NO CLOTHES JUNKIE

WHEN I READ that Nancy Reagan was still on the borrowing circuit, I immediately started worrying about such things as dress shields and red wine.

How do you explain to Galanos if you spill ketchup on the $20,000 evening gown he lent you? What sort of an apology do you make to the Winstons if the back comes off one of the $800,000 diamond earrings and you can't find it anywhere in Buckingham Palace?

This train of thought revealed three things about me: (1) I am hopelessly bourgeois; (2) the only person I borrow clothes from is my sister; (3) I wasn't surprised.

I never thought the Reagans were cut from the old Republican cloth coat. Ronnie's $200,000 salary makes him a pauper in his set. If he had been such a creative cost-cutter—borrowing a few tanks, for example—we might not be in the deficit hole.

But within days of the news that the first lady had broken "her little promise" of 1982, I began to hear a curiously therapeutic line of criticism.

"What we have here is a striking example of fashion compulsion," one New York magazine editor told a reporter. "That woman is a clothes junkie," exclaimed a more political friend. A third, upon hearing that Nancy had worn eighty outfits since 1982, costing between $1,500 and $20,000 each, sighed, "She's got a real psychological problem."

There it was. Compulsion. Junkie. Problem. Infusing the talk about Nancy was the sort of drugspeak that has become, well, habit-forming. When anyone, not just Nancy, behaves outrageously we are likely to nod our heads and speak of this behavior as the symptom of an addiction.

Even our most barbed and personal criticisms have begun to sound more medicinal than moral. We simultaneously translate human weaknesses into this new tongue.

A bore at the party is a compulsive talker. A woman who lives at the mall a compulsive shopper. A friend found with her hand in the fudge sauce admits sheepishly, "I'm addicted to chocolate." A wife talking of her husband's endless office hours says, "He is a workaholic."

I am hooked on macadamia nuts. The kids are hooked on television. You are hooked on potato chips, *Thirtysomething*, Susan Sarandon or cherry-vanilla ice cream.

Even our gossip is exchanged in drugspeak. In any fern-infested restaurant, a casual eavesdropper can hear about a woman who is addicted to married men or a man who is addicted to 20-year-olds. She is now suffering from relationship withdrawal. He keeps going back for a fix.

It reminds me of the Bloom County penguin standing before his support group confessing, "Hi. My Name is Opus and I am a Herringholic. I admit I am powerless over fish innards and that my life has become unmanageable." Give that bird a fish.

The way we use the language of addiction is sloppy to say the least. Addictions are real. Ask a smoker. Ask a drinker. Ask someone with tracks up his arm.

But having a fantasy life rich in chocolate doesn't qualify as a drug problem. You can indulge in a series of bad love affairs without having a chemical dependency. And you can actually do something wrong without being certifiably sick.

Drugspeak is at once damning and forgiving. The subtext is the excuse as well as the admission that "I can't help myself." The way that notion has crept into our everyday conversation, infesting our criticism and self-criticism, undermines the sense that average people are in control of their own lives.

This is especially ironic in the case of Nancy Reagan, whose whole pitch against drugs—real drugs, not love potions and clothes fixes—has been to encourage kids to make the right choice: no. It's more than peculiar to find her judged and diagnosed in a language she surely wouldn't approve of.

The first lady doesn't need to be sent to Borrowers Anonymous. I suspect that she rationalized her loans and their secrecy. I'm also sure she was wrong.

She lied about it. She was caught. She's embarrassed. But it's a Galanos on her back, not a monkey.

OCTOBER 1988

HIGH-TECH FAMILY

WHAT A LONG, long way from May to October. In May, Patti Frustaci gave birth to America's first septuplets. In October, she and her husband Sam filed a lawsuit against the doctor and clinic that made her fertile.

In May, the excited father of six live babies told one press conference, "We at least have a basketball team." In October, the attorney for the parents of three remaining infants told another press conference: Sam and Patti "are literally prisoners in their own home."

In the spring, the cover of *People* magazine proclaimed, OH, WHAT A BIRTH-DAY!" In the fall, there was a small item carried on the wires: PARENTS OF SEPTUPLETS SUE.

In some ways the progression from delivery room to courtroom was as predictable as the transition from spring to fall. But hardly as natural. The Frustacis' story is a modern high-tech drama, a tale of human nature and sophisticated medical technology, of high expectations and deep disappointments.

At one point Sam Frustaci called his children "a gift of God," but there was human intervention in their creation and their care. Both the Frustacis had some form of fertility problem that might have left them childless a generation ago. With the aid of a drug, Pergonal, they had a son. They went back to the same drug for a second child, but this dosage produced a bounty of eggs. With proper monitoring, the couple claims now, with ultrasound imaging, they might have avoided the "catastrophe" of septuplets by waiting for a less fertile month. Instead of one fetus, she got seven.

Together the Frustacis decided against abortion. She went through with a carefully monitored pregnancy, much of it spent lying on her side in a hospital bed. Then, at twenty-seven weeks, she delivered by cesarean section.

Patti would never have conceived these babies in another era, or delivered them. Surely, none of them would have survived in an earlier time. One was stillborn, the other six weighed from a little more than one pound to less than two pounds. The *People* magazine cover featured them in pink-and-blue ski hats. But it was the myriad machines and tubes—the aggressive neonatal technology—that kept any of them alive.

None of those tubes and machines could guarantee a happy human ending. Only three babies survived to go home. All three are on heart monitors. They are being treated for serious lung diseases, eye problems and hernias. The bills so far have been over one million dollars.

There is no reason to doubt Patti Frustaci's description of this "catastrophe." She wrote, "You simply cannot imagine how our lives have been totally and radically altered. . . . I can scarcely leave the house. . . . Life will never be what it was before." No one goes through such a pregnancy, the loss of four infants and taking on the care of three very injured babies without traumatic change.

But what is too familiar and too unsettling is their need to assess blame, get compensation. At some level, the Frustacis are suing for a breach of technological promise.

The experts in this case will duel over fertility drugs and ultrasound monitoring, over whether doctor and clinic were guilty of malpractice. The courts will decide whether the doctor sealed the "wrongful death" of four babies when he helped create their life. What is equally important is their and our own expectations of medicine.

I asked the Frustacis' lawyer, Browne Greene, whether his clients would have sued if all seven babies were alive and healthy. He answered, "If it was not what they bargained for, they would have had one hell of a grievance." The phrase *not what they bargained for* echoes with me now.

What do we bargain for when we bargain with reproductive science? One perfect child at a time? Risk-free ventures? Just what the patient ordered?

When something goes wrong with our bodies, we turn to medicine to make it right. When something goes wrong with medicine, we turn to the law to make it up to us. We are less accepting today of accidents, frailties, even "acts of God," because we depend less on nature and more on technology.

The path from the treatment room to the courtroom is well trod. It's a direct line from hope to disappointment, from belief to dismay, and from May to October.

RACING TIME

THE OTHER DAY, a woman I have known intimately since birth suffered a bout of what can only be diagnosed as self-loathing. This is not, I assure you, a common condition in her life. It only comes occasionally, unexpectedly, rather like an attack of hypoglycemia.

During these bouts, she is unusually vulnerable to the hawkers of self-improvement. I will not embarrass her by reciting the list of leftovers from earlier self-loathing. Let's just mention the exercycle and the ten-pound bag of brewer's yeast and leave it at that.

This time, she found herself at the checkout counter of the bookstore with Jane Fonda's mid-life missive on health and well-being, *Women Coming of Age*. Mind you, the woman might have been suspicious of any author who opens a chapter with the following line: "In the course of writing this book there have been times when I've actually hoped I'd have a hot flash."

But it turned out that the advice therein was written in the sensible, home-medicine, everybody-up-for-volleyball style that she had come to know and love from her other attempts at healing. To wit: "We all have to work a little harder if we want to burn rather than store fat, if we want to be fiery furnaces rather than cold storage."

On the whole it was a solid, even convincing, manual for the care and maintenance of mid-life. Which, of course, made it worse.

You see, this woman figured out that if she followed all eminently worthwhile plans and prescriptions written by Jane, it would take a minimum of two hours per day. This did not include the time to drink the requisite eight glasses of water, or to put the recommended wet tea bags on her puffy eyes.

This veteran of so many literary excursions into self-health decided at this moment that health has become the ultimate consumer industry of the middle-aged. It consumes more and more of the time of the middle-aged.

The major portion goes to what is called fitness. The most modest program of back and heart maintenance involves no less than five hours a week, if you skip the shower. You cannot do your "abdominals" in the car on your way to work, the way you can, for example, learn French from tapes. You cannot lower your blood pressure running for the bus. That you know.

Today there are any number of other regimens, each requiring only minutes a day, which are added one by one along with each birthday until you are into holistic overtime. By age forty, the admonishments to keep your body together are a bit like the old warnings to keep your marriage together by applying makeup before hubby gets home. It's a grand idea, but you can only get the time if you tie the kids to the bedpost.

Fast food, for example, has been condemned by the nutritional board of health. That leaves slow food. This is the era of shop and chop. The cult of high fiber and low fat and fresh everything has increased the number of trips to the market, not to mention the cooking and chewing time, by an estimated 30 percent.

Add to that the care of the eating machine, i.e., the teeth. The woman in question has arrived at the stage of life where dental hygienists warn, "Your teeth are fine but your gums will have to come out." The average American hygienist, a major stockholder in floss, today prescribes a salvage plan, a middle-age evening ritual that has become the new national vespers.

This is to be followed by an elaborate skin-conservation program designed to roll back the tide of wrinkles. There are as many steps to the process of cleaning and lubricating the human face as there are products to be sold.

Of course, we have not yet added to this health and beauty clock the time required for meditation, biofeedbacking, memorizing the entire list of polyunsaturates, and deciding which sunscreen to apply when you leave the building to do required running.

No doubt there is some time to be saved in this health regimen. The moments you used to spend brewing coffee, for example, or shaking salt on your food.

But the overall principle is very simple. The older you get, the more time you are expected to spend on preservation. All this leads to a peculiar set of choices. The woman in question figures that she can spend her entire mid-life in a full-time effort to extend that life. Or she can live it.

OCTOBER 1985

THE HUMAN FACTOR

IN TECHNICAL TERMS, I am what is known as the "human factor." So are you.

Once upon a time we were just plain people. But that was before we began having relationships with mechanical systems. Get involved with a machine and sooner or later you are reduced to a factor.

Today, for example, I am interacting (this is what it's called) with a word processor and an entire computerized system. No matter how perfect this setup is, I have the power to botch up the results. From the point of view of the machine, I am the loose cannon, the dubious and somewhat unpredictable human factor in its life.

If the processor that I write on had a separate existence, it would probably send messages to its colleagues, saying, "You won't believe what my human factor did today. Coffee! Right down the old keyboard!" But on the whole, I am not very dangerous to the wider world. Indeed, the most common evil I spew forth from this machine into the environment is a grammatical error.

But what about the other human factors out there? Last week, the National Research Council reported with alarm that there is virtually no safety research being done by the Nuclear Regulatory Commission on the "human factors." The focus has been on the physical plants, they said, and not on the "people who design, operate, maintain and manage" nuclear plants. I suspect that it's like that almost everywhere.

The disaster at Chernobyl, the near disaster at Three Mile Island, each had its human factor and yet most of the original attention focused in on the buildings, the systems. The Challenger explosion one year ago initially was billed as a technological disaster. It was a while before the inquiry shifted from the state of the O-rings to the state of the decision makers.

At Bhopal, India, where some 1,700 people died, and at Basel, Switzerland, where the Rhine River was poisoned, we heard first of chemical leaks and spills, and impersonal safety "procedures." We heard only secondarily of workers who may not have sounded alarms or known enough not to hose chemicals. Even in the recent low-tech Amtrak disaster, the attention was first on the state of signals and only then on the signal-readers.

I suppose there's a reason for our reluctance to focus on the human factors. During recent decades, we have all become more conscious of the centralization of danger. We know that more lives hinge on fewer "things": on nuclear missiles and plants, on chemicals and computers. It may be easier to think of "systems" that can be perfected than of people who aren't perfectible.

But it is human factors who read nuclear-plant blueprints backwards. Human factors who cut corners to meet deadlines and use lower-grade concrete to save money. Human factors who try to cover up errors. Human factors who make those errors. Human factors who get cranky, careless, tired. Sometimes even fall asleep on the job. And when we try to design plants and procedures that guard against human error, it is humans who design them.

In my three-o'clock-in-the-morning fantasies of nuclear war, I have one that features a series of improbable mistakes in some silo deep under the North Dakota earth. I have another that shows a light going on in the White House and a single man who must, without a shower, without a cup of coffee, without time for consultation or double checking, decide whether or not to send the missiles up. Such fantasies are not reassuring.

But during daylight hours, most of us choose to think of the human role in our sophisticated technological society as a minor part of the equation. We accept a walk-on part in the modern world and give the machines, the systems, the lead.

Again and again, in the wake of a catastrophe, we look for solutions that will correct "it" rather than "us." The risks we live with, particularly those of chemicals and atoms, are so enormous that it is comforting to believe people can people-proof their lives. But it is illusory.

Consult my computer if you must, but no machine is more trustworthy than the humans who made it and operate it. So we are stuck. Stuck here in the high-tech, high-risk world with our own low-tech species. Like it or not, no mechanical system can ever be more perfect than the sum of its very human factors.

HIGH-TECH ANTIDOTE

THE TIDE has come in and filled up the cove. A fat, fuzzy bee has worked the last rose-hip flower in front of the cottage. I have been sitting on the porch all morning, sitting and watching.

It has taken me days to come down to this speed, to this morning of utter inefficiency. Only now am I finally, truly, totally unproductive. Able to just sit and watch.

This has been a rushed, high-priority, overnight-express, Fax-it sort of summer. It has been as scheduled as the airline timetable I carried in my pocketbook. By the time I left the city and office, I had reached a peak of impatience: The money machine at the bank seemed torturously slow. The traffic was impossible. The long-distance number that I had to redial was annoying. Too many digits.

Without actually knowing it, I had upped the quota on my own production schedule. It had begun to seem important to do two things at once. To return calls while unloading the dishwasher. To ask for the check with coffee. To read a magazine in the checkout line. To use rather than waste time. The pace of work had taken over the rest of my life.

Now I look at newspaper photographs of Michael Dukakis speed-walking with reporters at his side, accomplishing two tasks at once—aerobic interviews—and I am amused. Somewhere, surely, there is a commuter learning Japanese on the way to work. A child is being car-pooled from one lesson to another by a parent worried about being late for gymnastics.

Sitting here, idle at last, I am finally conscious of the gap between being productive and simply being. Of the wonderful, sensual luxury of being useless.

And its rareness. Do we need vacations now to learn how to do nothing, rather than something?

In front of me, the sides of an orchidlike wildflower open and close in the breeze like some cartoon mouth from a Disney character. I am amazed at the orange freckles that line its yellow throat. It is a wonderfully complex creation. I remember the line that accompanied that lush exhibit of Georgia O'Keeffe's paintings last winter. She wrote once: "Still—in a way—nobody sees a flower—really it is so small—we haven't time—and to see takes time, like to have a friend takes time."

Time. It is the priority and the missing element in our world of one-minute managers and stress clinics. But the artist knew it wasn't possible to sandwich in an appointment for awareness (from two to three this afternoon I will pay attention to the poppies) or to make friendship more efficient. They usually lose in the race of workaday life.

Not long ago, I read a report from Pittsburgh about how much time Americans waste in their lives. Five years waiting in lines. Six months at traffic lights. Eight months opening junk mail. The average married couple spends only four minutes a day in meaningful conversation. If only our tasks could be accomplished more quickly, the researchers suggested, we would have more hours for the things and people we loved.

Perhaps. But I am not convinced that inefficiency is our problem. Instead, it may be the passion for efficiency. The solution to the time crunch is not to move at a higher speed. It is too hard to shift out of that list-making, speed-thinking, full-throttle life into idle, the gear of human beings. The faster we try to move, the further we get from the rhythms of friendship and flowers.

When we rush through errands to clear a small block of free time for ourselves or families, we may end up rushing through that "leisure" time as well. In our most productive mode we are the least open to that slow, subtle pace of caring.

The great myth of our work-intense era is "quality time." We believe that we can make up for the loss of days or hours, especially with each other, by concentrated minutes. But ultimately there is no way to do one-minute mothering. There is no way to pay attention in a hurry. Seeing, as Georgia O'Keeffe said, takes time. Friendship takes time. So does family. So does arriving at a sense of well-being.

This is what I have learned on my summer vacation . . . slowly. On a porch in Maine, one American is carefully lowering the national productivity. And raising the absolute value of doing nothing.

PART SEVEN

CLOSE TO HOME

Home is where the hip are.

IT'S HIP TO HIBERNATE

WE STAYED HOME on New Year's Eve. Okay, I know what you are thinking. How trendy can they get? There she goes, flaunting her life-style. Always one step ahead of the crowd.

This is true. Let me add another tidbit. We wore sweat clothes for our New Year's Eve celebration. Yes, yes, call us slaves of fashion. Mine were olive green. My husband's were gray.

Eat your heart out, all you people who went out in black velvet strapless mini-gowns and tuxedos. How many of you discovered to your great chagrin, just as the champagne was crossing your lips, that it was now officially declared "out" to go out.

To be frank, I might not have known that I was in the right place, home, at the right time, midnight. We had, after all, been staying in long before it was the in thing to do. But days ago I heard the news on television from a professional trend-watcher.

Faith Popcorn (I did not make up that name) said that in her professional judgment everybody who was anybody would be staying home in 1988. Ensconced there, they will be found eating "mom" food, putting on a few pounds, and in general doing the very latest thing trendwise: "cocooning."

According to Faith Popcorn (does she have a coworker named Hope Cheeseballs?), cocooning and home cooking are "exactly and perfectly on trend." In short, it is now hip to hibernate.

You may wonder how this happened. How did the trend curve move right along from cocaine to cocoon? When did the chic switch from sushi bars to home-mashed potatoes? When did the *Saturday Night Live* set start falling asleep after the ten o'clock news?

I have a theory about "cocooning" which, you will be pleased to know, has absolutely nothing to do with the End of the Reagan Era or the Beginning of the AIDS Era. It has to do with age.

The bulk of the American population, that enormous demographic blip called the baby-boom generation, is at last entering middle age. Tired. At thirty, they wanted to have it all. At forty, they are exhausted from trying to do it all.

But alas, any bona fide member of the eternal youth generation can't come right out and say publicly that they're suffering from an energy crisis. It's bad enough admitting that you've quit running and taken up power walking.

I know this because I was born just before the boom, one step ahead of the generation that has lived the stages of its life in neon letters. We got adolescent rebellion. They got the greening of America. We settled down. They got the big chill. We had kids. They returned to family values. The baby-boom generation teethed on its own trendiness. By sheer force of numbers, everything they've done has been heralded as *the* thing to do. It's been dressed up and marketed in flattering packages that invariably disguise any breath of bad news.

So if baby-boom women are gaining weight, it won't do to call this middle-aged spread. Better to call it the return of femininity. If baby-boom men can't digest nachos and salsa after 8 P.M., let's not chat about emerging ulcers. Better to herald the renaissance of good-ole down-home comfort food.

And if hats and horns and hangovers no longer seem worth the effort, it can't be because of such mundane concerns as baby-sitters and money. Nor because they've lost the old ability to rebound. That would be too depressing, too down and too downscale. How much more fun to convince baby boomers that they are once again on the cutting edge of a massive cultural change.

Are you longing to stay home and go to bed early? Not to worry. It's official now. This is the year of the cocoon. Home is where the hip are.

JANUARY 1988

Time and the Tomato

LET ME ADMIT, right off the bat, that my offspring are not perfect. How many people will say that in public? Though I have raised them from infancy, nurtured them, spared neither expense nor affection in their upbringing, they have their flaws and I know it.

Take the two before me, both thoroughly mature. I must confess that their shape and complexion are just a bit off. They bear some scars, a bit of discoloration. They are a touch misshapen and carry internal marks of a genetic background that is, well, anomalous.

But when you are in the tomato-raising business, looks aren't everything. Taste is everything. These are my Big Boys. They are real tomatoes. The luscious natives of my sixteenth acre, watched over, waited for, picked in their prime, about to be devoured.

Years ago, when I first planted a victory garden (a victory over rocks, bits of glass, and carbon monoxide), I brought forth from the reluctant urban soil a much wider variety of species. I cared for an entire nursery of eggplants, green peppers, lettuce, snap peas, green beans. I had my successes and failures in this venture, and must hold myself responsible for the unforgivably neglected toddler who grew into the Zucchini That Ate New York. It had to be stuffed.

But two years ago, it occurred to me that all I really wanted anymore were tomatoes. And more tomatoes. This being the era of reproductive targeting, I decided to get what I wanted. I went back to basics and Big Boys, not to mention Beefsteaks.

Now I spend my late-summer weeks harvesting and devouring the only fruit that you salt, the once designated "love apple," the crop that Thomas Jefferson introduced to America: the glorious tomato. The kind that actually smells like a tomato. For some six weeks, I become the abominable tomato glutton. I have been known to put a tomato on virtually everything, with the possible exception of ice cream.

Yet when this orgy ends, I shall again retreat, and just as abruptly, to my winter policy of tomato abstinence. A committed cultivator of the real thing, I have come to regard unseasonable and migrant tomatoes—"their" tomatoes—the way our forefathers once regarded the entire species: as inedible; possibly poisonous, at least to the soul.

Witnesses who watch my annual rite of passage from orgy to abstinence report that from October to August, I inspect any tomato that finds its way onto my restaurant plate as if it were a hamster dropping. My husband believes that I reserve my most severe moral judgment for these salad invaders. They receive a one-word death sentence: "plastic."

I do not tell you this merely to prove that I suffer from tomato pride and prejudice. Nor do I wish to regale you with the entire and tragic history of tomato production—*manufacture* is a better word—in America. We all know how the innocent *Lycopersicon esculentum* has had its hide toughened, how it has been pushed around, squared, even gassed to death.

But every year the tomato becomes less of a fruit and more of a metaphor for our dissatisfaction with limits. Our consumer impatience is such that we regard seasons as nothing more than an arbitrary barrier to overcome. We have come to expect, to demand, year-round, uniform access to the things we like. We want everything, everywhere and always.

The marketplace whets and fills this demand. The agribusiness moguls end up spending enormous time and energy in order to create and distribute a strain of corn suitable for starching shirts, a cantaloupe useful for bowling and an entire orange shotput collection. We have more and more fruits and vegetables whose only claim to life is their shelf life. Color them plastic.

The desire to shatter the seasonal barrier doesn't just affect edibles and inedibles. It is the assumption behind Yuletide decorations in Key West and tanning salons in Burlington, Vermont, not to mention that ultimate aberration, football in August. In Miami.

My ultimate out-of-season experience, the sort of parapsychology trip that people write about, occurred in an air-conditioned shopping mall on a humid day in Houston. There, this New Englander stood transfixed, watching people in shorts and halters going around and around an ice-skating rink. Yes, I said to myself, they were skating on ice. No, this was not ice skating. Not the real thing.

As for tomatoes—the fruit, not the metaphor—I am grateful for the failure of agribusiness to market a palatable winter variety of the species. The tomato is not a fruit for all seasons, but that rarity of modern life: something rooted in its natural space, a backyard on a warm August afternoon.

So today, looking at my slightly flawed crop, I renew my pledge: I shall eat no tomato before (or after) its time. How nice that its time is now. Come here, Big Boys.

AUGUST 1987

105 AND STILL WALKING

IT IS 7 A.M. and I am about to take my dog Sam out for her walk. I know what you are imagining. A frolicking dog straining at the leash, ears flapping, racing back and forth, eager to hit the pavement. Not exactly.

I approach Sam slowly with the leash. She raises her head from the rug. I attach the leash. She lowers her head. I clap. She opens her eyes. I plead. I tug. She gradually—we're talking truly gradually—rouses herself. Finally we are off and walking at a pace that rivals the last straggler in the Boston marathon.

My dog Sam, you see, is nearly 15. By my calculations this makes her the canine equivalent of 105 years old. (I will shortly be sending her picture to Willard Scott.) At 105, Sam regards the prospect of these exercise routines with all the enthusiasm of a veteran of the Bataan death march.

Why, then, do I do it? Why do I pursue these half-mile, half-hour forced marches? How did I become this canine's aerobics instructor? This poodle's drill sergeant? The cheerleader of the four-footed geriatrics class?

Some months ago, my family decided that Sam was deteriorating, falling apart. She needed to get into shape, keep the old legs moving, the old lungs expanding, the old aerobic rate up. My family decided that it was important to put her on an exercise regimen.

About the same time, one of these alleged dog lovers also decided to monitor her diet. Cut out scraps of eggs, cut back on chicken skin. We're talking cholesterol. We're talking heart disease.

Quite frankly, I didn't approve of this plan. It seemed to me that falling apart was an entirely reasonable thing to do at 105. This is a dog that had spent her life in high-stress professional work. She'd been a career companion and vigilant watchdog.

When the youngest member of the family left for college, Sam simply retired. She stopped barking. She gave up her midday mail attack. She ceased inspecting strangers. It seemed to me that she deserved to spend her golden years in the sun spot on the dining room rug, which I came to think of as her St. Petersburg.

Now, however, as I put the poodle health program into effect—up, Sam, up—I have begun to regard her exercise regimen as an omen for my own and very human future.

My generation is the first in my species to have put fitness next to godliness on the scale of things. Keeping in shape has become *the* imperative of our middle age. The heaviest burden of guilt we carry into our forties is flab. Our sense of failure is measured by the grade on a stress test.

On television, the thirty-second morality plays of mid-life revolve around the portion of bran in our breakfast. The newspapers teach us to separate the good cholesterol from the bad. We are supposed to watch what we eat with a vigilance that once was reserved for religious shamans. Tobacco is our taboo; the exercycle is our totem.

Does anyone actually believe this will ease up in our sunset years? Does anyone believe that Richard Simmons will revert to a couch potato?

When my generation is finally allowed to retire in our seventies—having been exhorted to work that long to save the Social Security system—I am sure we will immediately be transferred from one treadmill to another. At Senior Citizen fitness centers, we will begin each day walking our stationary miles under the watchful eye of a trainer armed with a stopwatch and aerobics rate-calculator. Time will not weigh heavily on our hands. Weights will.

Remember rest homes? Remember rocking chairs? Forget them. In renovated elderly homes, complete with gym facilities, they will hold no-impact aerobics classes. Should we lag at 85, someone will immediately show the tape of Jane Fonda at 95. And when we ask our children to sneak chocolate in, they will smile regretfully but protectively and remind us to eat our high-calcium broccoli.

No, my species will no longer be allowed to go gently into that good night. We will go huffing and puffing. Take it from Sam, 105 and still in training. Left . . . right . . . left . . . right.

JUNE 1988

NETHING TO EAT

AS A PARENT who works with words for a living, I have prided myself over many years for a certain skill in breaking the codes of childspeak. I began by interpreting baby talk, moved to more sophisticated challenges like "chill out" and graduated with "wicked good."

One phrase, however, always stumped me. I was unable to crack the meaning of the common cry echoing through most middle-class American households: "There's Nothing to Eat in This House!"

This exclamation becomes a constant refrain during the summer months when children who have been released from the schoolhouse door grow attached to the refrigerator door. It is during the summer when the average taxpayer realizes the true cost-effectiveness of school: It keeps kids out of the kitchen for roughly seven hours a day. A feat no parent is able to match.

At first, like so many others, I assumed that "NETH!" (as in "Nothing to Eat in This House") was a straightforward description of reality. If there was NETH, it was because the children had eaten it all. After all, an empty larder is something you come to expect when you live through the locust phase of adolescence.

I have one friend with three teenage sons who swears that she doesn't even have to unload her groceries anymore. Her children feed directly from the bags, rather like ponies. I have other friends who only buy ingredients for supper on the way home so that supper doesn't turn into lunch.

Over the years, I have considered color-coding food with red, yellow and green stickers. Green for eat. Yellow for eat only if you are starving. Red for "Touch this and you die."

However, I discovered that these same locusts can stand in front of a relatively full refrigerator while bleating the same pathetic choruses of "NETH! NETH!" By carefully observing my research subjects, I discovered that the demand of "NETH!" may indeed have little to do with the supply.

What, then, does the average underage eater mean when he or she bleats "NETH! NETH"? You will be glad to know that I have finally broken the code for the "nothing" in NETH and offer herewith, free of charge, my translation.

NETH includes:

1. Any food that must be cooked, especially in a pan or by convectional heat. This covers boiling, frying or baking. Toasting is acceptable under dire conditions.

2. Any food that is in a frozen state with the single exception of ice cream. A frozen pizza may be considered "something to eat" only if there is a microwave oven on hand.

3. Any food that must be assembled before being eaten. This means tuna that is still in a can. It may also mean a banana that has to be peeled, but only in extreme cases. Peanut butter and jelly are exempt from this rule as long as they are on the same shelf beside the bread.

4. Leftovers. Particularly if they must be re-heated (see 1).

5. Plain yogurt or anything else that might have been left as a nutrition trap.

6. Food that must be put on a plate, or cut with a knife and fork, as opposed to ripped with teeth while watching videos.

7. Anything that is not stored precisely at eye level. This includes:

8. Any item on a high cupboard shelf, unless it is a box of cookies, and

9. Any edible in the back of the refrigerator, especially on the middle shelf.

While divining the nine meanings of "NETH!" I should also tell you that I developed an anthropological theory about the eating patterns of young Americans. For the most part, I am convinced, Americans below the age of twenty have arrested their development at the food-gathering stage.

They are intrinsically nomadic. Traveling in packs, they engage in nothing more sophisticated than hand-to-mouth dining. They are, in effect, strip eaters who devour the ripest food from one home, and move on to another.

Someday, I am sure they will learn about the use of fire, not to mention forks. Someday, they will be cured of the shelf-blindness, the inability to imagine anything hidden behind a large milk carton. But for now, they can only graze. All the rest is NETHing.

AUGUST 1986

HOMETOWNS

THE TALK on the island is of change. People who have summered here two years or twenty greet each other on the road these days and swap tales full of the evil omens of progress.

Can you believe that the town hall has put a quota on clam licenses? Pretty soon you'll need a license to pick berries. Did you see the big-city papers for sale at the store? *The New York Times,* for gawdsakes. Did you hear about the old Hamlin cottage that sold to some highlander for $75,000? It's not even on the water.

There is much headshaking, followed by an exchange of memories of "what it was like when I first came here." Finally, one says to another in rueful parting, "Someday they'll be building condominiums down at the point." The word *condominium* is uttered slowly like a five-syllable obscenity.

The scene is reenacted up and down the Gold Coast of Maine and, I suppose, up and down the shorelines of the Atlantic and the Pacific. It's like this in every rural refuge that attracts its own loyal tribe of summer people.

For the most part, these summer people have spent their winter work lives in offices that must be reached by elevators. Many have moved two or three or fifteen times until some cannot name their "hometown" anymore. They telecommunicate or travel or high-tech most of the year in a fast-paced world.

But in July, even those who consider themselves progressives in their fields resist the advances on their summer retreat. In August, they rail against each subdivided potato farm, each new onslaught of convenience, each inch of pavement that encroaches on their turf.

They want this hometown at least to stay the way it exists in their winter imagination: warm and full of clear light, with an ancient red flannel shirt on the hanger, a mackerel jig in the top drawer, beach glass in the bowl, a wonderful, waiting quiet broken only by the sound of gulls. They want it to stay the same, even if "it" is a view.

It's to be expected, I suppose. Summer people are not like the other vacationers who pick up roots each year and pack them into Winnebagos. They don't want to go somewhere different, new, unusual. What is unusual to them is a sense of place. What they want in a transient world is a right to return.

So it happens in a hundred summer places. The very people who come from the world of instant-money machines and twenty-four-hour convenience stores are warm-weather boosters of inconvenience. Having found a place of their own, summer folk become its most fierce conservators.

Let others call them regressive. But it is the inaccessibility, the unreliability, the wonderful, quirky, haphazard independence of rural life that insulates a community where children can still hitch rides, where adults can leave doors open, where a crime wave is a midnight rider knocking down mailboxes. They know from experience: What a place does not have protects what it does have.

I suppose that those who go to islands like this one are a hard-core subspecies of summer people. Water is the last line of defense against malls and modernism. The ocean may be a saline preservative against change. Those who choose islands choose also to believe that the fog can protect their refuge the way the mists and magic protected Brigadoon.

Yet there is an irony to all this that does not escape the people who measure and talk of change. Each year the world of their winter lives creates a greater demand for this small summer supply.

There are more Gypsies who follow work from one city to another and try to put down roots in summer. The special attraction of country, space, quiet, water, entices the crowds who inevitably transform them into subdivisions, neighborhood, noise. The growing need for retreat impinges on each retreat. There is a fragile ecology that separates shore from suburb.

It hasn't happened here. Not yet. Not really. There are no condominiums. People still look up from their hammocks in greeting when someone walks by their cottage.

But lately there are tourists on the main road who do not know to return the island wave. And someone, or so I am told, has just installed an answering machine.

AUGUST 1985

TOO CLOSE TO FOOD

THERE IS A NOTE inside my egg carton. It is nicely printed, slightly larger than a business card. The message it carries is a formal introduction to what I am about to eat.

"We think you will find The Country Hen very special in regard to: taste, yolk color, the way the yolk stands up and the whites don't run, and in shell strength. Our reasons for these differences are listed on the reverse side."

Dutifully, I turn the card over. There I discover that the chicken-mother of my eggs is a "floorwalker in a building with windows." Not only does this hen eat organic feedstuff, but she eats marigold petals and alfalfa, fish meal and oyster shells.

Of course, I am delighted to get to know my egg donor up close and personal, although alas, there is no photo. I am happy that she is leading a life far healthier than my own windowless office existence. I am glad she is dining, California style, on flowers, and getting the proper amount of exercise.

But looking down at the eight brown eggs before me, I don't wonder whether they are good for me to eat. I wonder if I am good enough to eat them. If so, would my country hen prefer that I scramble or fry them? Shouldn't she have some say in the matter?

As I crack two of the floorwalker's offspring into a bowl, I divine a decidedly unhappy trend in the very yellow yolks. I am being encouraged to become intimately acquainted with life-style and family of the things I devour. This violates a fundamental rule of life. Never eat anything that has a name.

By now you have figured out that I shop at one of those earthy places where the foods are marked with small placards detailing the farming practices and the overall condition of the acre upon which each navel orange grew up. It is a store that offers, if nothing else, a cornucopia of information.

Indeed, I have been waiting to find a personal footnote in the avocado bin: "John and Josie grew these very avocados on their small organic farm in California. The couple, who met at U.C. Berkeley in 1970, use their own compost and would like you to know that their youngest boy, Sam, planted this row of avocado trees in solidarity with the people of El Salvador."

But I never expected that I would be moving toward a cuisine in which each lamb roast would come certified as to how much Farmer Mary loved it. That each egg would carry a testimonial about the happiness of its parent at the moment of delivery.

I, too, am leery of chemicals and squeamish about factory farming. Yet I have the sense that the advent of friendly farming will get out of hand. We are entering an era when the very best people will only eat food that's been well-bred, hand-raised, indeed, scratched behind the ears. Purveyors to the finest will be required to prove that they were kind and caring to all the little piggies who went to market.

It does not take much of an imagination to see where this is leading. "This flank steak comes from Bessie, who was hand-raised by the Johnsons after a difficult labor. Bessie spent her first year of life frolicking around the crystal-clear pond behind the Johnson's Vermont house where she became a favorite of Pearl Johnson, who always slipped her the finest of grains."

Will the restaurants that now wheel raw platters of meat and fish for our choosing bring along testimonials about how well each item was brought up? Will our leather shoes require a certificate proving that the animals were all volunteers?

I know where you think this is heading: toward vegetarianism. But sliced tomatoes are said to scream, and even zucchini may need a certificate attesting to a happy summer in the sun before they were killed with kindness.

The truth is that I don't want to get any closer to my food. It is bad enough to have to know the cholesterol content of eggs, the country of origin of grapes, the chemical content of apples. I do not want to feel responsible for the workplace conditions and psychological profile of my dinner.

Pass me two more eggs. Crack them. Cook them. Eat them. Just don't tell their mama.

APRIL 1989

REVENGE OF THE THINGS

O N MY DESK are two articles I diligently clipped and saved from this week's papers. They lie side by side on my desktop and, I must admit, in my brain.

The first is about time, or the lack of it, in our lives. If people drew up a January list of wishes instead of resolutions, suggests the author, our first wish would be for more time.

The second article is one I should file under home maintenance. In it, an expert warns that any decent germ-fearing owner of an ultrasonic humidifier should clean the tank every day with a cup of bleach.

As a certified humidifier owner and a bona fide citizen in pursuit of elusive free time, I find myself making a connection between this incongruous pair of messages.

Maybe the infamous time crunch of the eighties is not just a product of work and family pressures. Maybe we are not all just overachievers who feel lazy unless we are listening to Swahili tapes while running three miles in a event sponsored by a worthy social cause. Maybe part of the problem is the demands put on us by the burgeoning number of *things*. Maybe we consume things that, in turn, consume our time.

Every thing, even the so-called timesaving device and energy-efficient machine, comes these days with an elaborate set of instructions for its care and feeding. Buying a machine has become more and more like buying a pet.

You get the feeling that you aren't worthy of owning a humidifier unless you promise to clean it with bleach. You don't deserve a coffee maker unless you faithfully give it doses of white vinegar. You don't warrant a VCR unless you run the head cleaner through it routinely.

And I haven't even mentioned the car.

As an owner, I am often guilty of thing-neglect. I am about as likely to get up every morning and pour bleach in my humidifier as I am to shave the pills from my sweaters. I have enough trouble remembering to floss.

But I am subject nevertheless to the ultimate way that *things* devour time. By breaking. Without doubt, the two words that strike the deepest terror in the heart of a person whose life is contained in an Hour-at-a-Glance book are these: "It's broken."

This announcement conjures up two horror scenes. One of them is a classic rendition of waiting for the Godot Repair Company. This is an outfit that estimates its time of arrival in your city as alternate Tuesdays between dawn and dusk. The other is a road tour that leads you to the remote and highly specialized factory-service representative. This is located handily next door to a motel where you may check in and wait.

In my experience, the amount of time spent transporting broken television sets, answering machines and personal computers surpasses the amount of time spent transporting preschoolers to gymnastics classes they will not remember when they are in analysis. The amount of time spent waiting for a repairer to come fix a disposal or automatic icemaker surpasses the amount spent in a meat line in Warsaw.

And still I haven't even mentioned the car.

My own major culprit in this department is the vacuum cleaner I live with and for. This is a machine that breaks down so routinely I am trying to enroll it in an HMO.

I know that I am not the only person who wastes time on the things that were supposed to free time, or enhance time. We have all become machine caretakers in one way or another. We buy some thing in the flush of desire, the rush of romance; it's only later that we realize we've made a commitment to it.

It insists on being cleaned. It demands to be fed bleach or vinegar. At the very best it sits there nagging you to make use of it for the manufacture of yogurt or popcorn or videotapes. At the very worst it forces you to take it to be fixed. It not only gives, it takes . . . time.

This is one of the ironies of a thoroughly modern life. We are time-crunched. Not just by the number of things we have to do, but the number of things we have. In the late twentieth century, things have become our new dependents.

Now, then, let's talk about the car.

REAL-LIFE MOMS

IN THE PREMIERE of the TV series *Baby Boom,* there was a moment when the single working mother of the 1980s met the fifties mothers of her dreams. Literally.

The star of the show, J. C., fell into bed after another hard day, failing to achieve a perfect score as mother, worker and woman. From deep in her subconscious she conjured up none other than June Cleaver and Margaret Anderson. But this time, the flawless mother of the Beaver and the perfect wife for father who knows best let her in on a little secret.

Margaret: "J.C., you know we were just actresses playing parts." June: "We reported to work and they tied aprons on us." Margaret: "In real life we were working mothers putting in a twelve-hour day."

In this refreshing encounter, June Cleaver and Margaret Anderson were played by the actresses from the original show, Barbara Billingsley and Jane Wyatt. It was reassuring to discover in a nonfiction moment in this fictional meeting that even Barbara Billingsley felt inferior to June Cleaver: "I was forever comparing myself to the character I was playing and I always came up short. . . ."

But the most crucial part of these confessions was embodied in three little words: "in real life." This presented in its most pristine form my favorite test on the images about women that have floated up and around for all these decades. I call it the Real Life Test.

I was first inspired to apply the Real Life Test long after June and Margaret were in reruns. It was back in the seventies when Phyllis Schlafly was extolling housewifery as the only virtuous role for women. But what was she in real life? A lawyer and political activist.

Then there was the woman who published a particularly judgmental book about how she had quit work—and others should follow—to stay home with her children. In Real Life, the woman had become a writer.

In the early eighties, there were all those superwoman stories about top executives who led seamless lives balancing home and office, without ever wearing panty hose with runs stopped by nail polish. In Real Life, they had housekeepers and gobs of money.

Now, I find myself using the Real Life Test to judge the next generation of ads that have incorporated late-eighties fantasies of working motherhood.

One is the United Airlines ad that opens with a young mother dropping her child at day care and flying to a meeting in Chicago. While her child plays happily, she works with no more than a casual glance at her watch. After a calm flight home, she picks the girl up right on time. Courtesy of United.

The other is a Macintosh computer ad that shows a very pregnant woman talking about her plans to be back working one week after her baby is born. "Do you think you can run a $10-million business from the nursery?" a friend asks. She answers, "No, I think I can run it from the den." The computer makes it possible.

I don't know much about the stars of these ads, except that in Real Life the women are both actresses. But the test comes in handy anyway.

After all, in Real Life, we all know women who travel for work have more backup childcare plans than generals had for the invasion of Normandy. In Real Life, I have sat next to a mother of a waiting child when our plane was number twenty-three for takeoff out of O'Hare and watched her hands begin to sweat.

I also know enough about Real Life to envision the baby formula dripping onto the Macintosh keyboard. I certainly know about trying to concentrate on work with a newborn in the next room.

There is a somewhat more honest tilt to the eighties. Shows like *Baby Boom* are about stress and the well-dressed single mother trying to hold it all together. (Although in a Real Life role reversal, the star Kate Jackson doesn't have children.)

But there is still a notion running like a theme song through these decades that somebody (else) is doing *it* perfectly. In the fifties, June Cleaver and Margaret Anderson were perfect mothers because they had the right temperament. In the eighties, the women in these ads lead perfect lives because they have the right technology.

In real Real Life, there is no perfection. So the best, most enduring line of all came from the fifties mom, June Cleaver, to her eighties counterpart: "Aren't you being a little hard on yourself?"

NOVEMBER 1988

JAYBIRD IN MY BACKYARD

FIRST LET ME admit that it is at least half my fault. I cannot entirely blame the blue jay, the one I have come to call "Nemesis," for his lengthy criminal record.

After all, I am the one who originally planted the blueberry bushes in the back forty (feet). A court-appointed defense attorney for Nemesis would undoubtedly describe these urban bushes as "an attractive nuisance." Berries are to birds what a swimming pool is to an asphalt jungle or a BMW to a deserted street. He might even convince a jury that this was a classic case of entrapment.

I maintain, however, that any enterprising, self-respecting creature who didn't merely want to rip off the labor of others and had some respect for private property could have found other sources. Mine are not the only blueberries within several city blocks. There is a supermarket right down the street.

If Nemesis chose my market it was probably because he liked the hours better. It was open twenty-four hours a day, seven days a week. An aviary convenience store. Besides, the price was right and there was no check-out line.

But I am getting ahead of the story. Until recently, I considered Nemesis to be a decent enough neighbor. A bit noisy now and then, but you get used to that in the city. A touch aggressive, but up here we like a tough bird. Frankly I respected him because he didn't escape south every winter.

As the bushes began to bear fruit, Nemesis began to hang around a bit, but I had no way of knowing that he was casing the joint. I thought he was admiring my day lilies.

Then, on about July 6—we must be careful with dates in criminal charges—

the jay began his career in larceny. The moment the berries turned blue, he turned greedy. The other birds in the neighborhood might have one for dessert, but Nemesis seemed to regard these bushes as all-you-can-eat night at Howard Johnson's.

Some members of the jury will say that I should have bought a net. Well, I did buy a net. This raised the cost of the berries to approximately $12 a pound and the charge to grand larceny. The net barely slowed him down.

But it wasn't the money that finally got me mad. It was the sheer gall of the bird. He had the cool that characterizes a sociopathic personality. I can call an expert witness on this. Any other bird would flee when I came outdoors, but Nemesis would not even flutter until I came within three feet. To describe him as cheeky is not enough. He had the nerve of the leader of a street gang. All he needed was a leather jacket.

Now as any poll-taker from the American Enterprise Institute can tell you, a neo-conservative is a liberal who's been mugged. The swiftest way to harden someone soft on crime is to trespass on her turf. So it was that I became a card-carrying member of the law-and-order ranks, wing-and-beak division.

Indeed there were moments these last weeks when my family feared that I would put a National Rifle Association sticker on the fence and buy a Sunday afternoon special. I took to charging at this fly-by-day criminal, screaming at him like someone in Marine boot camp. At the very least I was hoping to give him indigestion.

Finally, one glorious morning last week, I went outside to get my allotment of berries and there he was. My Nemesis was trapped under the netting. He couldn't find his way out. I had him cold.

As I approached, the bird lost his cool and began flinging himself nervously from one side of his prison to the other. And what did I do? Hopeless recidivist in the ranks of the bleeding hearts, I lifted the netting and let him go.

I wish I could tell you that Nemesis learned his lesson and went straight. This is not the case. He has been back for his regular breakfast. Twice in the past week he has been caught again in the netting and twice more I have let him out. The last time I had the distinct impression that he had been sitting calmly, waiting for me to help him out.

The reality is that I have become his accomplice if not his advocate. Let out on bail, he commits another crime. Allowed only one telephone call from his prison, I am sure he would dial my number.

I have now decided to retreat to the last resort of liberalism. If I cannot reform Nemesis, I can decriminalize him. I shall deed him the right to eat my berries—I mean, our berries—that is, if he doesn't mind sharing them with me.

JULY 1985

THESE SHOES WERE MEANT
FOR WALKING

I BEGAN WALKING before it was popular. I was, you might say, a step ahead of the times, right there at the infancy of this trend, or at least its toddlerhood.

Before I was a year old, I just sort of picked it up all by myself, without a coach or a single lesson. I don't mean to brag, but apparently I was a natural and, within a matter of weeks, had more or less mastered the trick. I can't prove this because second children don't get their shoes bronzed, but I have witnesses.

It is remarkable, I know, to find someone that trendy before she had ever read a single word, let alone a fitness magazine. Before she could say "aerobics" or anything else. This was at a time, mind you, when people still thought her baby fat was adorable. Where, sometimes I wonder today, did I ever discover the old get-up-and-go?

Now I no longer walk. I am "into" walking or, if you prefer, power walking or striding. Indeed, the child who walked to get from one place to another has become an adult who walks merely to keep her waistline in place. The person who once did it barefoot has just become the owner of a scientifically constructed, brilliantly marketed and redundantly named pair of "walking shoes."

How did this happen? I ask myself regularly, as I lace myself into these specialized pavement pounders. How is it possible that the same soul who once owned exactly one all-purpose pair of sneakers has now added her fifth pair of "shoes" to the tennis shoes, running shoes (two styles) and squash shoes that form a small community on her closet floor? Did the sneakers beget over the years while I wasn't looking?

For many years we have watched American entrepreneurs learn to make extraordinary profits selling expensive textbooks, lessons and equipment to help us do what we previously did naturally. This was, needless to say, the success story behind the sex industry from Masters and Johnson to the Playboy Channel to Victoria's Secret.

Now we are at the peak moment of a second cycle. I have joined the league of entirely willing, even eager, victims of a different marketing trend. I am another consumer who has been broken down into the sum of her activities, each requiring another set of shoes.

Remember when the baby boom receded and the population started to stabilize? In those yesteryears, the market moguls already knew that there was only one way to keep the sales chart growing. They would have to transform a constant population of consumers into an expanding market. They would have to multiply the existing number of consumers by a growing number of fully equipped "life-styles."

Alas, individual consumers were only inclined to own one car at a time. But accessories were something else. We were gradually sold, for openers, entirely distinct sets of clothing for everything from leisure to success. Every time we grasped an all-purpose outfit, like jeans and sweats, the market subdivided them into designer jeans and evening sweatsuits. We eventually stopped wearing clothes and began wearing costumes.

The fitness boom added whole new frontiers to explore, at least for those who were properly equipped for exploration. (See the Banana Republic catalog.) Today the savvy would no more wear aerobics tights on the golf course than fins on a treadmill. Anybody who would run in tennis shoes would probably play racquetball with a baseball bat. The more you did, the more you bought; one pair of shorts begat another.

The problem, of course, it that every complete set of costumes requires a quick-change artist. Consider the new entry into my fertile sports-shoe wardrobe. In order to go away for the weekend, I need to bring along my entire shoe collection, not to mention the Heavy Hands and headset. Before lacing up any one of these two-footed creatures, I have to plan. What speed? What distance? Is this a job for the walking shoe? The running shoe?

Merely striding to the tennis court has now become a two-pair operation: one to get there, another to play. Even crossing a street, I have to calculate the speed and whether it would be wiser for my back, heels and knees to change into running shoes for the dash across traffic.

I do take some comfort in the fact that the walking shoes in my possession are surely the very outer edge of this technological trend. This is the last frontier of the frantic, fragmented consumer.

After all, having sold this consumer shoes to walk in, what is left? Sitting shoes? Shoes to watch television in? Costumes for the couch potato? What color do you think they'll come in? Robin's-egg blue would be nice.

JULY 1987

PART EIGHT

MEN AND WOMEN

Ours is an era of marriage until love do us part. People once found their security in the institution. Now they seek it in the emotion. They long to witness and believe in lasting love.

MEN-O-PAUSE

I HAVE A FRIEND who is in his late forties and trying to decide whether he wants to have children. This is not exactly a new question in his life. He has talked about it through ten years and ten relationships. Talked about it with women who weren't quite ready, with women who were eager and with women who'd already had their fill.

I have another friend who is just past fifty, just past one divorce settlement and three college tuitions. The current and younger woman in his life now wants to begin what he has just finished. He has to decide whether to recycle his life cycle.

I have listened to these two for some time now, and have come to the conclusion that middle-aged men suffer from a distinct biological disadvantage: They don't go through menopause.

I know, I know. This is not a widespread opinion. The average man does not rage at the heavens because he has been denied the growth experience of hot flashes. Wishing menopause on men sounds like the sort of curse once uttered by covens of radical feminists at meetings in lofts in lower Manhattan.

Indeed, if women could vote on their biology, they might well outlaw the "change of life." It seems like a leftover from another age, an appendix of inequality. If men can have babies into their seventies why can't women?

I know more women who resent the midnight on their biological clock than men who would welcome it with hats and horns. Menopause just doesn't fit our social calendar. It certainly doesn't fit the all-American notion that we have interminable choices and unlimited options in life. The fertility deadline forces women to make those choices and take up those options.

Which is, when you come to think of it, an advantage.

If a number of single American men suffer from what the pop psychologists call the Peter Pan syndrome, it may be biology that has destined them for Never-Never Land. There is, for some, rooted in this lifelong fertility, the sense that as fatherhood is open-ended so is life. It allows some men to postpone so much, even maturity.

I don't want to exaggerate this. I don't believe that fertility makes most men less aware of mortality. But it makes it marginally easier for men than for women to be alienated from their own life cycle. It makes it marginally easier for them to postpone paternity and also to push off the realization of age.

The physical symptoms of male menopause in the current jargon include a pulled muscle, a gray hair, an elevated cholesterol count. At mid-life, men wrestle with limits. A 45-year-old will never again be the "youngest success" at anything; indeed, he may never live up to his own expectations.

But this is not a demarcation line. There is no clear change of life. There remains, at least in theory, the biological ability to start, or start again, to create. This possibility dangles over some men's lives in ways that do not always work in their favor.

Women are hardly without biological options. They have, for the most part, thirty or thirty-five years before they run out. But the knowledge that fertility is finite gives a contour to a woman's life. It heightens her sense of timing. It may even help her to feel more in sync with each stage.

In this age, our psyches are not as tied to our biology as in the past. There are millions of us who choose to close options by sterilization. But I suspect this biological difference lingers.

What I have witnessed is not only the indecisiveness of my two middle-aged male friends, but the shock that senior citizenhood brings to their elders. It seems to me that men have a much harder time coming to terms with retirement and old age.

Age seems to spring upon some men. Women, on the other hand, have an earlier warning system built into their biology. It may be easier for men to postpone the realization of age and harder to cope with it when it inevitably arrives.

I offer no solution for this imbalance and, no, I do not wish menopause upon my friends. They will have to make do with their minds. But for most of time, menopause has been looked upon as a female disadvantage. From my listening post, I am not so sure. Not so sure at all.

NOVEMBER 1986

PG-RATED COED DORMS

SHE WENT TO college last fall, carrying with her two family gifts: a sense of humor and an answering machine. By midwinter she had put together these two weapons and produced a salvo intended for her elders.

This is what her mother heard when she called. A male voice in the machine stuttered, "Um, uh, you called at a bad time. We're, um, in the shower right now. But we'll be out in a few minutes, so just leave a message."

The unsuspecting caller was not freaked out, as her daughter might put it. She waited for the beep and the giggles to subside and left a return message. After all, the mother said to herself, it was only 10 A.M. The bathroom on her daughter's floor was all female in the morning. It only became coed after noon. Or was it the other way around?

Well, never mind, this is dormitory living 1987. The national fantasy of coed showers, and the reality of coed friendships. Much less heavy breathing than laughing.

What the mother had witnessed when she visited this campus was not a seething caldron of casual sex. It was rather a comfortable atmosphere of casual friendship. Young men and women live with each other not in a state of permanent arousal but of permanent disarray.

In the morning, they lurch past each other, oozing the same unwashed charm they had in their high-school days. Day and night, they walk in and out of each other's rooms dressed in their finest sweatpants and T-shirts, faces dotted with ritual zit cream. They borrow each other's clothes and cut each other's hair and listen to each other's complaints. They are, in short, at home with each other. Male and female.

Running through her own impressions, it occurs to this mother and tuition payer how much has been written about college students and sex. Sex is easy to study, to quantify. It's also sexy.

Less has been said about the incest taboo that arises on a dorm or a floor where people live together like brother and sister, where the family dynamic depends on avoiding the storm and stress of romance and breakup. And still less has been said about friendship, plain old friendship.

When the mother was in college in the early sixties, a male friend was someone who was shorter than you. Or maybe your boyfriend's roommate. He was called, carefully, a platonic friend, as if there were something ancient and idealistic about nonsexual relationships between the sexes. And something altogether rare.

Even in coed schools like hers, where she studied with men, went to class with men, they did not live together in the real daily sense of that word. For the most part, women and men had to venture out to meet each other. They dressed for the occasion.

As her classmates went into the work world, it took time for them to develop anything like camaraderie. It isn't easy to learn to be buddies late in life. Like learning a new language, it happens most fluently when you're young.

To this day, men and women of her generation who travel together, work together, have to get through the flack of male/femaleness. When the business literature talks about this, it stresses the woeful lack of experience women have as teammates in their college years. Those who never played team sports, they say, have trouble in the corporate huddle.

But maybe the best turf for learning how to work together isn't a playing field; maybe it's a dormitory. Maybe it's not in competition but in the easy give-and-take, the naturalness of living together.

Men and women marry one by one, or a least one after another. But we work together in droves. We have far fewer lovers than coworkers. We tend to focus on the coed dorm as a breeding ground. The value of this learning laboratory of relationship may be in graduating men and women who are natural with each other in the work world.

As for the young man in the recorded shower? The mother cannot resist asking. The daughter laughs at their recorded prank. He lives a couple of doors down the hall, she says, you met him. Oh, yes, says the mother, he's your friend.

WHO PAYS FOR THE KIDS?

IT IS PAYDAY and the working mother is counting her wages. After taxes, after Social Security, after health insurance, how much is left to show for her work week?

If she is typical, the working mother goes home and pays her baby-sitter, or stops at the day-care center to deliver the weekly check. Sometimes more money changes hands from the mother of the children to the caretaker of the children than remains with the mother.

Every once in a while, the working mother and her husband hold one of those conversations about family finances. They casually or formally calculate how much her work is worth, really worth. From her take-home pay they subtract transportation, clothes, lunch, and then the biggie: child care. At times, stressful times, she reruns these numbers in her head. And invariably she concludes this arithmetic exercise with a diminished sense of the value of her job.

But rarely does either parent wonder why child care is taken as an automatic deduction from the maternal side of the ledger. Why do the overwhelming majority of married working mothers pay for day care out of their pockets and paychecks? Why is the care of their children her business expense?

The Census Bureau may categorize couples like these as partners in a two-parent working family. But in the everyday life of these economic units, the partnership is psychologically divided in a way that puts children under her masthead.

In the majority of American families, women are no longer the full-time caretakers of their children. But they remain the managers of that full-time care.

The mothers of preschool children are usually the ones who search out that care, write the ads, conduct the interviews, make the choices. It is their jobs that hang by the thread of the day-care center opening. By and large, they are the ones who stay home from work when a baby-sitter or a baby is sick. And by and large, the price comes out of their purses.

Often when a woman pays for child care, directly, exclusively, she is also making a statement. She is paying someone to do "her" work, not her husband's; paying someone to replace her, not him; to perform her role, not his.

There are any number of reasons why mothers, even professional women with high wages, assume this arithmetically traditional role. Many in these transitional times may be comforted with the sense of control over child care that comes to the person who holds the purse strings.

For other mothers, perhaps most, it comes from their image as a marginal worker, a secondary, expendable earner in a family. Mothers of young children often and anxiously reassess the relative values of going to work and staying home. For them, child-care costs are part of their ongoing tally.

But when women take this expense as their own personal burden, it inevitably costs something in terms of both self-worth and net worth.

In strictly economic terms, child-care expenses are generally highest at the time of life when wages are lowest. Most of us have children when we are young, during the early years of our employment. It is easy to reckon the cost of day care from our current paychecks, even to decide that it isn't worth working.

But it's harder to calculate these costs as an investment for the future. The women who remain at work are likely to stay in line for the promotions that later offset the temporary expenses to a young family. It's hard to reenter, harder to catch up.

As for the emotional equation, women generally earn less than men in the work force. Subtracting child care from the female side of the ledger doubles the price of being female, lowers her contribution to the family income. Child care looms larger as a portion of her check than of theirs.

It's also true that as long as child care remains a cost of female employment, many men may go on assuming that it costs them nothing. They can maintain the attitude toward day care their fathers once had toward diapers: hands off.

Very few married people keep his and hers bank accounts. Our paychecks go into one pot. But families do have these psychological accounting systems. How simple a mathematical step it would be to recalculate child care as a cost of two parents rather than one mother. How simple to share the job of paymaster, the person who hands over the money. There are large and maybe crucial messages that would come in those modest changes.

Children are, after all, a joint creation and a joint concern. The parents who pay together, pay attention together—to this delicate and critical enterprise.

MAY 1988

A LITTLE ROMANCE

DROP THE old-time old-tyme marching band and send out for the string quartet. The soul-stirring, crowd-pleasing music for political life this year isn't martial, it's romantic.

Love, palpable, and above all else, publicly displayed, is becoming a requirement for political success. The national candidates, once expected to kiss babies for the camera, are now expected to kiss their wives . . . on the lips and in prime time.

This is the way it goes in the up-close and personal politics of the post-Reagan era. When Ron and Nancy walked offstage holding hands this week at the Republican National Convention, they left behind a national legacy of White House bliss.

For more than seven years, adoring stares, declarations of mutual affection flowed within the First Couple in full view of their viewers and voters. The final stanza of their love song Monday, romance under the Superdome, came complete with real violins. The President-husband said unselfconsciously of his first lady-wife: "I can't imagine life without her." The people who long for a happy marital ending got the price of admission.

In post-Reagan politics it isn't just fidelity that is expected. That, as Gary Hart found out, is a minimum. It's love in public—absolutely marital and totally safe, peppered with an occasional touch and feel—that has become the new standard.

Last month, when Michael Dukakis finished his acceptance speech and hugged his wife with more than wing-tipped passion, it raised his standing with the emotion watchers. Much was made of their love match. Were those just naps in Atlanta? Is he really cranky when they're apart?

This week, George Bush, who was raised never to chew with his mouth full or reveal his feelings to strangers, told Dan Rather that he was trying to show and tell a bit more of what was in his heart. He tapped his wife's fanny on network television. He even shared his fantasy life. If he couldn't be himself, Bush said, he'd choose to be Barbara's second husband.

What is this political lovefest? Why are Americans looking for love in all the high places?

Nobody expected George and Martha Washington to dance cheek to cheek. If Adlai Stevenson lost points on account of his divorce, it was among the folk who believed that marriage was a sacrament, not an eternal delight.

For most of our national campaign history, the woman was seen standing behind her man, not in his arms. Marriage and children made the candidate appear trustworthy and staid, not love-blissed and sexy.

Now we ask our candidates to reveal themselves emotionally. We expect them to have a rich internal life. We want full disclosure on their histories, even their psychohistories—although heaven help them if they've seen a psychiatrist. We have upped the ante on the amount they are expected to expose.

We also judge them in terms of home life. National politics is a family affair. In Atlanta, the Jackson family, even the Dukakises' grandchild in utero, made featured appearances. In New Orleans, the entire Bush clan, sixty members strong, is present and accounted for.

If the width of relationships matters to the public, so does their emotional depth. A solid marriage ranks as an achievement. The guy who can balance a political career without leaving a personal wreckage may get a special due.

But at the crux of our passion for passion at the top is probably our own anxiety about love. Ours is an era of marriage until love do us part. People once found their security in the institution. Now they seek it in the emotion. They long to witness and believe in lasting love.

So, like kids, we seek comfort in the couple of grown-ups in the big house who love each other demonstrably. The old G-rated political couple is now getting a PG. Keep posted. Any day now, they'll be soul kissing in the streets.

AUGUST 1988

MARRIAGE STUDY I

THIS IS getting spooky. One week the cover of *Newsweek* offers up the shade of Richard Nixon. The next week it resurrects the specter of old maidhood. The only news from the Great Media Beyond that could terrify more readers would be an amalgam of both stories: "Richard Nixon's Back and He Wants to Marry *You!*"

The tale of the unmarrying maidens came wrapped inside a chart showing the slim prospects for any college graduate to get to the altar after age 30. A never-married 30-year-old has only a 20 percent chance of wedding. By 35, she has only a 5 percent chance. And by 40 (this is *Newsweek*'s phrase, not mine), she is "more likely to be killed by a terrorist."

These figures come from a demographic study that entered the media bloodstream like a hit of caffeine right around Valentine's Day. The message sent a lot of 35-year-old hearts into instant arrhythmia. Now in its second life, the study has reappeared not only in the newsweekly but in an ABC nightly news report, and a *Wall Street Journal* front-page feature. Stop it before it kills again.

The *Journal* had the decency and balance to report that more men than women were still single in their thirties and likely to remain so. But collectively, the pieces did little to dispel the belief among biological clock-watchers that all the "good men" were taken. As a Berkeley sociologist told *Newsweek*, "When you look at men who don't marry, you're often looking at the bottom of the barrel. When you look at the women who don't marry, you're looking at the cream of the crop."

As a married woman I find that vaguely insulting, but never mind. The chart readers are too reactionary for my taste. How gleefully they warn that an uppity woman may be overqualified for the marriage market. Reach too high, young lady, and you'll end up in the stratosphere of slim pickings!

The scare stories about Success and the Single Woman don't answer the most interesting questions. They don't say, for example, whether success makes a 35-year-old woman unmarriage material or whether staying unmarried is what made her successful.

If the highest ranks of female achievers are disproportionately single, it may be because marriage has not, in general, boosted a woman's career. When a young woman marries, she's less likely to get a helpmate than a second job. The opposite has been true for men.

The sense that marriage may come with a lopsided work load has not escaped the notice of ambitious, educated young women. From what they've seen of it, marriage is more likely to siphon than save their energy. It looks like something else to manage.

Those college graduates who want careers and families—and almost all do—think they can solve the problem by postponing it. In the new chronology, putting first things first means putting the career first. Many figure that once their work life is launched, they can switch gears into a more wifely mode.

But I know very few careers, male or female, that get "established" and stay there, like a well-trained dog, while your attention wanders. Anyone who waits for work to settle down, waits for a placid moment to walk down an aisle, is heading for the skinny end of the chart. Marriage isn't a second career, but a relationship.

There's nothing wrong with the stretched-out life plan. I'm all in favor of growing up before hitching up. With the current divorce rates, a lot of us hope that later marriages have more sticking power.

But sooner or later a lot of unmarrieds realize they want the same things at 35 they wanted at 25. A balanced life. A marriage that offers more than a labor-intensive way of avoiding loneliness. It doesn't get any easier.

This rash of articles make the post-30 crowd of single women sound simultaneously desperate and picky. In fact, young women no longer have to marry or burn, let alone starve. If they are as choosy as the charts suggest, it's because there are choices, even second-best choices.

Marriage, when it works, is a mutual-aid society. Two people can make life a little less rocky than one. But when it's a bust? I've got a chart that shows the highest rates of depression are among unhappily married women. It's pretty scary stuff. Somebody ought to put it on a cover.

JUNE 1986

MARRIAGE STUDY II

HAVE YOUR PARENTS been sending you veiled messages that read: Sweetheart, you aren't getting any younger?

Did the creep down the hall tell you last night that he might be your very last chance?

Do you find yourself wondering whether it would have been wiser to invest in a hope chest than an M.B.A.?

Did one of your married friends suggest that maybe it was time to place an ad—very discreet, of course—in the personals column?

If so, you are suffering the long-term effects of fallout from *the Study.* You know which one we mean.

By 30 years of age, the Study projected, a never-married woman had only a 20 percent chance of marrying. At 35, she had a 5 percent chance. At 40, the infamous *Newsweek* cover on the Study warned, she was "more likely to be killed by a terrorist." (A fate we might wish on the writers.)

The results of the Study, annointed as the Harvard-Yale Study, were carried nationwide on wings of ill-will as swiftly as radioactive debris from Chernobyl. They fell silently all over the population and settled into the marrow of women in their thirties. Since then, the singles set has been glowing with anxiety: "Say it ain't so."

Well, guess what? Somebody says it ain't so.

The figures looked funny to several people in the Census Bureau, including

Jean Moorman. Unlike the great unwashed mathphobics among us, Moorman is an analyst of marriage and family statistics. She did not genuflect to the three Ivy League statisticians.

At 36, and married only three years ago, Moorman said to herself, "I just didn't believe that the current 30-year-olds were not going to get married. There is an awful lot of marrying going on right now."

Moorman and her colleagues did what statisticians do. They ran the numbers. Here is what they came out with.

Of college-educated, 30-year-old, never-married women, 66 percent will eventually marry.

Of 35-year-olds, 41 percent will marry.

Of 40-year-olds, 23 percent will marry.

Of 45-year-olds, 11 percent will marry.

The above information is offered to you in a form suitable for framing. Or for passing around at parties. One of Moorman's colleagues has found this a more effective mood brightener among her peer group than unlimited amounts of chardonnay.

Is this just a case of dueling statistics? It's more like a case of dueling mathematical models.

The Harvard-Yale people got into this whole catastrophe as an experiment; for the first time they used something called a parametric model. I will spare you the details, but it is regarded by its designer as risky for these sorts of projections. The Census Bureau people used the standard model.

"They think I'm wrong and I think they're wrong," says Moorman philosophically. But she points to other weaknesses in the Study That Would Not Die. The sample, divided and subdivided, was rather puny. The dimmest prospects for black women were based on about 100 in each age group.

Moreover, what separates these two sets of statistics—the difference that produced the Old Maid Revival—is a dispute over whether educated women are postponing the marriage option or closing it out. Here, too, the trends are in the Census Bureau's direction. Not only has the median age of women at first marriage been rising rather dramatically, especially for educated women, so has the overall marriage rate.

The statisticians behind both the Study and the Rebuttal do agree on one thing. One of the Harvard-Yale team attests, "The bottom line is that we really don't know what will happen in the future."

These are statistics, not tea leaves, projections not predestination. Nobody predicted the baby boom itself and nobody can predict when, how and whether the boomers will marry.

The appalling part of the media hype of the Study is that it transformed marital choices into marital chances. We have analyzed the glee that accompanied this feat. It struck with the power of a backlash.

How nice now to have a second, user-friendly set of numbers that add up to one message: Relax.

SEPTEMBER 1986

WHAT EVER HAPPENED TO
THE HEEL?

ABOUT HALFWAY through the movie, just as the unfaithful Jack Nicholson told his pregnant wife Meryl Streep that the whole business "is hard on me too," I had this odd sensation. Somebody was missing from the film version of *Heartburn*. The cad was gone.

The novel by Nora Ephron had the brave wit of a woman whistling her way through a catastrophe. It rested on the shared assumption that everyone could tell the wronger from the wrongee. A guy who embarked on a love affair while his wife was having their baby was a certifiable louse.

But the designated villain wasn't wearing a black hat in this movie. It was a gray hat over his thinning hair. When Rachel finally smashed the key-lime pie in Mark's face, the audience didn't break out into applause. There was quiet, as if she'd done something unseemly—overreacted, you know, in public.

This transformation from print to film may be what happens when an author's ex-husband (Carl Bernstein in this case) gets approval rights to a script about their breakup. It may be what happens when Jack Nicholson gets hold of a part. It may be what happens when the kids of a messy divorce get old enough to be part the audience. Or it may just be what happens when the whole social concept of a heel gets worn down.

Good old-fashioned terms like *cad, louse,* and *heel* have disappeared from everyday use. The people who pay $4.50 to witness the dissolution of Mark and Rachel's cinematic marriage are no more likely to call a man a "cad" than to challenge him to a duel with pistols at twenty paces.

We have become uneasy with these judgments. The most dreadful behavior of husband or wife is seen more often as a psychiatric symptom than a character flaw.

In the immediacy of post-marital partings, men and women may tell their own "story" to smaller audiences, cast as classic mythology, full of good and evil, dark and light. But the friends who shake their heads in sympathy use a different language. "He has serious problems." "She must be sick."

There is a sense that any partner who has misbehaved is more to be analyzed than judged. Certainly more to be self-analyzed than self-judged. It is no coincidence that so many who leave the marriage bed make their next stop the psychiatric couch.

Not even the courts, which are in the business of judging, take sides anymore. Like our friends, they are uncomfortable with it—too sophisticated, too experienced, too rational to try and assign marital blame.

Husbands and wives now come to court pleading "no fault." It is a reform that takes into account absolutely everything except the human desire for revenge and absolution. How many couples leave secretly longing for a verdict that declares their ex to be: Cad! Heel! Louse! By order of the court.

But publicly and privately, we are urged to come to terms with disasters. Even terms. We are told to take 50 percent of the blame for every broken relationship, even if we believe, deep down, that our half was asphalt and their half was steamroller.

And if, by some heinous behavior and some social accident, someone we know is actually ever labeled a cad, it is only a temporary decree. It took just about a decade for Richard Nixon to return from disgrace. The half-life of caddism is much much shorter. This month's louse is the next month's extra man.

The informal legislature of contemporary life has decreed a statute of limitations on these things. We even grow intolerant of the victims. "You want monogamy," says Rachel's father, "marry a swan."

One of the delights of *Heartburn* as a novel was its contrariness. Hers was a novel that didn't try to "understand" him. It was deliciously one-sided. Literary revenge, they called it in Washington.

I know that if you keep it too long, revenge, like one of Rachel's favorite rice puddings, turns rancid. But at times I miss a nice clear case of the cads.

In the movie, Mark kept losing his socks. In real life, the rest of us keep losing our heels.

AUGUST 1986

STAND BY YOUR MAN, LEE

H**E WOULDN'T** be where he is today without her. Not in New Hampshire. Not in Iowa. Not in the running at all.

I don't say this as a political nicety, the words that any candidate would employ as he tipped his hat to a loyal wife. In the case of Gary Hart, it is the absolute truth.

Maybe the second time he can do without the media consultants and campaign strategists and pollsters. But there is no way he can do without Lee.

So she can be seen these wintry days, standing by her man, in photographs and newsfilm, in the coffee shops and drugstores and high-school auditoriums. They are inseparable. He even introduces her to the toll taker at a turnpike booth.

Lee Hart has become her husband's talisman. She is a portable shield against the Question. A living rebuttal to those who would attack him for wife misuse.

Who would be so rude as to badger him with questions about Donna in front of Lee? If someone in an audience or on late-night television criticizes his behavior as a husband, Hart has his defense close by. "She's actively campaigning for me," he can and has said, "so I don't think this caller has the right to interpose himself in my wife's defense." If his wife doesn't feel abused, surely we shouldn't feel it for her.

Today Lee Hart holds the key to his comeback. And more than that. She holds the key to her own comeback as well.

Last May, when photographs of Gary and Donna Rice seemed a permanent fixture in the papers, when everyone in America was speculating on the impact of "womanizing" in politics, the candidate's wife looked as if she were held together with chewing gum. She was the national image of a wronged wife.

Their marriage became public property. Many made bets on how much longer they would last. Three months? Twelve? People who had never met Lee Hart asked each other why Gary didn't just get divorced. People who knew nothing of their relationship asked each other why Lee didn't just ditch the guy.

When Lee Hart looks back to those days in May she says, "It was hell," and nobody doubts it. But she chose to join her husband in portraying that hell as a media creation.

After twenty-eight years of marriage and two separations, she said: "I know Gary better than anyone else and when Gary says nothing happened, nothing happened." She was not a wronged woman. They were a wronged family.

When, in turn, Hart wanted to reenter the race, the decision hinged on Lee. As he put it coolly, "It got down to how much abuse she was willing to take." Not from him, mind you, from the press.

Why did she do it? Why does she do it? Why does she shake hands every day with people who are often uncomfortable in her presence, people who shared her public humiliation, who see mental images of Donna Rice on her husband's lap when she comes into a New Hampshire hall? What makes Lee run?

I don't think it is masochism or unblinking ambition for the White House. If Gary Hart believes that he can overcome the image of philanderer and retrieve his dignity, I suspect that Lee Hart believes she can save her self-respect *and* her marriage. She can campaign as a partner, not a victim.

Her public image may have been as hard to live with as his. After all, we once applauded spouses for stoicism, for keeping a marriage together no matter what. Now we are as likely to wonder why someone "takes it." Divorce was once a political kiss of death and indiscretions overlooked. Now we condemn infidelity and accept divorce.

Clearly this is not a Golden Era for wronged wives. We are less admiring of long suffering. We tend to believe that suffering and sufferers are foolish. We aren't comfortable with wives as victims.

But the woman Lee Hart tries to offer New Hampshire and Iowa, perhaps even herself, is not the wife left at home while her husband went cruising. She is, rather, the unflagging campaigner. *The* crucial member of the Hart team.

I don't know whether the voters will buy a new Hart brigade or a resurrected marriage. But for now, the candidate, a true loner, defiantly self-reliant and at times blindly self-centered, has taken on a real partner. This Gary Hart needs his wife. It must be, after all this, a good feeling for Lee.

In Love Fornow

THEY ARE IN their twenties and in love. Not in love forever. In love fornow.

They haven't said this exactly. But as a certified FOF (friend of the family) I have heard it in their silences. Certain words don't come up when we talk. Words like *our future* or even *next year*.

They are sharing their plans with me. But these are not shared plans. She has applied to East Coast graduate schools, he has been interviewing for West Coast jobs. They tell me this casually, their limbs familiarly entwined on the sofa in the position they adopted a year ago to tell everyone they were in love.

As an FOF, I quietly take in this scene. Have my young friends mastered the ability to love in the now? I ask myself. Or are they missing the romantic glue of futurism? I wonder if this is what it's like to be young lovers today.

Sitting with them, I am reminded of my reading trip through this year's Valentine's Day cards. I flipped through dozens of messages. The poetic pledges of forever love were almost all marketed for old lovers. The mush quota was highest for the cards marked: To Grandma.

But the Valentines for young lovers were, by and large, careful, cool. Some risqué, some even raunchy, but not emotionally risky. The Valentines I read carried no promises that would last longer than flowers or chocolate. They were about love fornow.

The woman who had dubbed me the Friend of this Family stands beside me. At her son's age, she had been married for two years. She was the example she didn't want her two children to follow. Married at 22, divorced ten years later.

"We were too young." How many times had she said so to the two children of this marriage and divorce? Children who had watched her start a career at 32. Children who had watched their father start another family at 40. My friend had told her sons, "Wait a while. Get to know several people, including yourself."

This young man had listened. His whole college generation had listened to some variation on that parental or societal advice. They had learned to put reason over romance. This young couple were like the graduates in that Dow Chemical ad last year. They were able to say—"I am going to miss you next year"—and accept parting as the given at their stage of life.

"So what," I ask my friend when we retreat to privacy, "do you think of this reasonableness now? Is it not just what you wanted?"

"Yes," she says, but slowly, and goes on. "I think they are doing the right thing. There are too many changes ahead for them. They are too young to limit their options—jobs, schools, cities—for each other." Then she adds quietly, "But what about the option to have each other?"

We sit quietly with each other, thinking about the dramatic reversal of life patterns in two decades. The young people we know have a passion for finding the right work. And caution about finding the right relationship. Those in their twenties pursue careers wholeheartedly. And embrace love halfheartedly. The half that is missing may be the part that pulses with the idea of a future, the desire for forever.

My friend and I, FOFs for a dozen or more young people, figure that on average these began their first love affairs between 18 and 20. If our small statistical sample holds up, they are likely to be single until 28 or 30. The time lapse between intimacy and commitment, between first love and marriage, has expanded enormously from our twenties to theirs.

In the interim these young may become very good at conditional love, love "until," love fornow. But it seems to us that it is hard to love fully in a limited time zone. Love without a belief in a future is like a chocolate heart made of skim milk and Sweet 'n' Low.

The timing of our revisionist notion is probably lousy. This is the Love Carefully era. A balanced life is more prized than a sudden disorienting fall into love. On campuses, this Valentine's Day is celebrated by distributing condoms, not commitments.

Yet my friend and I, harbingers of realism, proponents of caution, survivors of one or more disasters, have, to our great surprise, discovered that we are more romantic than the young lovers in the next room. We wish them wholehearted-ness. And the rich flavor of forever.

FEBRUARY 1988

A POSTMODERN DIVORCE

THE BARE OUTLINES of the O'Brien story are familiar, classic, even banal. Two young people get married. Nine years go by. He studies. She works. He gets an M.D. She gets a P.H.T. (Putting Hubby Through). Then he files for divorce.

In the old days, five or maybe fifteen years ago, couples like Michael and Loretta O'Brien probably got a Traditional Divorce. The law back then was drawn by its architects to ask a moral question: Who was at fault for the breakup of the marriage? It was a messy design, but after a bit of wrangling, perhaps some perjury and a whole lot of moral judgment, a divorce was usually granted. To the "innocent" went the alimony.

More recently, such a couple faced a Modern Divorce. Between 1970 and 1980, the courtroom was trimmed of baroque moral judgments, streamlined for contemporary life. Fault was banned from the law because it was an anachronism, rather like a gargoyle on a glass skyscraper.

The thoroughly Modern Divorce, with its pristine, hard-edged outlines, divvied up the past and the visible property—a car, a bank account, a house. It was designed with a wistful belief in fresh starts.

But Loretta and Michael O'Brien are part of the avant garde of legal architecture. Last week, they became the owners of a Postmodern Divorce. A new pillar, a new touch had been added to the modern structure.

Loretta O'Brien claimed, and the New York Court of Appeals agreed, that Michael O'Brien's medical degree was just another piece of property. Since that property was gained during the marriage and with the financial investment of his partner, Loretta was entitled to a part of her ex-husband's future income. It is now up to a lower court to determine how much money will be hers.

The decision was not unique. There are now at least six states with similar cases on the books. In Michigan, a wife was awarded a share of a law degree. In Washington, a wife got a share of her husband's license to practice dentistry. There are also six states that have ruled the other way.

The argument is intriguing because it comes out of the recent attempts to reform the divorce reform. Modern Divorce looked wonderful on the drafting board, but it has provided little shelter for women and children. As Stanford's Lenore Weitzman points out in her utterly convincing book, *The Divorce Revolution,* divorce reform has been a financial disaster. Today, on average, the standard of living for a divorced woman and children goes down 73 percent in the first year while her husband's goes up 42 percent.

Under the roof of Modern Divorce laws, courts have treated husbands and wives, fathers and mothers, even M.D.s and P.H.T.s with an evenhandedness that is, in effect, unfair. Property has been divided both equally and inequitably.

Now, the Postmodernists want to remodel a more livable space. Today, they argue, the major financial worth of a middle-class American family may not be in the bank account but in the company pension balance, may not be in a house but in an insurance plan. A couple's time and energy and money may not go into stocks and bonds but into a license or a degree. The courts are being asked to think about "career assets" when they tally up the property for any divorce settlement.

The trickiest of all those "career assets" has to be the one featured in the O'Brien case. The P.H.T. was always an honorary degree, a loving tip of the hat. It is the rare professional who doesn't believe at heart that he or she got that degree by individual labor.

One person studies. One name appears on a license. It isn't easy to price an investment in education when one doctor goes into brain surgery and another chooses missionary work, when one lawyer goes to Wall Street and another to Legal Aid.

At the same time, as Loretta O'Brien said, "I feel I should be compensated for the blood, sweat and tears of those years, when I had the whole financial burden on my shoulders." What is marriage if one person makes all the investment and the other is allowed to leave with the rewards? How different is her financial interest in a medical license from her interest in any other business?

On the whole, I approve of this new pillar of Postmodern Divorce because it may shore up the fragile status of some divorced women. But it is still flawed. Indeed, the architecture of divorce has been under constant renovation for the past twenty years, but it never seems quite right. Fairness is as elusive as ever. Have you noticed how hard it is to find a sturdy structure when the one called marriage falls apart?

JANUARY 1986

EX-HUSBANDS AND LOVERS

SOMEONE FROM Geraldo Rivera is on the line. This is a sign. Carla Parrillo, you understand, does not ordinarily get a chance to chat with talk-show hosts. They do not usually reach out to mothers of three from Johnston, Rhode Island.

But this month, Carla's family life became a precedent for the divorced parents of Rhode Island and maybe the country. The state Supreme Court upheld a ruling that prohibited Carla from having a man sleep overnight when the kids were home. Now she is a shooting star in the courtroom-to-television trajectory of modern life.

As she takes the call on the other line, I try to imagine the way Geraldo would pitch the show to the audience, which angle he would take. Sex and the Single Mother? An Old-fashioned Judge and a Newfangled morality? The Good Mother, Part II? Groan.

Before the Parrillo story became a national soap opera, it was just a nasty post-divorce wrangle like a thousand others. Maybe ten thousand. Carla and Justin Parrillo, twice-married with three kids, had finally called it quits in 1986.

When Carla started dating a man named Joseph, when he stayed overnight with her and the children, she says her ex-husband began harassing her. She accused him of making unscheduled visits to his old home, smashing the guy's car windows.

So Carla went into court to restrain this behavior. There, she found her own sexual behavior questioned. Her ex-husband raised the matter of the boyfriend.

And the judge said, in essence, we can't have that sort of thing going on.

The judge talked to the children. He didn't find them troubled: "The court cannot fault the mother in any way for not taking good care of the children." Nevertheless, he declared, "The court must infer that this situation is not conducive to the welfare of the children." No guests allowed.

It is this ruling that still sticks in Carla's craw. It took over two years for the case to get up to the Rhode Island Supreme Court. Joseph, the boyfriend, is long gone. But when the court ruled, she was angry all over again.

"The court is trying to tell me what to do in my private life," said the 33-year-old mother whose children now range in age from 10 to 15. "They have no proof of adverse psychological effects on my children. My kids liked the guy. I discussed it with them before he slept over. The judge was imposing his values on my life."

Indeed, this is the first time a state Supreme Court has limited the behavior of a custodial parent. This was not a custody fight. The father was not trying to win the children; he was trying to control what went on in his children's home.

Implicit in the decision is the notion that (1) unmarried sex is misconduct and therefore intrinsically (2) bad for the children. In both of these judgments, the decision flies in the face of current legal and social trends.

Cohabitation, which was once illegal, is now commonplace. There are some 2.3 million unmarried couples in the United States. They do not regard themselves as living in sin.

There are surely many more millions of divorced parents who go through a time of trial marriage and error, integrating new partners into their children's lives. Even Justin Parrillo, who praised "the old-fashioned morals" of the court went through some variation on this theme before he remarried last fall.

Some make this transition better than others. Few ex-wives or ex-husbands like it. Typically, women try to control their ex-spouse's behavior by withholding children; men by withholding money.

Sometimes a parent's sexual behavior or indeed the arrival of a new partner in the house is profoundly disturbing to a child. Sometimes that partner is or becomes a real plus. But the notion that a judge can automatically "infer" that it is bad for the child is psychologically and legally off-base.

As Sanford Katz, a law professor and former head of the American Bar Association's family-law committee, says: "Unless you can show a connection, show that the conduct of the parent has an effect on the child, the parent should have the freedom of association."

What happens next? Aside from a starring role in Talkshowland.

Carla and her lawyer, Patricia Hurst, are trying to decide whether to appeal to the United States Supreme Court. Carla would like to. Hurst worries that the current conservative court could turn a bad state decision into a bad federal case.

For now, Carla Parrillo has to decide whether some guy is worth risking a $500 fine and a year in jail. The rest of us can be grateful that Rhode Island is a very, very small state.

MARCH 1989

CARING HARRY

SOMEWHERE in the middle of *Heartbreak Ridge*, the movie camera pans in on Clint Eastwood poring over a women's magazine. The die-hard Marine officer is struggling, lips moving like a slow student in a language class, to pronounce the foreign phrases he deciphers from his reading: "Sensitive dialogue . . . sensual communication."

When Eastwood meets up with his ex-wife, he awkwardly sputters these phrases in her direction. "Tell me something," he says. "Did we mutually nurture each other? Did we communicate in a meaningful way in our relationship?"

Hello? Has Clint Eastwood become the new sensitive man? Are we about to see a series of movies about Caring Harry?

Not to worry. By the end of this generally appalling film, he has grunted through the Rolodex of obscenities, whupped the raw whippersnapper recruits into shape, and won the great American victory in Grenada. (Grenada? Yes, Grenada!)

Nevertheless, sitting in a movie theater surrounded by a mob of adolescent males, it occurred to me that I had seen a small window of vulnerability. Even this caricature of a macho sergeant who insults his men by calling them the worst thing he can think of—"ladies"—is showing signs of change. He says to his ex-wife, "I was just wondering, what went wrong?"

A Clint Eastwood character who wondered what went wrong was once about as likely as a Woody Allen character who felt sexually secure. Not anymore.

The reigning male image of the 1980s may not be Alan Alda. The "sensitive man" may have wilted under the word *wimp*. But we haven't reverted all the way back to Conan the Barbarian. The image is now someone between Alda and Conan. It's Clint Eastwood, coming in from the dark ages, to begin "wondering." And on the other side it is Bruce Springsteen, coming in from the seventies to pump iron.

Ten years ago, Springsteen had the tortured look and triceps of Bob Dylan. Now this massively popular singer looks the way he sounds: strong. His new record is filled with a muscular sensitivity. The rock and roll carries enormous physical energy and yet the lyrics speak for men who were inarticulate a generation ago.

As Ralph Whitehead, Jr., the University of Massachusetts professor who coined the phrase *new collar voter,* put it in our conversation: "Think of the characters played by Marlon Brando or James Dean. Thirty years later those characters speak in Springsteen's songs."

What these stars suggest is something that men are trying to work out in their own lives: a way to combine strength and sensitivity, action and introspection. A way to be strong and no longer silent.

It is no coincidence that the prime-time TV drama that draws the the highest share of male audience features Frank Furillo of *Hill Street Blues.* Furillo is a man who knows and says what he's feeling and also acts decisively. It's a combination that men (and women) admire but fear they can't pull off.

As Whitehead describes it, "Men are trying to combine sensitivity and strength in precisely the way women are trying to combine work and family." It is the male variation on having it all; a massive rewiring of men's inner lives that parallels the restructuring of women's outer lives.

This change may not come in a neat, precise, linear way. The nostalgia for a "simpler era" heightens the popularity of cartoon figures of masculinity like Rambo. Nothing wins male ratings like the Super Bowl; all action, no dialogue. Indeed, much of the impetus for this change comes in response to women.

Clint Eastwood's own dim "wondering," for example, is inspired by the loss of his wife. *Heartbreak Ridge* touches, if only lightly, this dichotomy: The hero must be tough enough to succeed in war, yet sensitive enough to keep peace at home. Eastwood's Marine is hardly the first, and surely not the last, man to experience this conflict in public and private expectations.

By the end of the movie, the star wins both the battle and the woman. Are we to believe that the prizes go to the warriors, that the old ways work? I don't think so. The pivotal moment came much earlier when she watched this fighting man wrestle with new words and emotions. His ex-wife looked at Eastwood as many women have looked at changing men—surprised, even suspicious, but for the first time hopeful—and said, "You really are trying to understand."

PART NINE

TAKING
LIBERTY

Our car alarms announce that we value private property over public interest. We support the right of citizens to protect their cars even if their false alarms steal our sleep.

Dying with Their Rights On

I N T H E M I D D L E A G E S, Europeans would confine their lunatics between the city gates. They would stay there, locked behind iron grilles, forming a symbolic human way station, marking the fragile edge of civilization.

Later on, mad people were loaded onto boats, "ships of fools," that were set on the waterways. These boats carried their human refuse from one city to another.

We don't do such things anymore. In the late twentieth century, we let many of our mentally ill wander the city streets. We step over them, walk around them. Unless we hear them talking with characters in their own psychotic world, we may not even distinguish them from others who make their "home" on the sidewalks.

But now we have a new celebrity among the homeless. Her name is Joyce Brown. And with her fame comes a set of questions about our cities' obligations to the mentally ill.

Joyce Brown, alias Billie Boggs or Ann Smith, had a chic address in Manhattan's high-rent district. She lived on a grate beside a restaurant at 65th Street and Second Avenue.

On October 28, Brown became the first person picked up under a New York City program. The mayor had created a plan to round up some of the homeless mentally ill and take them to hospital shelters.

But in a real way, this story began much earlier, before Joyce Brown's own life began to fall apart. Back in the fifties and sixties it was easy, too easy, to commit people to institutions. Then, in the seventies, as Dr. Darold Treffert, the Wisconsin psychiatrist who has written widely on this subject, says simply, "The pendulum swung too far."

In 1972, a Wisconsin federal court ruled that the state could only detain people if they were dangerous, and dangerous meant suicidal or homicidal. It became harder to hold people against their will. And remained harder to help people.

There were a large number of people who were not suicidal, not homicidal, but gravely disabled—people who just didn't know enough to come in out of a snowstorm. Dr. Treffert collects some of their stories under the title: "People Who Died With Their Rights On."

Now, in urban America, many wonder whether the respect for rights isn't also an excuse for neglect. The feisty mayor of New York, Ed Koch, is one of the few who decided to push the pendulum back a bit.

It is too bad for the mayor and for the program that Joyce Brown was its first target. He would have had a better case with the man who willingly shares his plastic-bag "house" with rats in Central Park, or the woman acting out her own sexual hallucinations in the Port Authority.

Joyce Brown, however, resisted the city's "help" all the way to court. There, one group of psychiatrists portrayed her as a psychotic who defecated in the streets and ran in front of traffic. Another portrayed her as a rational survivor who could take care of herself.

The 40-year-old former secretary, shored up by all the attention or in a respite from mental disorder, was her own best witness. The "professional" street dweller, as she called herself, was hard to distinguish from other homeless we are conditioned to ignore. So, the judge ruled last week that Brown be allowed to return to her homeless home.

Make no mistake. There are no victors in this case. The civil-liberties lawyers who protected Brown's right to be "free" know that the streets provide a mean sort of freedom. The judge who ordered Brown's release also wrote pointedly, "There must be some civilized alternatives other than involuntary hospitalization or the street."

Joyce Brown herself, "choosing" street life, was asked in court where she would like to go. She wanted to go to an apartment. Could she afford it? No, she answered.

In reality, there are very few civilized alternatives. Today there are fewer institutions and more mentally ill people on the streets. Brown may go on coping. Or, like so many others, she may have to deteriorate to the point of real danger to get help.

The homeless celebrity provided a poor test case for the city. But even the judge called the program a first step in the right direction. It won't cure high rents and homelessness. It won't end psychosis. It won't produce a community mental-health program. But New York is offering a small antidote to urban callousness. At the very least we can provide emergency help to some of the mentally ill before they, too, die with their rights on.

NOVEMBER 1987

RELIGION IN THE

TEXTBOOKS

HERE WAS A TIME when people who wanted to keep the peace and keep the crockery intact held to a strict dinner-table rule: Never argue about politics or religion. I don't know how well it worked in American dining rooms, but it worked pretty well in our schools. We dealt with religion by not arguing about it.

Children who came out of diverse homes might carve up the turf of their neighborhood and turn the playgrounds into a religious battlefield, but the public classroom was common ground. Intolerance wasn't tolerated.

In place of teaching one religion or another, the schools held to a common denominator of values. It was, in part, the notion of Horace Mann, the nineteenth-century father of the public-school system. He believed that the way to avoid religious conflicts was to extract what all religions agreed upon and allow this "non-religious" belief system into schools.

I wonder what Mann would think of that experiment now. Was it naive or sophisticated? Was it a successful or a failed attempt to avoid conflict in a pluralistic society?

Today, textbooks are the texts of public-school education and their publishers are, if anything, controversy-phobic. Textbooks are written and edited by publishing committees that follow elaborate guidelines to appease state and local education committees. They must avoid alienating either atheist or fundamentalist. And still these books have become centerpieces, controversial sources of evidence in courtrooms.

A judge in Tennessee recently allowed a group of students to "opt out" of reading class because the textbooks violated their religious beliefs. Their parents had managed to read religious subtexts, even witchcraft, into such tales as "Goldilocks," "Cinderella" and "The Three Little Pigs." Nothing was safe enough or bland enough to please them.

At the same time, a group of parents in Alabama went to court protesting that textbooks are teaching a state religion masquerading as "secular humanism." Not to teach about God is to teach about no God. The attempt to keep religion out of the textbooks was no guarantee against controversy either.

There is still a third argument about religion in the public schools that doesn't come from fanatics but from educators. They maintain that the attempt to avoid conflict has pushed textbook publishers to excise religion altogether, even from history class. It is not just the teaching *of* religion that has become taboo, they claim. It is teaching *about* religion.

Sources as diverse as William Bennett's Department of Education and Norman Lear's People for the American Way have reported in the past year on the distortions that result. There is a history book that tells about Joan of Arc without mentioning her religious motives. Others explain Thanksgiving without discussing the religious beliefs of the Puritans or to Whom they were giving thanks.

"The result of wanting to avoid controversy is a kind of censorship," maintains Diane Ravitch of Columbia University. "It becomes too controversial to write about Christianity and Judaism." Ravitch is involved in creating a new history curriculum for California that would incorporate teaching about people's belief systems and their impact on society. It may be tricky, she admits, to teach about religion without teaching religion, but then all good teaching is risky. So is learning. And that's what is at stake.

The common ground of values, neutral turf in the religious strife, threatens to shrink to the size of a postage stamp. In Tennessee, the court agreed to protect the religious beliefs of a set of parents whose own beliefs included intolerance of other religions and the importance of binding a child's imagination. These are ideas that are profoundly hostile to the American concept of education.

If textbook publishers keep retreating to a shrinking patch of safe ground, they will end up editing chunks out of "The Three Little Pigs." The task is not to shy away from our diversity, but to teach it to our children, and proudly. The strength of our system, what's worth telling the young, is not that Americans deny their differences or always resolve them, but that we have managed, until now, to live with them.

NOVEMBER 1986

A STRANGER AT A FAMILY
TRAGEDY

THE PROTESTORS are gone now. The legal hit team has wandered off in search of another target. The television crews have moved to other sites and other stories.

The people who surround Nancy Klein these days are those who care about her. Not as a case study or a political focal point, but as a wife, a daughter, a mother. Her husband Martin visits with her as he has every day since the 32-year-old woman went into a coma. He tells her the simple things, how his day went, what he did, what their 3-year-old daughter did.

If some spark leads Nancy Klein out of the shadows of her coma, her husband and parents will eventually also tell her how strangers tried to wrest control of her medical care away from them. They will tell her how these intruders, men she had never met, sued to become guardians of her and her fetus, to make decisions about her life and death.

The story of the Klein family began on December 13 with a car crash that left this woman, pregnant with her second child, in a coma. In the weeks that followed, doctors at the Long Island hospital told Martin Klein that his wife might have a better chance of recovery if she had an abortion.

These doctors offered opinions rather than promises, and odds rather than certainties. But Nancy's family held to those opinions and pinned their hopes on those odds. They opted for the abortion.

If this had been any other medical procedure, there would have been no further delay. It is virtually automatic to allow family to make decisions for an incompetent patient. This hospital, however, spooked by right-to-lifers, refused to perform an abortion without court permission. The administrators invited intervention and they got it.

Two men, anti-abortion advocates both, came to wrangle for power over the body of the comatose woman they had never met and have never yet seen. Their lawyer was A. Lawrence Washburn, Jr., a regular on the right-to-life legal circuit.

In 1984, in the famous Baby Jane Doe case, Washburn was the one who sued to force surgery on the handicapped baby against the will of her parents. Since then, he has represented more than one estranged husband trying to prohibit his wife from having an abortion. In June, he was briefly appointed guardian of the fetus inside a client's wife's body.

Washburn eventually lost the Klein case, as he lost those others. After two bitter weeks, three New York State courts ruled that only Martin Klein was the proper guardian. On Saturday after the Supreme Court refused to overturn that ruling, the abortion was performed.

The crucial sentence in all of this judicial maneuvering came from the appeals court ruling that stated unequivocally that these "strangers" had "no place in the midst of this family tragedy."

All but the most hard-core right-to-lifers in the country seemed to identify with the family and against the invaders. Even Barbara Bush came out of her silence on abortion. Not only she but her husband sided with the Kleins. "I agree with my husband on that," Mrs. Bush said. "The life of the mother was at risk. I'm very grateful that it worked out as it did."

Is the Klein case then such an exception in the annals of abortion that even a pro-life President and an ambivalent populace can separate it from the others? I don't read it that way.

The question in this case was not whether an abortion would save Nancy Klein's life. The medical evidence was less than conclusive; sadly, she is still in a coma. What was at stake in the court was who had the right to make that determination.

This is not some peripheral issue. It is the central question of the entire abortion debate: Who decides? The answer of the anti-abortion activists is: "Strangers."

Martin Klein eventually won the right to choose abortion because his wife had that right. It was protected in the Roe v. Wade decision. He was merely the guardian allowed to exercise his wife's rights. If abortion were illegal, he might not have had that right. It is notable how much more support there was for the family of a comatose woman facing these decisions than there might have been for the woman herself.

What we have seen here is a preview of what the world would look like if Roe is overturned, a grave and imminent possibility. It's a world in which the Washburns would decide the fate of the Kleins and the rest of us. A world in which the government would become the "guardian" of every pregnant woman, of every fetus. A world in which "strangers" would weigh the evidence of everywoman's health and life.

So I wish Nancy Klein a full recovery and a return to her husband and child. In a coma, this woman may have helped to wake up the country.

FEBRUARY 1989

SMOKING ADS: A MATTER
OF LIFE

IMAGINE WHAT would happen if some modern entrepreneur came up with a nifty idea for a new consumer product. It was an item that had no notable benefits, was addictive and would be implicated in the deaths of some 350,000 Americans a year.

What precisely would be the response of his corporate superiors? Beyond stunned silence? Would the Food and Drug Administration give his brainchild a seal of approval? Would the government allow it to be extolled and sold to citizens? Hardly. If cigarettes did not exist, we might invent them, but never in the wildest scenario would we let them loose on the legal market.

But what do you do once cigarettes are in the marketplace? What do you do once you have a hooked population, a hooked economy?

This is the raw-throated question that plagues the anti-tobacco coalition. When you cut right through all the arguments by lawyers and doctors and public-policy makers, what we have are fifty million addicted Americans. We know two things about them with absolute certainty. That smoking is bad for their health, bad for everybody's health, not to mention health bills. That banning cigarettes at this moment in time would be a social disaster, turning smokers into criminals and farmers into bootleggers.

The actions of the anti-smoking people can be seen as an attempt to get around this central conflict, an attempt to wean the country from smoking without going cold turkey. So far, they have tried putting warnings on cigarettes and rotating those warnings. They are backing legislation to raise cigarette taxes and to eliminate the industry's deduction for advertising. Even the movement toward a smoke-free workplace and public space has, as a subtext, the hope that smoking will gradually become socially unacceptable.

But nothing has elicited quite the level of controversy as the proposal to ban all forms of cigarette advertising and promotion. The latest bill, introduced February 24 by Mike Synar (D-Okla.), would outlaw the whole $2 billion boodle: newspaper and magazine ads, billboards, posters, match advertising, samples, sponsorships of athletic events—virtually anything with a cigarette name on it except the package itself.

Synar, who smoked for ten years, became convinced after watching the non-effect of labels that, "You cannot compete with $2 billion worth of advertising and promotion." The ban is seen as a better way to stop companies from recruiting new and young customers, to make up for the ones who have died or quit. With no new recruits, ashtrays will gradually become heirlooms.

The American Medical Association agrees. The American Bar Association disagrees. First Amendment lawyer Floyd Abrams calls it censorship and warns: "Censorship is contagious." American Civil Liberties Union Director Ira Glasser says: "We have always been against bans of advertising [for] any products that are legal to sell."

I have watched this argument emerge with some trepidation. I no longer worry that banning tobacco ads today will make it easier to ban liquor ads tomorrow and then salt, beef fat, even automobiles. Tobacco is unique. As Synar put it, "We are dealing with the only product that when used as instructed is destructive." Moreover, each ad that portrays the glamour of healthy young people smoking is intrinsically false.

But I agree that there is something contradictory in the message that it's okay to sell cigarettes but not okay to tell people about them. The Supreme Court ruled that Puerto Rico could permit gambling and prohibit advertising for it. Such a duality is apparently constitutional but also contradictory.

Nevertheless, what are our choices? Cigarettes are deadly. It isn't okay to sell them in any moral sense, but we allow it. Fifty million addicts make a ban on cigarettes impossible. Does that mean we are stuck forever with this historic health disaster? Because we can't forbid cigarettes, do we have to allow the industry access to new addicts, allow them to keep their numbers up, keep their constituency intact, maintain the smokers' clout? I don't think so.

This is perhaps the most powerful place to interrupt the cycle. A ban on advertising is an imperfect and unstable compromise. But the alternative is grim in its consistency: the seduction of yet another generation into disease.

DRUG TESTING: JAR WARS IN WASHINGTON

THIS IS WHAT the crusade against drugs has come down to: Jar Wars. All summer long, politicians have been overdosing on polls and political anxiety about the drug issue. By September the climate in Washington was still humid with hysteria. And now it appears that the one analysis of the drug problem that will really count is urinalysis.

On Monday, the President ordered mandatory drug testing for federal employees. "This," he said with a flourish, "is the federal government's way of just saying no to drugs."

The order applies to all law-enforcement officers, to anyone with access to classified information, indeed to anyone who has what is loosely described as "public health or safety or other functions requiring a high degree of trust and confidence." It is estimated that more than a million federal employees may now find their job security rests in a jar.

I am not entirely surprised by this political pursuit of bodily fluids. Ever since drugs replaced pornography on the front pages, there has been a growing obsession with filling little laboratory vials.

First, the President of the United States volunteered himself as Chief Donor of the nation. Then, in the congressional race in Atlanta, John Lewis challenged his opponent, Julian Bond, to dueling samples and matching test scores. Any day now I expect to see a political ad boasting about a candidate's specimen instead of experience.

All this is the stuff of satire, but there is also something menacing about wide-scale mandatory testing for drugs. The initial response of Americans to the idea of drug testing may be favorable, but I don't think we'll respond the same way to the reality.

Under this order, employees would receive a general warning two months before the drug-testing program begins. Agency heads would decide who is to be tested. To be at all reliable, the drug testing has to be random and has to be supervised. As an expert in the field said, a trusted worker "must watch each person urinate into a bottle."

If a pop quiz at the official specimen-collection center doesn't seem like an invasion of your privacy, consider this: A lot of other information goes into the jar. By analyzing urine, a superior can also find out whether you are pregnant, whether you are taking medication for your heart or for your mental health.

Americans have always been sensitive, indeed Reagan has always been sensitive, about government intrusion. The Fourth Amendment to the Constitution protects us against unreasonable searches and seizures. The Supreme Court has ruled that the government can't "search" and "seize" our bodily fluids without cause any more than they can our homes and possessions. A federal employees union is trying to block the order on these grounds.

I have no argument with drug testing when there is a genuine, compelling safety concern. As far as I am concerned, the military can test the people who work in nuclear-missile silos every time they heed the call of nature. If there is probable cause to suspect workers of drug use, test them. But the majority of workers who have "nothing to hide" do have something to protect: privacy.

Setting up a $56 million federal program to collect and analyze urine from as many as a million federal workers is not only unseemly, not only unconstitutional, it's a wasteful diversion. Urinalysis doesn't affect the crop of coca leaves. Nor does it catch the big-time drug pushers. It doesn't keep crack out of schoolyards.

The administration knows that. What they want is an easy showcase, something to prove that the government is cleaning up its own house. What they are funding is a lineup for workers who must prove their innocence at the washroom door.

That is not the stuff of a great war against drugs. It's the comic tragedy of a little, bitty battle of the bottles.

SEPTEMBER 1986

HOMOSEXUAL CRIMES

THERE ARE TIMES when you can only get to the heart of the matter the long way around. You have to begin with the footnotes and work your way up.

Last week, a slim majority of Supreme Court justices upheld, 5–4, a Georgia law against any sexual act "involving the sex organs of one person and the mouth or anus of another." The Court declared that the state can criminalize sodomy between homosexuals even in their own home.

This week, it's time to read the footnotes. At the bottom of Justice White's opinion, in the offhand way you might brush something under the rug, there is a notice. The court, he writes, is expressing "no opinion" on the constitutionality of *heterosexual* acts of sodomy.

The Georgia law itself contains no such neat distinctions. It makes the act of oral or anal sex illegal, no matter what the sex of the actors. The legislature there and in seventeen other states has no qualms about telling husbands and wives what they cannot do with each other.

Not to worry, though, if we believe the footnote. The Court has "no opinion" on whether the law applies to heterosexuals. Not yet.

Homosexuals are the targets of the Court's attention this time because Michael Hardwick, the man arrested by police, is homosexual. They entered his bedroom to deliver a warrant for a fine and found him engaged in oral sex with another man.

If they had found him with a wife, I assume they would not have arrested Hardwick for sodomy. They might have just closed the door and given them privacy. This, however, is precisely what the Court says homosexuals do not have: the right of privacy.

Justice White insists that the people who brought the Georgia law to the Supreme Court want nothing less than "a fundamental right to engage in homosexual sodomy. This, we are quite unwilling to do." The Court bolsters its argument against homosexual sodomy by tracing history back to the days of Henry VIII, when sodomy was considered an offense of "greater malignity" than rape. Is it any wonder that in Georgia today, oral sex between consenting adults may still carry a greater penalty—one to twenty years—than sexual violence?

I do not agree with Justice White. The Court was not asked to create "a right to homosexual activity." Hardwick did not request the seal of government approval on his bedroom door. He asked, rather, to be protected from government intrusion. In the words of Justice Blackmun's impassioned dissent, Hardwick wanted "the right to be left alone."

What is chilling in the Court's ruling is not just its limp reliance on tradition. It's the vigor with which it closed down the borders on the "zone of privacy."

Over the past decades, in one case after another, the Court marked out a certain territory of personal decision making, a turf where individuals could lead their lives without interference from the government. The choice of a marriage partner, of birth control, of abortion. "We protect those rights," explained Justice Blackmun, "because they form so central a part of an individual life."

What is more private than the sexual act itself? "The right of an individual to conduct intimate relationships in the intimacy of his or her own home seems to me to be the heart of the Constitution's protection of privacy," writes Blackmun. Yet this centerpiece has been declared out of bounds by the majority of justices.

Would the Court have drawn the same bold line around the zone of privacy if Michael Hardwick had been arrested with a wife? Maybe not. It is homosexuals who the Court, and much of society, want to keep beyond the pale.

But if a state has the right to tell man and man how to behave sexually with each other, it has the right to tell man and woman. If homosexuals have no privacy in bed, then neither do heterosexuals. If a legislature can criminalize oral sex, it can criminalize any other practice considered "deviant" by any political majority. Never on Sunday?

When we limit rights, it is easiest to start with a minority. It's easiest to draw the line that defines "them" as outsiders. But it rarely stops there. Check the footnotes.

JULY 1986

MIXED SIGNALS ON

SMOKING

SO WHAT'S THE latest flight plan for all the folks in the anti-smoking section? After last week, there are enough mixed signals to cause a midair collision.

On one day a jury in New Jersey decided for the first time that a tobacco company was liable in the lung-cancer death of a smoker. They said the Liggett group had $400,000 worth of responsibility for the fate of Rose Cipollone. The disease that came from smoking was 80 percent her fault, 20 percent theirs.

But the very next day a federal appeals court in Cincinnati ruled that R.J. Reynolds Co. had no responsibility for the vascular disease that resulted in the amputation of Floyd Roysdon's leg. His smoking-related trauma was entirely self-inflicted.

If these two cases didn't exactly collide, they were a near miss. Neither was decided by a careful medical evaluation of the effects of the evil weed on the human body. They were determined by another measurement: responsibility. These days, the courts are being asked who is to blame for the health disasters that come from smoking. The companies that market or the people who consume cigarettes? How is that blame to be distributed?

The difference between the two verdicts was in part a matter of timing. Two years ago, an appeals court ruled that 1966 was a watershed year for consumer information. It was the year Congress put warnings on cigarette packages. The court said that anybody who smoked after that year was duly warned, taking the coffin nails in their own hands. They couldn't sue.

In the Cipollone case, Rose's widowed husband was only able to wrest a share of the blame from the tobacco people because Rose began smoking during those wonderful postwar years when ads boasted "Just What the Doctor Ordered" and "Play Safe—Smoke Chesterfields." Roysdon, on the other hand, could only claim damages dating to the mid-seventies. He lost because, the court ruled, "Normal use of cigarettes is known by ordinary consumers to present grave health risks."

Do you get the feeling that we're locked in a holding pattern here? Circling the issue of blame?

There is a legitimate question about responsibility. The tobacco companies don't stuff cigarettes between smokers' lips and force them to puff until they die of it. On the other hand, they do entice anyone within sight of an ad to light up.

There should be some sharing of the blame. The principle of joint responsibility established in the Cipollone case—whether it's 80–20 or 50–50—makes a lot of sense. The notion that warning labels protect cigarette pushers doesn't.

Even in the turbulent legal air over these cases, there really is a new sense of direction. It comes curiously enough out of this debate about taking blame.

Until recently, the tobacco companies defended themselves by denying their product was dangerous. Even when they introduced the smokeless cigarette last year, they didn't say it was safer. They said it was cleaner. To this very day, they ardently challenge evidence that cigarettes cause cancer, emphysema, heart disease.

But now the legal strategy is the so-called "free-will defense." The tobacco people are saying that people are smoking with full knowledge of the very risks the companies deny. As expressed by one of their regiment of lawyers in the Cipollone case, "Individuals who make informed choices have to take responsibility for those choices."

There is something truly sleazy about all this. The tobacco merchants are allowed to spend $2 billion advertising and promoting cigarettes and then hide behind the Surgeon General's warning. As Richard Daynard, of the Tobacco Products Liability Project, says sarcastically: "What they're saying is that anybody who's sucker enough to believe us deserves to die. I find that a very elegant, morally attractive position."

But in the long run this free-will defense is a public-relations disaster, and a public-information success. Not even the tobacco companies can go on denying health hazards while claiming that everybody knows about them anyway.

From where I sit, the estimated time of arrival for a smoke-free society has just gotten a bit closer.

JUNE 1988

THE LAST BASTION CASE

THOSE WHO HAVE never entered the inner sanctum of an all-male club are likely to envision it as the exclusive, wood-paneled retreat of the elite. There the very late George Apley and his cronies, resplendent in tweeds, still sit in leather wing chairs, puffing pipes, rising only occasionally to toast good fellowship and lament the loss of the gold standard.

But this vintage nineteenth-century scene has been updated. On any given day, such a club is not just hosting George and his unreconstructed pals. It's probably serving breakfast to the law firm of Biddle, Biddle and Fiddle, lunch to the monthly meeting of the investment bankers and dinner to the state insurance association.

In the twilight of the twentieth century, the most vaunted private clubs are also in the business of business. The women excluded from membership or banned from the premises, women who aren't allowed to sit in the lobby or walk through the front door, are penalized in doing business with the boys.

So, on Tuesday, the Supreme Court is going to hear what might be called The Last Bastion Case. It is listed formally as New York State Club Association v. City of New York. It will test the constitutionality of a law, already copied in at least half a dozen other cities, that would force these clubs to choose—gasp—between admitting women or giving up money.

This choice is not just an arbitrary one, your money or your manhood. Under the Constitution, any group of Americans has the right to private association. If the blue-eyed, right-handed, bird lovers of Wisconsin want to form an exclusive club for the purposes of warbling, the government cannot force them to open up the premises to brown-eyed, left-handed cat fanciers.

More to the point, any group of males, young boys or old boys, can freely build their plywood clubhouse and post a sign: NO GIRLS ADMITTED. Any group of girls can do the same thing. But if a private club gets involved in public, commercial activity, how long can it go on claiming the rights of "private association"?

The New York law says that a club stops being private and starts being subject to public laws—including those against discrimination—if it has more than 400 members, provides regular meal service and gets regular money from non-members "in furtherance of business or trade." Most of the rich and famous clubs do just that.

In 1980, 37 percent of city-club income and 26 percent of country-club income in America came from memberships that were paid by businesses. Companies paid men to belong to clubs that barred their female colleagues. It's estimated that 85 percent of the money spent at these same clubs was treated as business expense, so that taxpayers also supported "private clubs."

Columbia Law Professor Jack Greenberg, author of the law, made this careful distinction: "If it's a club where people hang out, are affable and drink port it's not covered." But if it's the Century Club and assorted other last bastions of New York business, it is.

This case goes to the Supreme Court at something of an historic moment. Justice Blackmun recently resigned from one all-male club. The brand-new Justice Kennedy resigned from another all-male club. A third Justice, O'Connor, was once barred from an all-male club.

It was Justice O'Connor who wrote the decision that opened up the Jaycees and Rotary: "When a club enters the marketplace of commerce in any substantial degree, it loses the complete control over its membership that it would otherwise enjoy if it confined its affairs to the marketplace of ideas." Do I hear a bell knolling over the Century Club door?

The issue of integrating clubs is often seen as one of those elitist matters of importance only to a handful of already privileged women like the late George Apley's granddaughter, a Princeton graduate and corporate lawyer. But as any woman who has ever been excluded from a lunch meeting or forced to go through a side door to join her companions can tell you, they are a real part of the fabric of business in America.

In that sense, this is not an attack on single-sex associations, the kind many of us choose for friendship. There are all-male and all-female environments, segregated retreats, coffee klatches and clubs, that sustain many of us. But business is not private and professions are not an all-male club. And clubs that pocket profits from business cannot run for the protection of privacy. The law before the Supreme Court says simply: They can't have it both ways anymore.

FEBRUARY 1988

SAVING CARS, KILLING
SLEEP

I T IS 3 A.M., a happy hour for creatures of the deep REM, the time of night when pillow and posture have found their natural resting state and the mind is free to dream. But somewhere from the middle distance, a sound is piercing the plot line of one urban sleeper's dream.

Waaaah. One long loathsome note in the night. It is the well-known cry from the modern beast of burden, the car alarm.

In our sleeper's city neighborhood an automobile is shrieking. Like a watchdog in front of the ranch, the car howls on and on, announcing some perceived intrusion on its territory. Probably the prowler is the wind, or a faulty electrical wire or a branch that has touched the high-gloss sensitivity of its surface, but the car is relentless in its screaming self-defense.

Behind a brick wall, our sleeper gradually and reluctantly is roused from the kingdom of deep REMs. One eye opens onto the green numbers of the digital clock: 3:15 A.M. She estimates the distance of the offending vehicle. A block, maybe two. She calculates the timing. Five minutes, maybe ten.

She is a veteran of many such nights in a city where car alarms are more common than cat howls. So she offers a small prayer to the Saint of Slumber: Let this be the kind that goes off automatically. Her prayers are answered. Pillows and posture are rearranged. But with a cruelty yet to be ranked on any torture list, as she begins to drift off, the alarm springs back into action.

On again, off again. The digital clock reads 4:34 A.M. Her dreams have now been replaced by fantasies of revenge. If it weren't so cold and dark, ah, what a time she would have. A spray can, a deflated tire come into her mind. She would wait in hiding for the owner and handcuff him to a chair with a six-hour tape plugged into his brain. Have a nice day.

By 5:07, she has begun a more serious computation. There are a minimum of a thousand people within range of the offending vehicle. Of that number surely half have had their sleep shattered.

What is the productivity of that small community, what are their salaries, what is the cost in crankiness and exhaustion due to loss of sleep? What on the other hand is the relative value of the car? How many of these alarms are true and how many more false? How did the shrieking of the four-wheeled night creature become an accepted fact of life?

Our former sleeper, now fully alert, thinks back to the recent Saturday when, in full daylight, a false alarm polluted an entire downtown block and hundreds of people passively walked around it. They accepted the right of that car owner to disturb their peace in his efforts to protect his property.

Does the shrieking of the night represent the victory of crime over community? Our would-be sleeper is a veteran of one stolen tape deck. She lives in a city where car theft is a major hobby. But it occurs to her that our self-defense budget has escalated automatically. We rarely calculate whether this defense has affected community life more than the offense.

Our car alarms announce that we value private property over public interest. We support the right of citizens to protect their property, even if their false alarms steal our sleep.

Is it too much to suggest some comparison to guns? After all, in defense of the right to bear arms of self-protection, we allow easy access to weapons that shatter whole communities.

What she is proposing now—it is 5:45 A.M. and counting—is a reassessment of the value of property over community. If we can pass rules for private space—don't dump garbage on the front lawn, or don't keep a chicken coop in the city—then why allow a loaded car ready to go off at any minute? If we can zone everything from the height of fences to the behavior of pitbulls, surely we can insist on a no-siren zone.

It is six o'clock in the city. An owner's hope to scare off a thief has instead robbed a neighborhood of quiet. The woman chalks a victory for the things that go *Waaaah* in the night. She rises now to sound the alarm about alarms. Quietly, of course.

FEBRUARY 1989

DID THE RAPIST HAVE

AIDS?

FIRST, a stark dose of reality: Rapists don't use condoms. They don't follow the Surgeon General's guidelines for safer sex.

So today the brutality of sexual assault has a whole new dimension of anguish for the victim. Did the rapist have AIDS? Do I have it now? Did I survive the attack to die of the disease he left behind?

Questions such as these have become routine to rape-crisis counselors and victim-assistance programs. And with them have come a new series of conflicts. Can we force every rape suspect to be tested for AIDS? Must we protect the privacy of a man who may have deposited a deadly calling card?

This intensely emotional issue was placed before a Connecticut court this month. Under state law, a victim could have a suspect tested for syphilis or gonorrhea. But the Bridgeport judge ruled she wasn't entitled to have the suspect tested for AIDS. In a tortuous bit of semantics, the judge declared that AIDS was not a venereal disease.

No other court will likely have the luxury to sidestep this matter in such a peculiar way. The legal, ethical and medical issues still lie out there, waiting to be resolved.

In our legal system, we presume that a man is innocent until proven guilty. The pressure to test rape suspects comes smack up against that presumption. There are enormous risks to civil liberties when any man accused of rape, rightly or wrongly, could be forcibly tested.

But what of men who are already convicted of rape? Should we be allowed to test them at least?

Those who say "no" do so often on technical grounds. They remind us that there is no absolute certainty in test results. There is a lag between the time of infection and the time antibodies develop. If an assailant comes up negative, he may yet harbor the virus. If he is found to carry the virus, the victim still won't know whether he transmitted it to her.

"The sad fact is, you can't know by testing the perpetrator," says Beth Weinstein of the AIDS office in the Connecticut Health Department. The woman still must test herself. Nevertheless Weinstein describes herself as "torn" on the question of testing rapists.

Her ambivalence is echoed by many for a simple reason: On the other side of this conflict is the victim. Even if the knowledge to be gained by testing isn't perfect, it is better than nothing and she may want it. Isn't she entitled to whatever margin of comfort or caution it would provide her and her family?

Ronald Bayer, a bioethicist at the Columbia University School of Public Health, says carefully: "In the situation of rape, if the woman believes that her sense of well-being would be enhanced by information, however ambiguous, then her claims ought to take priority over those of the rapist."

That, it seems to me, is the humane minimum. At bottom, the victim's right to know is greater than a convicted rapist's right to privacy.

There are some who disagree, who want to build a Maginot Line against any form of mandatory testing. But these absolutists lose their moral footing. There is a difference between massive testing such as the premarital screening going on in Illinois—a model of absurdity—and a careful program for rape victims.

At the same time, there are limits when you only test convicted rapists rather than suspects. Many believe that a rapist with AIDS commits an even greater crime. How do you make that charge before you know whether he carries the virus?

There is also the cruelty of the waiting period. It takes a year for the average rape case to come to trial—a long year of anxiety. Indeed, the AIDS epidemic lends special weight to the longtime demand of victims' groups for a speedy trial.

These are the murkiest of waters. We are just now wading into them. Even victims' rights groups like the National Organization for Victim Assistance offer a two-sided argument on this issue in a newsletter with the neutral headline: A DEADLY PROBLEM IN SEARCH OF A POLICY.

But there is a place to begin. Yes, a convicted rapist can be required to take an AIDS test and give the results to his victim. This is, after all, the very least he owes her.

OCTOBER 1988

ALCOHOL AND EXCUSES

I DON'T KNOW when the town drunk was officially transformed into a victim of alcoholism. It is still only thirty years since the American Medical Association first declared that chronic drunkenness wasn't a sin. It was, rather, a disease.

Now, according to polls, some 87 percent of us accept alcoholism as a sickness. But our attitudes toward the "ism" of alcohol are not as clear as this figure suggests.

We may no longer want to condemn alcoholics for their addiction. On the other hand, we don't want to excuse them from responsibility for their behavior.

This ambivalence about the semantics and social policy of alcohol abuse is now coming before the Supreme Court. Next week, the high court will hear the cases of two men, both veterans, both recovered alcoholics, both suing the Veterans Administration.

The two men missed the VA deadline for college benefits. They were drunk during their eligible years. They complain that under the VA guidelines, disabled veterans would have had longer to apply for these benefits. But the VA doesn't call alcoholism a disability. It calls alcoholism "willful misconduct." So these two have accused the VA of illegally discriminating against them on the basis of their handicap: alcoholism.

The case may finally turn on some minor point, but it raises major questions. Is alcoholism a disease? Is an alcoholic disabled in the sense that, say, a paraplegic is? Does he or she deserve an extra hand from society, an extension of benefits, a special ramp into life? Must we then agree that alcoholism is a legitimate excuse for misbehavior, even for a crime?

In a curiously parallel case, the President's friend, Michael Deaver, is using alcoholism as a defense against charges of perjury. He was too sick to know what he was saying. The disease, not the man, done it.

These lines between sick behavior and bad behavior are not always clear. Leonard Glantz of Boston University's School of Public Health offers another example: "If you have a brain tumor and attack me because of this tumor, is it fair to send you to jail? Most people would think not. But if you ran me down with a car because you were in the throes of alcoholic delusion, should you go to jail? Most people would say yes."

Our ambivalence toward alcoholism may be entirely appropriate, even accurate. We are often comfortable labeling alcoholism as a disease. There is medical evidence to match the terminology. We know alcohol can be addictive. We read that people can inherit a susceptibility to addiction. There may be a genetic link.

The semantics also fit our current social-policy desires. If alcoholics are "sick" instead of bad, they need, indeed deserve, help. This attitude has destigmatized the addiction, and put into place a vast array of programs on alcohol abuse.

At the same time, we know that alcoholism has an element of choice. You can't just say no to cancer. But you can say no to a drink. The cure is not in the hands of a surgeon. It is in the hands of the "victim." Indeed part of the cure is getting people to take responsibility for their actions.

Ultimately, says Glantz, "we still must make choices about how people are handled." Choices for the whole of society, not just a "sick" individual. Most of those choices are made in the courts, not the medical lab. Today, even a sociopath—someone who has no regard for the life of others—is not considered mentally ill for the purposes of criminal prosecution.

We can label alcoholism a disease to help those who are in need. But we shouldn't accept it as a defense, when the alcoholic's behavior threatens the rest of the community.

If Michael Deaver had blacked out on the highway and slammed into another car, we would not have forgiven his behavior on account of drunkenness. Nor should we forgive perjury on these grounds.

As for the veterans demanding their handicapped rights, I don't think we should extend benefits to alcoholics that are denied to the sober. Remember that these two veterans have recovered from their disease. They didn't do it by making excuses.

DECEMBER 1987

PART TEN

CAMPAIGN '88

*I don't know when the American public turned
permanently into the American audience. The citizen
is now the couch potato and politics has become a
spectator sport.*

MICHAEL WHO?

T HERE WERE NO Secret Service cars lined up along Perry Street last Saturday morning. The red brick two-family house in this Brookline neighborhood is no governor's mansion. The car in the driveway is not a limo but a 1981 Dodge Aries.

The man who answered the door in his corduroys led this neighbor automatically back to the hub of his home—the kitchen—for coffee, cornbread and conversation. Moving about the room, with a comfortable domesticity, Michael Dukakis knew he might be spending his last Saturday at home for a very long time.

"We've been able to achieve a pretty rare degree of normalcy around here," he said, and his wife Kitty agreed as we sat at the round wooden table. The Dukakises' youngest daughter came through the room in sweats, sneakers and Walkman on her way out for a jog. "If I decide to run for President, it is the end of life as we've known it and really enjoyed it," Dukakis said. "And that is something that one has to think about very hard."

Dukakis had other things on his list to think hard about it. Could he do the job? Could he win? Could he be a sitting governor and candidate? But finally, on Monday afternoon (March 16), the man they call the Duke announced: "With your help and your prayers, a son of Greek immigrants named Mike Dukakis can become the next President of the United States."

Out in the country, the voters paying attention this early in the game undoubtedly asked each other "Mike Who?" and "Mike Why?" The national media only offered him a slot in the second tier of candidates. But here, in this city-suburb, a mile from where John F. Kennedy was born, in the sort of town people choose "for the schools," the announcement was greeted with the bemused excitement people reserve for the high-school friend, the local boy who made good.

At the Longwood trolley stop where the Duke often takes the T, at the Stop and Shop where he goes grocery shopping, along the route where the former marathoner now does his speedwalking with hand weights, people who have known the man since he ran for state representative in the sixties shared one-liners about Mike Who.

"If he becomes President, Mike's so cheap, he'll save half his salary," says one old supporter. "I'll tell you one thing about Mike: There's nothing in his closet, no ghosts, no surprises," says another.

In the announcement Dukakis said he welcomed tests of "character and competence." A strength of the Dukakis candidacy is that there is no whiff of scandal, no weakness for law-bending in his twenty-four-year political career. If anything, he expresses genuine bewilderment at how an Irangate can happen. "I don't get it. What happens to people in that place?"

As for competence, Dukakis prides himself on being able to "make idealism work." He takes pleasure in the practical. In Massachusetts, where people voted for both McGovern and Reagan, this governor measures his successes in people programs that work: the much-touted welfare reform that turned recipients into employees, and the revival of this economy that meant jobs.

"When I was in Birmingham, Alabama," he remembers, "some guy said, 'Massachusetts has 3.2 percent unemployment? The only thing we know that's 3.2 down here is beer.'" Dukakis thinks he can make it all work nationally.

Character and competence. If the third C is charisma, this governor doesn't get much of a rating. Indeed, Dukakis seems charisma-aversive, almost suspicious of raising emotions in a crowd. In their marriage, it is Kitty Dukakis who carries the emotional baggage and the Tums.

Dukakis is Greek, but not Zorba the Greek. He is a man who once climbed the Acropolis in wing-tipped shoes. It has taken him years to feel comfortable publicly sharing the story of his father, a man who went from immigrant to medical student in eight years. When I asked him during breakfast to write his own bumper sticker, he said, "This is a guy who's strong, competent, caring," and then went on for minutes expanding the bumper sticker into a position paper.

But the man who admits he is "no smiling Jack" adds this thought: "A lot of folks are saying, 'We've had six years of charisma, maybe it's time for something else.'" Perhaps even time for a man who is just what he seems, exactly the same in private and in public, at the kitchen table or in front of the cameras, making cornbread or public policy. A centered soul.

Dukakis knows he is a long shot. He knows he has to translate local experience into a national vision. He talks about being President as "if lightning strikes." But in his hometown, there is something akin to presidential electricity.

"He already has four percent in the polls!" exclaims one old friend. "Four percent is the margin of error," cautions another. "Think about it this way," says a third, rattling off the list of Massachusetts Presidents. "Mike has less charisma than JFK. More charisma than Calvin Coolidge. And he's taller than John Adams." The Duke of Brookline is off and running.

MARCH 1987

GARY HART I: DOES
WOMANIZING MATTER?

IT WAS NOT the sort of headline that the Hart campaign wanted to paste in its media scrapbook. *The New York Post,* with its penchant for putting words in the mouths of politicians, had done it again. Page one blared: "Gary: 'I'm No Womanizer.' "

The *Post*-written quote was the low point of a week of more decorous discussion of "the sex issue." *Newsweek* had started it off with a line from John T. McEvoy, a longtime Hart adviser, who said, "He's always in danger of having the sex issue raised if he can't keep his pants on."

Having been sabotaged by one of his own, Hart then claimed and later recanted his claim that opponents were spreading these rumors. We were smack in the middle of another controversy about a public man's personal life.

Hart's marital and extramarital life may be set for the treatment that Ted Kennedy's got in 1980. Virtually every profile on the twice-separated Harts includes some line about their relationship. "Last time around he had to be reminded to kiss her in public," wrote a *Washington Post* reporter. "Today he touches her often and calls her 'babe.' "

Still, the question that interests me more than Gary Hart's past or present is this: What exactly do we know about any person when we know "everything" about his sexual life? What exactly does it mean if and when a man is a "womanizer," in terms of his ability to lead? Nothing? Everything? Do we need to know?

We can look at this information as gossip of the sort that follows British royalty or movie stars without ruining their careers. We can also regard it as a disqualification, evidence that a man is morally unfit for higher office. But historically, the record is very unclear.

In the past decade researchers have unearthed all sorts of examples of hi-infidelity. Was FDR's legacy diminished by his apparent love for Lucy Rutherford? What of JFK, whose amorous adventures have been chronicled, if not exaggerated, by a flock of women announcing, "Jack slept here." Did it, does it, diminish his moral claim, the clarity of his vision? How badly?

And what of another leader, Martin Luther King, Jr.? In David Garrow's moving biography, *Bearing the Cross,* the "sex issue" appears, delicately, as King's clay feet. Infidelity increased his own sense of unworthiness, writes Garrow. With the FBI trailing, he risked discovery and damage to the civil-rights movement. Does that mean that the cause, the dream, would have been articulated, pursued more effectively by someone whose private life was pure?

Sexuality has a different place, a different meaning in the lives of different public men, a Jim Bakker or a JFK. One "womanizer" may hate women, another love them; one may feel immune to discovery, another may be courting disaster; one may be following his father's pattern; another rebelling. It is possible to follow a strict moral code in public and not in private. The opposite is also possible.

Infidelity also suggests different things about the leader to different viewers, or voters. In the Ted Kennedy campaign in 1980, there was evidence that people who believed he was unfaithful were most uneasy with what they regarded as the political exploitation of his wife. We imprint our own ideas onto acts.

If sexuality doesn't mean *one* thing, if we cannot draw one lesson from private life about public performance, perhaps we have no need for this information at all. Perhaps it is just irrelevant, salacious gossip. Perhaps we should go back to the days when a gentleman's agreement kept this off the record.

But my own sense is that, finally, this is fair game. You do learn something important about the character of a man from revelations of his sexual behavior. The information may be no more important than how he treats his children or secretary, no more important than his stand on world trade and farm policy. It may tell little about how he'll deal with the poor or with arms control. Or how well he will run a government. But it becomes part of a whole portrait of a man.

You learn about fidelity to more than a wife. You learn about his capacity for deception. You learn about his vulnerability to exposure, fascination with risk-taking. You learn about impulsiveness, self-control, even the ability to compartmentalize ethics.

This does not excuse *New York Post* headlines or vicious rumormongers who claim dossiers on one candidate or another. But every President finally serves, not just as a chief executive, but as chief figurehead, chief role model, chief moral leader—in short, chief American. We ask a great deal. Anyone who runs for the office today has to know that there is no room in the job description for chief womanizer.

APRIL 1987

GARY HART II: A
QUESTION OF CHARACTER

ANYBODY WHO WANTS to know how private political lives became public territory in America can start the search with the gentleman's agreement that kept John F. Kennedy's infidelity off the record and follow the trail all the way to a car parked outside Gary Hart's house.

Inside the car were reporters from the *Miami Herald,* acting on a tip, staking out Hart's house as if they were waiting for a drug dealer. From their stakeout grew a story about the arrival and departure of Donna Rice, the woman who has become the ball and chain on Gary Hart's race for the presidency.

Hart and Rice deny that she stayed overnight. When it was revealed that they had gone to Bimini on a yacht named *Monkey Business,* they claimed to have slept in separate boats.

The campaign took the best defense in a strong offense against the reporters. Hart called the story "false and misleading." His campaign manager said, "Scrutiny and questions of character are one thing: Character assassinations are entirely another." The line, they said, had been crossed.

But it is not just the Hart people worrying whether journalists have become the new morals squad, the watchdog of a resurgent Puritanism, the people who point to the lipstick on politicians' collars. Nor is it just the Hart people who wonder whether there is any perimeter of privacy left around a public life.

We are deep into the era of up-close and personal reporting. The TV camera offers, as information to assess, the sweat on a candidate's upper lip as well as the words. Politicians are covered like celebrities and those who fear that political discourse has slipped to the level of *People* magazine worry that we are sliding down to the *National Enquirer.*

But if much has changed in journalism, it is in tune with the times, with changes in the wider world. Today the country is more accepting of divorce among politicians and—therefore?—less accepting of marital infidelity. The old-boy tolerance of dalliance—men will be men—has been changed by the admission of women into the system: the gentlewoman's disagreement.

More importantly, a slogan of the women's movement—the personal is political—has become a common sensibility. We are more willing to admit the importance of something we call character. And less willing to accept a character that is split between public and private life.

It may be that newspapers report on sex because it is, well, sexy. Certainly sexier than military-reform policy. But I don't believe that journalists have become obsessed with the candidates' sex lives. The profession has, rather, taken sex out of the exempt category.

Imagine that the *Miami Herald* got a solid tip about a presidential candidate meeting with a drug dealer at his home. Imagine that a candidate had a cancer specialist making a house call. Imagine that a candidate was to be visited by a foreign agent. Would we still say that a stakeout violated his privacy?

What if a reporter can prove that a candidate is a liar? Is he or she allowed to follow every lead, except the one that might prove the candidate had lied about fidelity? Is sex the only thing that's off-limits?

Many protest that a person's sexuality, unlike his drug use or health, wouldn't affect the way he handles the presidency. We would surely prefer a man who compulsively made love to one who compulsively made war. But I am not being coy when I say the issue isn't morality, isn't the clinical details, but character.

In a recent piece I suggested that the relationship between sex and presidential character was elusive. "Womanizing" was, however, a fair topic for reporters, because it revealed something about a man's capacity for deception, vulnerability to exposure, fascination with risk-taking. Even in his own best-case scenario we have learned a great deal about the man who invited investigation.

Was it worth the cost in invasion of privacy? The closer you are to the presidency, the smaller the circumference of privacy. I don't for a minute believe the media are now on a roll, that news organizations will compete with stakeouts of every candidate's hotel room. This is a special case. But they won't any longer automatically excise infidelity from the roster of things they can report.

It is too bad that we can't find out as easily about a candidate's penchant for foreign adventures or nuclear risk-taking. But the press is not guilty of the character assassination of Gary Hart. Call this one character suicide.

THE GEORGE BUSH
MANHOOD TEST

WHEN WE LAST tuned in to "The Story of George Bush: Macho or Mouse?" the year was 1984, the city was Philadelphia, and the event was the vice presidential debate. There, an effervescent candidate attested to the utter joy he felt at being Reagan's Veep, joy that ran from his toes to his tenor.

The morning after this debate with the diminutive Geraldine Ferraro, he told a longshoreman gleefully: "We tried to kick a little ass last night."

Now it is 1988, and the most recent scene in "Macho or Mouse" pitted George Bush against Dan Rather in a debate that achieved the intellectual level of a playground pushing match: Sez who? Sez me. Oh, yeah?

What did our boy Bush say this time off camera? "The bastard didn't lay a glove on me. . . . That guy makes Lesley Stahl look like a pussy." The next day he told a group of students that going mano a mano with Rather was "kind of like combat."

Now, with all due respect to the Vice President (and as journalists we are now required to show due respect), what is going on here? For days now, the newspapers have reported that the Bush camp was overjoyed at the confrontation. They regarded the verbal wrestling match with Rather as a shot in the arm for the campaign. The needle was full of testosterone.

Apparently, the George Bush Manhood Test for 1988 is taking the offensive against a television anchor. An aide called the incident a "defining moment." A supporter in Wyoming gave him a T-shirt that read Bush-1, Rather-0. The Dole people half kiddingly demanded equal time. As for the World War II naval aviator himself? George Bush actually said: "I need combat pay for last night."

Combat pay? From where I sat, it was less like a war and more like a fraternity house thumb-wrestling match: unseemly, and just a bit absurd. Yet it sated some peculiar desire to see the guys mix it up.

I don't know when the American public turned permanently into the American audience. The citizen is now the couch potato and politics has become a spectator event. This transition has elevated television journalists to the level of contestants, and lowered the whole level of discourse. It's more fun to watch the blood dripping on the floor.

Consider what's happening to the news-talk shows. Dan Rather, if I may paraphrase Bush, is a kitten compared to the clawed cast of *Crossfire*. Political opinions on *The McLaughlin Group* are expressed with all the grace of a food fight. At least one news show, under the aegis of Morton Downey, Jr., has transformed talk into a rabble-rouse. On the other hand, Bush was the only candidate who refused an hour of civilized persistence by Marvin Kalb on public television.

Is there a national hankering after a good fight? "For the Republican right," said ABC's Jeff Greenfield, "being attacked by Dan Rather is like being attacked by Gadhafi." In real life his wrestle with Rather may be a lot more like our real-life attack on Gadhafi. It felt great at the time, everybody stood up and cheered, but it turned out to be the wrong target.

I find this long-running play—Macho or Mouse—more than a little repellent. It grows out of an attitude that confuses the Halls of Montezuma with the Shores of Grenada. It's the attitude that asks whether a candidate can stand up to Gorbachev instead of asking whether he can sit down with him.

I remember another time last year when Bush spoke out of his frustration with the wimp question. Didn't it take strength to sit and watch your child die? He had done that. But now he gains points as the kick-ass candidate. The man who stood up to Dan Rather.

This may be the year when the candidates all have to pass a televised testosterone test. When they have to win a gold medal in anchor wrestling. But if I were writing the scorecard for this pugnacious political event, it would be Bush-o, Rather-o, Leadership-o.

FEBRUARY 1988

VOTERS AND VIEWERS

I AM SITTING on a podium next to Barney Rosenzweig when the genial producer of *Cagney and Lacey* refers to his television audience as a "constituency of thirty million viewers." The discussion moves on, but my mind sticks on that phrase. A "constituency of viewers"?

My dictionary defines *constituency* as a body of voters. By all accounts it is a political word. But the producer has used it deliberately in describing his campaign for entertainment victories. People, he says, vote with their fingers every week.

I might have expected Hollywood to fuse such terms. Viewers and voters. Consumers and constituents. But sitting here, I was reminded of the other way we've become part of the role confusion. To the television moguls, we may be constituents. But in the political world, we have become viewers.

This is not the first presidential race to be played out on the television screen. By now, we have accepted the campaign as performance. We have become sophisticated about thirty-second bites. We know that candidates fly from market to market instead of city to city. We've seen Presidents sold like products; we know what goes on the political screen.

But there is a more subtle impact of television on our political behavior. Not television as a series of images on a screen but television watching as an activity, *the* dominant political activity. We have become better viewers than voters.

The only thing that television itself asks is that people watch. There is something intrinsically passive about this. Eyeball participation seems to me quite different from the whole-bodied politics that a democracy is supposed to demand of its people. It may be as different as the word *audience* is from the word *citizen*.

I won't indulge too deeply in television-bashing. The up-close and personal politics of this era is not intrinsically worse than the grand old gestures of hall orators. There is no greater civic virtue in attending a rally than in watching one. More people see a candidate than at any time in our history.

But television has produced a couch-potato constituency. Sitting in front of the set, we expect to be amused, entertained, informed, inactive. Everything comes to us in the same one-way human channel: news and entertainment, political debates and sitcoms. Watching television we expect to be, rather than to do. The set permits no entry from home.

In some curious way, the most experienced political viewer becomes expert at one thing: television criticism. We become better equipped to criticize performance than policies. It is, after all, easier. Having done this for years, we are no longer even embarrassed at criticizing the star quality of a candidate. This has become our job as members of the audience/electorate.

In 1984, I remember Tom Brokaw's post-debate analysis vividly. He announced that a candidate had scored with two uses of humor. With that scorecard in hand, the anchorman became the critic, closing the political circle. Then it was notable. Now it is routine. We are comfortable watching, comfortable criticizing. We sink into our role as easily as we sink into the couch. It's hard to get up again.

I cannot prove that the rise of politics-as-television is responsible for the decrease of actual real, live voters. But how many viewer-voters have learned from television that they can reject politics because the program is boring? How many think they've done enough when they voted with their fingers?

In front of the television set, citizens are transformed into an audience. We can only, passively, receive the messages. Or we can turn off.

MARCH 1988

SELLING STEADINESS

JUST A YEAR AGO, when the first political reporters started drifting into my hometown to find out about this guy Dukakis, a Washington colleague of mine asked what the governor's weakness might be as President. I said then that it might be his deep, even irrational, belief in reason.

Dukakis is a man who might have trouble understanding the great emotional "isms" rocking the world. He is wary of public passions, doesn't entirely understand their power.

So it was with that domestic breed of "ism," Jacksonism: a powerful mix of populist sentiment, black pride and flat-out charisma. Dukakis was his most uncomfortable self in the days before the Wisconsin victory. The more Jackson seemed to expand—his voice, his embrace—the more Dukakis seemed to contract. Jackson hugged; Dukakis shook hands.

If Jackson demanded passion from a crowd, Dukakis visibly flinched from public displays. He wanted listeners, not lovers.

There has rarely been a starker contrast between candidates and I do not mean in skin color. Jackson pitches to the heart, Dukakis to the head. Jackson exudes: "I am somebody." Dukakis explains: "I am what I am." More to the point, Jackson plays to the impulse buyer, Dukakis to the cautious, unit-price-reading, comparison shopper.

So the victory in Wisconsin must be particularly sweet to Dukakis. Because in a sense, he won it his way.

Remember the marathon metaphor? For most of this season, the governor has compared the campaign to that endurance contest, that competitive sport of loners. But recently he has begun talking about boxing.

The campaign, he said, on the night of his Wisconsin victory, was going the full fifteen rounds and there would be no knockout, he would win on points. In Wisconsin he did just that. Point One: Who can beat Bush? Point Two: Who has the experience in government? Point Three: Who can do the job?

"After seven years of charisma," said Dukakis, "isn't it time for competence?" Not the sort of sentiment you usually find on a candidate's bumper sticker. But it dealt head on with the issue of emotion in politics.

Is it an imperative, as Jackson suggests, for leaders to physically connect with citizens, for candidates to attract voters into their circle of believers? Is the powerful emotional surge—including the one that comes from watching a black man breaking through barriers of racism—a compelling plus? Or is there also something to be wary of in a mass chanting of rhymes and slogans?

We have seen it work both ways. The energy and passion that impels a movement. The loss of individuality, the giving up of reason that empowers a demagogue. The Jackson campaign struck at the ambivalence many voters felt about the passion issue.

Dukakis was in the curious and yet genuine position of reminding voters to think about what they felt, to resist going with the flow, the big Mo, chanting the chorus of Jesse's compelling refrains. He asked voters not to be swept off their feet. Not by Jackson. And also not by him. It is an extraordinary request from any politician. But one that fits seamlessly into his own life.

Last week, I heard someone remark that Jackson would be a great date, but Dukakis would be a better husband. It's steadiness that he's selling. It is no accident that he chose the emotionally charged Kitty as wife, or that Kitty Dukakis chose his steadiness. In the years before his brother's accidental death, when that brother was quite simply emotionally ill, Dukakis was also the steady one.

There is another marital analogy I have heard. Who was it who said that George Bush reminded every woman of her first husband? There is no charismatic competition there. But a Brookline neighbor says that Dukakis reminds many a woman of her second husband. He's the one she got to know slowly. The one she looked at long and hard, picked carefully with her eyes wide open.

This is how Dukakis is wooing the Democratic Party. He doesn't expect to sweep her off her feet. He wants to win on points.

APRIL 1988

WHY NOT TAKE AN EASY JOB?

IN THE QUADRENNIAL spectator sport known as a presidential campaign there comes the inevitable and wonderful moment known as: The Search for a Vice President. For a few summer weeks, we get to watch prominent Americans exhibit their reluctance for the role of understudy.

With the notable exception of Geraldine Ferraro in 1984, nobody who is anybody admits to a passionate desire to be number two. Nobody says that he or she grew up dreaming about being Vice President of the United States.

This year we may indeed have more protesters than applicants. Just this week, Jeane Kirkpatrick insisted, "I don't want to be Vice President." New Jersey Governor Thomas Kean told the press, "I'm doing everything I can to make sure he [Bush] doesn't come to me."

Democrats such as Bill Bradley, Sam Nunn and Tom Foley have all taken their names out of the running. Those who are said to be "interested" in the job don't say much except a self-sacrificing willingness to help the party and/or country. Even Jesse Jackson, who wants to be asked, appears to regard the job as political slumming.

There is a general, national, snickering consensus that the vice presidency is the worst job in Washington, not worth a bucket of warm spit and all that. The current occupant has even disparaged the role, saying: "I'm George Bush. You die, I fly."

A job without much power, a job without much labor. Bob Dole uttered the ultimate slur. Being Vice President, he sneered, is "indoor work and no heavy lifting."

Heaven forfend.

It's notable that the worst insult inflicted on a job these days is that the post is too easy. Isn't this what every American secretly craves, if only we didn't mercilessly disparage it?

These are the facts: The Vice President of the United States earns $115,000 a year plus $10,000 in expenses. He gets a nice big house on Massachusetts Avenue and he doesn't have to mow the lawn. He gets a plane and a decent office or two. It isn't Iacocca, but it isn't shabby either.

In return for this, the Vice President has to preside over the Senate, break an occasional tie, take charge of a task force or two, show up at Cabinet meetings and travel abroad. All you need for the job, as Bush once said, is "a black hat with a veil." You get home in time for dinner.

If someone in your family got that kind of a job offer, would you insist that they pass it up for the sake of something much harder? Or would you spring for the black hat?

The rap on the Vice President may be the most public vestige of the lingering Puritan work ethic. Upwardly mobile Americans still have difficulty accepting the attraction of leisure. There is no public acclaim, no hat or horn, for the person who wangles an easy job out of life. When Dole described the Veep post as one where you don't have to make decisions, you just sit on the bench, it was not meant to be a job plus.

Since the work ethic reappeared in a Yuppie uniform, a new generation of scorn has been directed at anyone who chooses the hammock over the gym. Young lawyers today put in hours that were once relegated to sweatshops. The belief in the virtue of labor—the more labor, the more virtue—is something a coal miner would find depressing. And it's endemic in politics.

The power class can lust for money, but not easy money. They don't buy lottery tickets. Only occasionally when, say, a Mike Tyson picks up $22 million in 91 seconds, do they take out their calculators and figure wistfully, "That's $241,760 per second."

Not long ago, National Public Radio's Susan Stamberg was asked the inevitable question about her life. What did she want to do next? She answered crisply and wonderfully with one word: "Less." I thought then how rare it is to have any prominent person admit that. How much rarer it would be to hear someone openly yearn for a nice job with fat paycheck, minimal responsibility, moderate prestige and short hours.

That's the vice presidency, folks. Nice work if you can get it. But you can't admit you want it or like it. The only risk is that you could end up President. But as Reagan has proved, if you play your cards right, even that job, too, can be inside work, no heavy lifting.

JULY 1988

THE I AM SOMEBODY
CAMPAIGN

THIS IS THE image that lingers on. Jesse Jackson preaching before the NAACP on the night after Dukakis chose Bentsen. Jesse Jackson closing on an eloquent and haunting word: "One thing I know. I may not be on the ticket. But I'm qualified. That's what I know. I'm qualified . . . qualified . . . qualified."

The word echoed again and again in the hall until it was dimmed by applause. *Qualified.* It wasn't meant to be an epitaph or even a grace note to the campaign, but Jackson's emotional acknowledgment of what it was all about. One clarifying moment.

The Jackson campaign always had its own duality, a stereophonic message coming out of its single speaker: It was the Jesse Jackson for President Campaign. It was the I Am Somebody Campaign.

Jackson Action: It was about electing delegates and winning respect. It was about being nominated and being acknowledged.

The star of it was a man who wanted to be both a Democratic Party insider and leader of a movement of outsiders. A man who wanted to be accepted as a full partner of the powerful and a surrogate for the powerless.

The stereo sound was sometimes jarring, but it was also stirring while there were primaries to be won, delegates to be counted. When people asked "What does Jackson want?" he could display resentment. Why, he wanted to be President.

But there was always more to it than that. The other side. And when the delegate count was in, when Michael Dukakis won, when he chose Lloyd Bentsen, when he treated Jackson as if he were, say, John Glenn, the split became clearer.

Jesse Jackson knew all along he wasn't going to be chosen Vice President. Whatever the politics, the racial politics as well, it would have been a profound mismatch of man and job. Jackson as Number Two? Jackson as Yes Man?

A friend, a psychiatrist prone to such questions, wonders why Jackson said he would accept the job of Vice President the night before he surely knew it would not be offered. Could it be, she asks, that this illegitimate child who grew up on the outskirts of his own father's life had set himself up for rejection? Was this why he was still asking days later for some amorphous "respect and responsibility"?

Maybe so. A quest for entry, for acceptance, may have had its roots in such a personal history. "I am qualified," said Jackson. The search for legitimacy in its widest sense comes powerfully close to those words.

But politics is more than autobiography. In the emotional speech to the NAACP, Jesse repeated his memory of Thanksgivings spent waiting for his mother to come home with leftovers from the white folks' table. The personal experience of being kept "outside" a biological family may not be as important as the collective experience of being kept outside the mainstream society. That is also what has connected Jackson to black and poor America.

His teasing interest in the job of Vice President may well have been a way to keep the two Jackson campaigns in harmony a little while longer. He seemed genuinely surprised at the news of Bentsen. But was it, as he said, because he wasn't told directly? Was his "sense of indignation and . . . insult" roused only by the poor communication?

Or was it the recognition that the Jackson for President campaign was finally over. And he hasn't yet charted a way to continue the I Am Somebody Campaign.

This is the problem facing Jackson now. How do you maintain a crusade after the election is over? It's one thing to stop running for office. But it's quite another to halt the machinery that is running for respect.

Running for President was a profound, prideful symbol of success. When Jesse says he is still running, it's because he hasn't figured out how to declare a victory that will fuel the continuing race for pride, acceptance, legitimacy. Not just for himself, but for his constituents.

The easiest thing in the world is to go back outside, disappointed, disaffected. Outside is a familiar place to many Jackson followers. It's far harder to hail a win in the race for respect and go on. But Jesse may have tested a victory speech before the NAACP. No, he said. He didn't win. But at last, "I am qualified . . . qualified . . . qualified."

JULY 1988

DAN QUAYLE: A
CO-ANCHOR FOR VEEP

THE SKEPTICS said it couldn't be done. Nothing could close the gender gap that stretches like a formidable canyon between George Bush and the White House. There it is: fifteen points wide; twenty points wide. But this didn't discourage the dedicated researchers at the Gender Gap Project. The very finest minds of the Republican Party gathered in their demographics war room to develop a plan that would win over the hearts, minds and votes of American women.

Would the child-care program do it? Would they have to show more sensitivity to the stress of women who spend weekends in the laundry room instead of on the golf course? Would they have to do more than sprinkle "family" through their speeches and photo opportunities? Might they have to—gasp—give up their jock-talk for the duration of the campaign?

Under this intense pressure, they came up with a concept so simple, so pristine, so elegant in its understanding of the female psyche that it's almost scary. Ladies and women, the secret weapon of the Republican Party has been unveiled, the one thing designed to make the fair sex swoon in the voting booth: *the pretty face!*

Danny Quayle, young and handsome, conservative and cute, right-winged and blue-eyed. He has been presented as the new co-anchor of the Republican Party.

From Jerry Falwell to campaign manager Jim Baker, there was more than an intimation that the Indiana baby boomer was chosen for his ability to attract women. Of all the candidates for the post, he alone ran equally well with women in his home state. If national politics is now Broadcast News, Danny Quayle was their William Hurt. Hire him and watch women change channels.

In describing the vice presidential choice, Senator John McCain of Arizona used the word *attractive* some seven times in one paragraph, "I can't believe," he said, "a guy that handsome wouldn't be attractive in some respect." At least to women. Baker seconded the thought with a more cryptic comment, "Regardless of where he is on the issues, he does very well with women."

Even the more enlightened or at least cautious conservatives here substituted words like *telegenic,* and phrases like *fresh face.* They carefully suggested that women in particular might be sensitive to the "human" side of the man.

Now I don't want to suggest that Danny Quayle is an airhead. Yes, Vanna, cute men can also suffer the slights of not being taken seriously. Deborah Steelman, the domestic policy adviser of the Bush campaign, recognizes that "If he makes a big mistake, his looks will turn on him and he'll never be able to get rid of the lightweight image."

Quayle calls this his "stigma." He lamented and fostered the "fact" that he looks like Robert Redford. George Bush allegedly chose him for his youth, not his looks. Together, they appear less like a hunting magazine, Bush and Quayle, than like a corporation, Bush and Son.

But there is something profoundly silly in the idea being bandied about that women flock to the best looker. They may date cute, but they don't necessarily vote cute. Even in 1960, more women voted for Richard Nixon than John Kennedy.

Moreover, this gap is, as the pollsters like to say, issues-driven. Quayle the young and handsome is on the other side of most issues. He did file a child-care bill in the Senate and helped create a job-training bill. But he is opposed to parental leave, supported cuts in Social Security cost-of-living allowances, voted against the plant-closing bill and the Civil Rights Restoration Act. As for standard women's rights issues, he is anti-ERA and anti-abortion. He is also a major hawk, while most women tend toward dovishness.

In polls and focus groups, women repeatedly express the feeling that Bush is too removed to understand their daily lives. Linda Divall, the Republican pollster, thinks that Quayle will appeal to them as warm and a listener. Indeed, Quayle the father, with three children and a wife who practiced law, may be closer to their lives. But Quayle, the millionaire, isn't sweating the mortgage.

So the question for the Gender Gap Project is: Will women drop their issues like a parasol to run off with Danny because he's adorable? Don't count on it.

The Pretty Face Factor doesn't sound like a campaign strategy at all. It sounds like a chapter from *Smart Women, Foolish Choices.* And isn't this how the Republicans got in trouble with women in the first place?

AUGUST 1988

IS THIS A CAMPAIGN OR A
COMIC STRIP?

I GREW UP in an era when the most profound political thought was: "I like Ike." So I never expected a presidential campaign to be like a graduate class in good government.

But after the back-to-school week of the 1988 campaign, I know how teachers feel when they get some new and simpler set of textbooks. What we are witnessing is the "dumbing down" of politics.

Forgive me if I reject the polite school jargon. This campaign isn't "special," nor is it "remedial." Even *simpleminded* is too kind a word. It has become just plain dumb.

Consider what we've been taught so far. That civics is solely a matter of pledging allegiance to the flag. That history is a matter of opinion: One side can blame every problem on the seventies, the other on the eighties. That math is something to be manipulated: You can add to the budget and subtract from the deficit.

The Bush campaign has had a heavier hand in the dumbing down process. In Bush's class you don't have to be the brightest boy to be the teacher's pet. Danny Quayle was already proof of that. But now Bush, who cannot parse a sentence, and Quayle, who speaks in Germanic word order—"it is an issue that I have not spent thus far a great deal of time on"—are trying to reduce the campaign to a patriotic pop quiz.

As for history, the Vice President misplaces more than Pearl Harbor Day. His geography class has maps that put Brookline, Massachusetts, in the Soviet Union and that cover up Iran. His best English compositions are by speechwriter Peggy Noonan. His worst are a litany of snide attacks. And in Bush's advanced economics class on taxes, all he asks is that we read his lips.

This man wants to be the education President?

Dukakis for his part looks shell-shocked by this streak of silliness. But he, too, has been warned against sounding professorial. Instead he has sounded elementary: leading drills in the American dream and refrains about "good jobs at good wages." He is now urged to put up his dukes by lowering his sights.

In this long-term dumbing-down process, all the pictures get bigger while the texts get smaller. The 1988 presidential campaign is a cross between a comic strip and a video. Bush goes to Disney World; Dukakis to Ellis Island. Balloons abound. The analysts grade campaigns as if they were MTV awards: one point for Concept, another for Special Effects, a third for Choreography and the ultimate for Viewer's Choice.

Is there anyone to blame for such political sliding? Surely Reagan had a role. It was more than a slip of the tongue, when he told the GOP convention that "facts are stupid things." Reagan's campaigns convinced a generation of handlers that the most successful candidate is the one who says the least of substance.

Few of us thought that elections would (or could) actually deteriorate in the post-Gipper era. But this year, it is considered brave and downright risky when a candidate "goes specific."

In one way or another, everyone has played a part in the downward spiral. The media do not go into a "feeding flurry" over economics or disarmament. We do not dog the candidates in their driveways until they sweatily explain how they would reduce the deficit. The networks, geared to the attention span of *Sesame Street* viewers, are easily manipulated, even as they report on their manipulation.

As for the voters, we are told that the legions of advisers do not go broke underestimating them. Negative advertising works. If voters find it hard to sort out messages, they choose an image. We have settled into a pattern of responses nearly as simplistic as last week's wave of boos.

My hope is that this campaign has bottomed out. Surely, if the public were to raise hands, the question we would ask is: "How?" How would the next President lower the deficit, live in peace, manage families and work, secure the future? Please give us more than a "sound bite" or a hint.

I wish I had more faith that an hour-long debate, or two of them, will answer these questions, satisfy the longing for real knowledge. But candidates care less about what we learn than how we rank them.

The next set of grades will be out in November. The most important news may not be which man passed and which failed, but how many more voters, once and for all, dropped out.

SEPTEMBER 1988

No "Gaffe" on Abortion

LET'S BE FAIR to the guy. Poppy was right the first time.

Dig back through the week of damage control and instant policy revisions. Watch a replay of the precise moment when George Bush was asked whether a woman who had an abortion, or a doctor who performed it, should go to jail.

His answer began with a flustered admission, "I haven't sorted out the penalties. . . ." But it ended with the truth: "Of course, there's got to be some penalties to enforce the law, whatever they may be."

If the alarm buzzers went off in the Bush war room, it's because they know how to count. By any estimate some fifteen million American women have had abortions since it's been legal. Everyone knows someone who's had one. Would they be criminals in Bush's America?

By morning, the handlers had "clarified" his position. No, no, the women wouldn't be prosecuted. They would be treated lovingly (not to mention patronizingly) as victims.

That, said the Bush people, should "close" the question. Indeed the media praised the Republicans for getting this "gaffe" out of the way and not letting it fester.

Well, not so fast. Credit is due to Poppy for being right and I intend to offer it. The man may get his syntax screwed up, but this time he got his facts right.

If, as Bush hopes, the Supreme Court should overturn Roe v. Wade, the states would have the right to ban abortion. Any law passed would come with penalties.

What would they be? In 1958, before the reform movement, eighteen states had penalties for any woman who survived an illegal abortion. As late as 1972, before the Supreme Court decision, fifteen states made performing abortion a crime, and eleven states made the woman a criminal. In nine states, it was even illegal to aid or counsel a woman to have an abortion.

Back then, a doctor who did an abortion in Connecticut was subject to as many as five years in prison, the woman as many as two. In Idaho, they could get five years in jail, in Minnesota four years.

That was even before the anti-abortion forces had mobilized and radicalized, crying "Murder" at every political rally. Does anyone believe that the penalties would be lighter today? Would there be a murder charge? Would there not be?

Of course, we could "just" prosecute doctors and counselors. But with new technologies, illegal abortions could be performed without medical people. How safely, we don't know. In 1968, five thousand women died from illegal abortions. That would of course be one of the "penalties." But the figure seems small to the right-to-lifers who regard every fetus as a human being. The Republican platform this year clearly places the rights of the fetus above those of the mother.

Today, we have abortion pills as well. Just this month, France and China legalized the one called RU-486. In Thursday's *New England Journal of Medicine,* there was a report about Epostane, a similar drug for early abortions from Holland. There would unquestionably be a black market in such pills. Would we chase after these "drug-runners"?

In a patchwork of state laws, would a woman who had an abortion in a "free" state be prosecuted in a "criminal" state? What if there were a constitutional ban nationwide? Would a woman who went to Canada or Europe be extradited? Would women be watched at the borders? What of a woman who miscarried in this country? Would she have to prove it?

This is not the stuff of science fiction or political alarmists, although there is surely an un-American air to it. In Romania today, where abortion is illegal, there are pregnancy tests given in factories and women who miscarry have some explaining to do.

Bush is a great believer in the free-market economy. He has said that if women would only deliver their babies and give them up for adoption, supply and demand would take care of the rest. Finally he was forced to think about the real consequences in real life, not in theory.

This was no blooper, no misstatement, no misunderstanding, nothing demanding "clarification" from his aides. Nor is it something we should let slide down the memory hole.

If abortion were illegal, it would be a crime. Every crime has a criminal. Even George Bush, who hadn't "sorted out" the issue, knew that right off the bat. "Of course there's got to be some penalties to enforce the law . . ." Of course.

OCTOBER 1988

CLOSING THE GENDER GAP

LAST JUNE, a group of pollsters rounded up some women in New Jersey for a sophisticated game of Knock-Knock.

Let's imagine the candidates coming to your front door, the pollsters said. Knock-knock, who's there? First comes Dukakis. What do you think would happen next? Well, said the women, he'd come in, have a cup of coffee, sit down and talk.

Okay, Knock-knock. This time it's Bush. What happens? One of these women answered for the group: Bush would come in and say hello, but he'd keep the car motor running.

This is the way it was in the early days when the women's vote ran deep and swift for the Democrats. There was the sense among a majority of women that Bush didn't understand their lives, didn't make a connection with them.

But what a long, long way from June to October. In the last polls, a modest gender gap remained, but the advantage among women had slipped away. By the end of Thursday night's debate, the images of the two candidates had almost flip-flopped.

What happened to the women's vote was simple: The Democrats took women for granted. It was the Republicans who came knocking at the door.

From the beginning, the Republicans knew that Bush needed a biography that women would relate to and so they presented it. The Republican National Convention was a Bush family reunion. He was no longer the man with the résumé but the grandfather.

They knew he needed a language that resonated in women's ears as well, something better than "the value thing" and so they scripted one for him. His speechwriter, Peggy Noonan, crafted a speech that presented him as caring, a man who wanted "a gentler, kinder nation."

The original fuel behind the women's vote, what prejudiced them in favor of the Democratic camp at the outset, was their sense of economic vulnerability. It is not news that women suffered more from the Reagan era cuts and profited less from the Reagan era prosperity.

The gap between the rich and the poor would have been greater if women hadn't kept their families above the line by going to work. But it came at a cost in anxiety about family life, about good jobs, about their children.

"On a whole set of issues, women have a Democratic profile," says Ethel Klein, a Columbia University professor who has tracked the women's vote. "But the campaign's silence on the domestic agenda really hurt."

The Democratic pitch to women's sense of economic vulnerability was slow and haphazard. The Republican pitch to women's sense of personal vulnerability was hard-hitting.

Using the language of values, Bush spoke to their fears of crime and environmental pollution. He issued one proposal for day care and another to encourage public service in young people. However specious an attack, however dubious a fact, however modest a proposal, he was in the kitchen, talking.

Dukakis, on the other hand, continued to present himself as the son of immigrants rather than the father of a modern family, a man who knew firsthand the cost of food at the supermarket and the difficulties of finding time for your family. He said that he cared "very, very deeply." But women in particular look for other clues and didn't find them. They have been harsher than men in judging the Democrat as unlikable.

Every piece of the Republican strategy for the women's vote was telegraphed well in advance. But the Democrats in '88, like the Democrats in '84, ignored the signals or directed their message elsewhere. When they came out with a plan for college tuition, a plan for home-buying, that margin of women was no longer as eager, as attentive.

Even in the debate Thursday night, Dukakis talked about "tough choices" while Bush again talked about "values." When asked a "hot" question—how would he feel about capital punishment if his wife had been raped and murdered?—Dukakis answered much too coolly for the wives listening.

If, despite all this, the race remains close, it's because women remain suspicious of Bush and of Republicans as well. There are ten million more women voters than men, and some 13 percent are undecided compared to only 8 percent of men.

Dr. Klein says the candidates at this point are like two potential suitors. "Here's a guy, Bush, who's not offering women much, but he's still asking them out. And here's another guy, Dukakis, who's asking them to stay home and sit by the phone. He may be the guy they really want to go out with. But you get pissed off waiting."

Knock, knock.

OCTOBER 1988

ELECTION DAY

I T WAS ONE of those sunny election days that poll workers pray for when they begin a thirteen-hour shift in the great outdoors. At 7:30 A.M. on Perry Street, a single Secret Service man was standing on the sidewalk sipping coffee, keeping an eye out and waiting for the candidate.

For Mike Dukakis, a man rooted in this community, it was time to come home. The marathon that had ended in a sleepless blur of campaigning was over. The reporters who'd flown through these last nights had already been awarded T-shirts that read: "I Slept With Mike Dukakis. Nov. 5, Nov. 6, Nov. 7."

Across the country, the enthusiasm was low for this hologram of a presidential campaign. But at Precinct 3, in the Theresa Morse Apartments for the elderly, the friends and neighbors of the governor were lined up to vote as if it were Sunday morning at Kupel's Bakery. Take a number.

Brookline is not big on self-deception. The conversation at the polls went along these lines. "What do you think? Any chance?" "Hey, you never know." "Yes, you do." One woman said to another, with only a glint of humor, that she had already been through five stages of mourning and was hoping soon to hit the one called "acceptance."

At 9:30, ahead of schedule, the motorcade came up to Precinct 3. The pool reporters raced ahead to the booth, and then the Dukakis family, looking slightly the worse for their all-nighter, came to vote: Mike, Kitty, John, Andrea. Nearing the doorway, the candidate stopped, smiled and delivered the last official baby kiss of the 1988 campaign.

The recipient was Zoe Jick, the daughter of the Duke's next-door neighbors. Her father Todd had been standing there to greet his friend, and Todd was quick to tell the cameraman that this wasn't just photo-op affection. How do you explain, he said later, that the guy next door, this "iceman" who ran for President, is really warm?

As a town, Brookline got mugged this year, along with the hometown boy who had been its state rep and its governor. Brookline, too, was dubbed as "way out there," not part of Bush's "mainstream," an ultra-L kind of place.

Bill Bennett trashed a town that has public schools he should have cloned. George Bush made it sound like a breeding ground for the sneering un-American elitism rather than a streetcar suburb with a history of intense public interest. The birthplace of Jack Kennedy, the urban suburb where the streets get plowed and kids can walk home without passing a crack den.

If a town could sue for slander, this one had a right. It had a right as well to feel disappointed that their guy didn't defend himself, didn't defend them, didn't make the case for their values as well as he should have. Or as early as he should have.

So, around Brookline, some of the folks hanging out, watching the national media come and go, said what all the analysts would say. Mike's reactions were too slow. He didn't believe the Bush attacks would stick. If only . . .

Those who know him best could tell you about the candidate's irrational belief in reason. Some worried that he'd have trouble understanding the emotional forces sweeping through the world. They were thinking of the Ayatollah. But it turned out that the whole Bush campaign—from Willie Horton to the Pledge of Allegiance—was the irrational force of 1988.

Those who know him best have seen both his stubbornness and his integrity. The grit they admire, the stiff neck they sometimes want to wring. So they know that the flaws of the campaign were his, not just his staff's. Those who believed he would have made a better President than candidate said to each other Tuesday: "That's Mike. What're you gonna do?"

By mid-morning, Perry Street was filled with kids bused over from the Brookline schools, some from Mike's old grammar school, some from Kitty's. The candidate, dressed in his telegenic red sweater although the cameras were gone, came out and teased them for cutting class. He said he hoped they'd think of public service when they grew up. Then he went back inside.

His neighbors began waiting, but not with much suspense. The Jicks talked about what they should say to Mike and Kitty in the morning. An old friend came by with a note, handed it to a Secret Service guy and asked him to deliver it.

For Mike Dukakis it was 557 days and half a million miles in the air. In the end he lost. It's lousy to lose. But it's good to know you can go home again.

NOVEMBER 1988

PART ELEVEN

IN A FAMILY WAY

The transition into motherhood came with such ceremony. But there is no shower for a woman when she completes the trimester of her life spent as a full-time mother. There is no midwife to help that woman deliver a healthy adult.

The New Father and the Mother's Secret

HE IS EVERY inch the new father. A family man. Close to his children. The full parenting partner of his wife. The very up-to-date image of the New Father's Day.

Maybe his own father was a remote figure who emerged from the office or from behind the newspaper only to lay down the law. But this new father can recite the full text of *Goodnight, Moon*. He has opinions on strollers and nursery schools. And when his children fall and scrape their knees, they are as likely to cry "Daddy" as "Mommy."

She is every inch the new woman. She brings home a paycheck. She doesn't defer to her husband's authority in making family decisions.

Maybe her own mother was a careful, protective authority who silenced the children when Daddy was home. But she is proud to be the wife of a new father, and will, if you ask, extol the values of having two who parent rather than one who mothers. She shares everything with him. Except, of course, her occasional, and decidedly retro, flashes of ambivalence.

When the children were born into this home, into this partnership, the woman had no idea that she would give birth to all sorts of assumptions about mothering. About how things should be done and who should be in charge of doing them. It turned out, to her amazement, that he found it easier to diaper than she to let him diaper his way.

Now, years later, there are the weekday mornings when he gives the children breakfast and she bites her tongue. They do not have, these partners, the same attitudes about hot breakfasts and sugared cereals.

There are times when he takes them clothes shopping and she turns pale. They do not have, these parents, the same attitudes toward fashion or toward chartreuse on rosy-cheeked four-year-olds.

And those vaunted moments when a hurt child yells "Daddy" instead of "Mommy"? To tell you the truth, which she does not tell the new father, her arms ache to be the only one her children run to. And when the six-year-old is upset and will only tell his father what happened at school, the new woman is—this is embarrassing to report—jealous.

In the past decades, how many people have heard much about the difficulties men have had adjusting to women's pressure for equality? We have had reports on how hard it is for men to share power in the wider world, to live with another and perhaps greater earner, to exchange the title "head of household" for "partner."

We have heard much as well in praise of the new father. He has gathered "firsts" like some champion in the changing life-style Olympics. The first man in his clan to participate in a birth. The first man in his family to stay home from the office with a sick child.

But we hear little praise when women accept these changing roles at home. It is, after all, women who recruited the new father, perhaps even invented him, and women who shored him up when he was still a fragile minority creature. If prizes aren't dispensed to the wives of these new fathers, it's because they are assumed to be the lucky ones.

Nevertheless, it turns out that sharing the work of raising children also means sharing the power over children's lives. Sharing the power—even the kind you didn't fully recognize—is harder than expected. Letting go of child power, giving up the central role in a child's life, can be as hard as letting go of purse power. It doesn't sound like a dramatic struggle. But it can come with a sudden, internal wrench.

Is this backsliding? I don't know a woman who would trade in a new father for his progenitor. Most mothers press for renovation, not restoration. There is something wonderful in seeing fathers and children together, really together. So, for the sake of this change, mothers hide their ambivalence as if it were a dirty little secret.

Maybe this Father's Day we could instead offer up the secret as a kind of present. Wrap it with a special card. The truth is that women have also given something up for the men in their lives. In celebration of the New Father's Day, they are learning to let go.

JUNE 1988

LEMON PIES AND FAMILY
TRADITION

ONE AUNT has called the other to ask for a Thanksgiving dispensation. Surely, she pleads, twenty years of lemon pies are enough for one family. She wants to make a new dessert. She has an entire Rolodex of recipes.

The senior woman (we may call her Number One Aunt since this is her family position) recoils, as if her sister-in-law had suggested rap music instead of Mendelssohn for a wedding ceremony.

Number One Aunt is, you see, the anointed keeper of the family Thanksgiving ritual. It is her job. The event takes place under her roof and her ministry. And she follows the book. Indeed, she has a generation of Thanksgiving dinners inscribed in a notebook which she guards, you might say, religiously.

There has never been a kiwi or Rock Cornish hen at her table. There shall be no nouvelle cuisine, no wild rice stuffing, no chocolate raspberry terrine. There shall be turkey and bread stuffing and sweet potatoes. And lemon pie. Thus it is writ.

Listening to this, I wonder: Does it sound like some ceremonial dictate? Is this a totem and taboo more fitting for the holy day of an ancient religious sect than for the celebration of a modern American harvest?

Thanksgiving is, after all, our most ecumenical national holiday, the most secular feast. Yet each gathering family, freed of scripture, seems to produce its own private set of traditions. The menu becomes a culinary liturgy, with ten thousand tribal variations on the theme of turkey.

Our particular family is not, I hasten to add, an authoritarian sect. We have had internal disputes about the ritual meal. There have been vast and uncompromising disagreements between the jellied-cranberry and the whole-cranberry factions. That divisive issue was barely muted by the acceptance of a two-sauce policy.

There has also been some debate over the occasional appearance of broccoli and string beans. But we have remained flexible on the subject of mincemeat and bundt cakes, adding and subtracting at the request or bequest of the membership.

Different opinions are even accepted on the matter of the prime Thanksgiving icon, the turkey. Some of our members regard it only as a decorative centerpiece, others as the culinary highlight. Although the majority of our sect consists of dark-meat eaters we are open-minded enough to look favorably on acolytes—fiancés, guests, roommates—who profess to like white meat.

But the core, the absolute center of our traditional offering, doesn't waver from one year to the next, or one decade to the next. Untouchable recipes handed down from one generation to another arrive on the table bearing the names of these ancestors. We dine with their shadows and sauces.

Indeed each year the Number One Aunt replicates in exquisite detail her own mother's stuffing. She produces it in a tearful ceremony brought on by equal portions of onions and memories.

Why does such a passion for sameness go on in this and so many other family menus? We have had our share of personal changes. I imagine we've seen the membership of our sect turn over by a half. We know our differences. We allow members to come bearing new points of view and husbands.

But there is something in favor of a feast that goes on proclaiming in the midst of change: This our family. This is the way we do things. This is our Thanksgiving. We are the people who put ginger snaps in our gravy. Like it or not. We are the people who like crisp sweet potatoes. We are the people who prefer lemon pie to pumpkin.

We savor, literally, our togetherness. And if we go somewhere else for Thanksgiving, it will never taste quite right. It won't be home. Who else will serve Grandma's stuffing?

We create our own traditions for the same reason we create our own families. To know where we belong. We like our holidays the way children like bedtime stories: predictable. We don't come together for something new. Families prefer the familiar. And that is why our Thanksgiving will have the same old ending: Lemon pie all around.

NOVEMBER 1987

ONE SMALL BOY

TERENCE KARAMBA may be too young to divine the importance of the term *diplomatic immunity*. At nine, any boy would find it hard to understand why such words would protect a father but not the son he may have abused.

Terence Karamba would be even more surprised to know that he has become the star of an international tug-of-war, a diplomatic custody fight. Yet the boy from Zimbabwe is just that: the central figure in a dispute before the U.S. Supreme Court that pits the best interests of one child against the interests of the international community in upholding a diplomatic code.

The eldest child of a Zimbabwean diplomat at the United Nations came to notice in the haphazard way that private pain sometimes becomes public information. One morning, it is alleged, he arrived at his Queens, New York, school bloody and bruised.

The city charged that his father, Floyd Karamba, "tied Terence's forearms and legs together with wire and repeatedly struck him with an electrical extension cord." During some of these beatings he was, they say, hung from pipes in the basement while his mother and two sisters were made to watch.

The Human Resources Administration, still reeling from the death of six-year-old Elizabeth Steinberg, allegedly at the hands of her father, gave this boy what they could not give Elizabeth. They gave him safety, a foster home.

Because the father was a diplomat, he was immune from prosecution but not from expulsion. The State Department ordered him to go home, citing unacceptable conduct. He went, followed by his wife and daughters, while Terence stayed in a foster home in New York.

Then Zimbabwe demanded its young citizen back. Officials prickled at the implication this boy would be safer in America than in his own country. More to the point, they prickled at a breach of diplomatic rules.

In this dispute, our own government has tried to sound a position at once in sympathy with the child and yet in support of international law. But in fact, the two conflict, and the State Department comes down on the side of diplomacy.

As Tom Merrill, who filed the government's brief with Justice Blackmun on Tuesday, puts it: "We wouldn't be happy if the officials of another country took a child of an American diplomat and determined that they had the authority to decide the custody of that child, or indeed whether the child had been abused."

We subscribe to rules precisely so our own diplomats or their children won't be at risk in other countries. There are questions of international law here. But there are also questions of one boy's psyche.

Terence is a fragile and frightened boy, his caretakers say. A boy who has tried to jump out of a car, out of a second-story window. When told in the gentlest terms he might return to Zimbabwe, they report that Terence crawled into a cardboard box and sat there, rocking back and forth.

So his Legal Aid Society lawyer, Janet Fink, asked Justice Blackmun to rule that Terence can apply for asylum in the United States. "To us," she says, "this is a children's rights case."

Even if the justices allow Terence to stay and plead his case before an appeals court, the odds are that he will be sent back to Zimbabwe. Even Fink admits, "What we're asking for essentially is time." But this is not a case that had to come to such a hard, unyielding, legal confrontation in the first place.

The charges that filled the air during the last weeks were full of acrimony. The authorities in New York were not "kidnapping" Terence, as the Africans claimed. They didn't intend to keep the boy permanently. Nor was Zimbabwe planning, as sometimes charged, to return the boy to his father. The government has one of the most elaborate child welfare programs in Africa. Child abuse is regarded at least as harshly as it is here.

The best ending to this story would have been a reassuring, careful transition smoothed by cooperating health officials on both sides of the ocean. But in this classic story, pride and prejudice intervened. The lawyers came next.

Now in New York there is a small boy, already bruised, who will learn again that he carries no immunity from pain in the world of international diplomacy.

JANUARY 1988

BABY PICTURES

HAVE YOU NOTICED a sudden rash of baby pictures? I don't mean the kind being passed around for approval by parents in the throes of their newborn love affair. I mean big pictures, cinematic pictures.

This winter there are so many diapers on the silver screen that I may sprinkle baby powder on my popcorn. In the language of *Variety*, babies are boffo biz at the box office. Two of the biggest hits, *Baby Boom* and *Three Men and a Baby*, star people who have babies unexpectedly dropped into their orderly, mid-thirties and midtown lives.

One of these instant parents is Diane Keaton, the Tiger Lady of her company who hasn't the slightest maternal urge in her briefcase. Indeed, she has told her boss: "I don't want to have it all." The others are Tom Selleck, Ted Danson and Steve Guttenberg, as an architect, an actor and a cartoonist respectively. Their pre-nappy attitudes to life are summed up in the opening theme song: "Boys Will Be Boys."

These movies follow one of the laws of nature: A Baby Abhors Order. In the most innocent way possible, the babies turn adult competence into parental bewilderment.

"I'm an architect, I can certainly put together a goddamned diaper," says Selleck in *Three Men*. "We're two summa cum laudes. We can handle one little baby," echo the baby boomers. Not necessarily.

But the adults whose lives are upended also collectively fall in love with the babies. And—this is the point—they all become better people by becoming parents.

The baby has a transforming effect. The Tiger Lady becomes a loving mother. The Boys become nurturing fathers. The message is that the way to grow up and grow out is to have a baby.

Listen to the dialogue in the pivotal scene in *Three Men* that occurs between the biological father among the trio, and his own mother.

Mom: "Jack, you've always run away from responsibility. Now you have to face it."

Jack: "Mom, I'm a screwup."

Mom: "You *were* a screwup. Now you're a father."

In some curious way, the baby becomes the savior. One baby saves Diane Keaton from a life of brittle workaholism. Another saves Ted Danson, "Jack," from a life of self-indulgence and philandering. Forced to deal with a real child, they are also forced to be the grown-ups. At last.

I see these as baby-boom movies in more than one sense of the word. The proliferation of babies in movies and in ads is just the most obvious offspring of the generation that has postponed commitments until the last stroke of the biological clock.

The youth generation delayed adulthood with a passion. They applied Retin-A to their life-styles. Some filled their lives with VCRs; others gave midnight feedings to their careers. They all had anxiety about how these lives would work with children. In the tense words of Diane Keaton: "I can't have a baby because I have a 12:30 lunch meeting."

Now the bulk of this demographic bulge has arrived at an awkward age. There is the sense among many that they haven't quite gotten on with it, made their own connection and contribution to the next generation. A sense that something is missing, and just maybe it is their own next generation.

Ironically, neither the three men nor the woman on the big screen actually made the choice to be a parent. This may indeed be another fantasy. How many have to cut through the ambivalence, to have the decision made for them?

Babies are indeed a transforming event in the life of any adult. Any parent can attest to that, although not every transformation is an improvement. Despite his mother's words, Jack can be a father *and* a screwup. He can even be a screwup *as* a father.

But the babies in these movies, like babies in real life, do expand their parents' emotional range by contracting the focus of their energy. In real life, too, babies take precedence. Babies steal the show. They take the center and hold it.

Who would have suspected that this would be so compelling to the people once tagged the Me Generation? The eternal-youth generation has outgrown the limits of "me." The message from the big-screen parents resonates more than a little with would-be, may-be, will-be parents. Have a baby to save yourself. From yourself.

A RIGHT TO FATHERHOOD

EIGHT YEARS AGO, Edward McNamara had what is described as a "casual affair." But in the way of the world, his brief romance had more than casual consequences. Unknown to him, the 20-year-old single woman became pregnant and gave birth to a baby girl.

On August 1, 1981, over dinner in a San Diego restaurant, she told him about the baby and how she had placed it for adoption. She asked him to sign away his parental rights.

That vivid scene between man and woman, the news announced over the neutral turf of a tablecloth—her revelation, his shock—was a vivid tableau of the essential difference between a biological mother and father. Only a father could be "stunned," in his own words, by the birth of a child.

Despite all the birthing classes and self-conscious descriptions of "our" pregnancy, not even married men and women are truly equal partners in pregnancy. Unwed and disconnected fathers haven't nearly the same investment as unwed mothers in a newborn child.

But does that mean there are no rights that come with a paternal set of genes? Does a mother have the unilateral power to put a child up for adoption? Can the state view unwed mothers and unwed fathers wholly differently?

These are some of the questions that came out of this casual affair. On November 28, Ed McNamara brought them to the Supreme Court.

McNamara never signed away his parental rights. He had them ruled away. Months after the baby girl—now a 7-year-old named Katie—was placed in a foster home, the court allowed Robert and P. J. Moses to adopt the baby over McNamara's protests. The girl had bonded with her new parents, the court ruled. Adoption was in her best interest.

McNamara claims that the law violated his rights, indeed all fathers' rights. An unwed mother could only lose her parental rights if she was unfit. But an unwed father could lose them "in the best interests of the child." He was denied equal protection under the law.

This is not an isolated or freakish case. One out of every four children in the country is born out of wedlock. Many of these children have a tenuous relationship with their fathers. There are more women trying to get men into the lives of children than trying to keep them out. There are more women than men trying to prove paternity in court.

Indeed, that scene at the restaurant might have gone differently if the biological mother had decided to keep the child. The result of McNamara's casual affair might have been eighteen years of child-support payments.

But can a state hold a man responsible for supporting his children one day and cut off his right to those children the next? Is a father who is liable for responsibilities to be denied rights?

At the same time, this or any woman who carries a child alone for nine months may assume that she can decide the fate of her newborn alone. Only 6 percent of babies born to unwed mothers are put up for adoption. Those mothers act in what they believe are "the best interests of the child." How would she assess those interests, make that decision, if the child could be claimed by a stranger-father?

The Supreme Court has ruled that biology isn't destiny for unwed fathers exactly the way it is for unwed mothers. If an unwed father wants to claim his paternity, he has to act like a father. But neither the mother nor the California law ever gave Ed McNamara the chance to act like a father.

This is a time of flux and confusion about families and the rules that regulate them. Family structures are more diverse, family law more complex. As a society we are trying to strengthen emotional ties while our institutions weaken. We are especially concerned about fathers and children.

Ed McNamara knows something about changing families and about maintaining relationships. A divorced father of two, an unwed father of one, he doesn't ask for custody of Katie but rather the right to visit, the right to be known and named as her father.

For all of its good intentions, the state of California was wrong to sever this or any father's rights before he can make a case for his responsibility. It may be rare, but a brief affair produced a tenacious father. There is nothing casual about Ed McNamara's fatherhood anymore.

CHILDREN LOST AND FOUND

I N A SUPERMARKET in Maine there is a poster of a girl. It says that she is missing. There are other such faces: boys and girls, three years old, eleven years old, eight years old, hanging like "the most wanted" in public places. Some are on the highway toll gates, others on the Chicago subways, or on milk cartoons, or on gas bills. All of them are missing.

In New Jersey last winter, they began fingerprinting 44,000 school children. In North Carolina, they put microdots into the molars of some children. At Tufts University, they developed a technique for toothprints. These are in case, just in case, children are ever missing.

Over the past year or more, the alarm about the abduction of children has been raised everywhere. A television special or two, a talk show or a hundred. A hot line: Dial 800-THE-LOST. Congress declared a National Missing Children's Day. The media rounded up the usual statistics: 1.5 million children missing, 50,000 a year abducted.

It has taken all this time for the facts to catch up with our bleakest fears.

Now, just now, we hear that there are not 50,000 children a year abducted by strangers. Child Find in New York has altered their estimate to 600 such kidnappings, and the FBI says 67 were reported in 1984. Nor are there 1.5 million missing children in this country. The FBI estimates, rather, 32,000.

Among the missing, the overwhelming majority—two thirds, three quarters, 90 percent (there are different figures from different people)—are runaways and, as they say now, throwaways. Of the rest, perhaps as many as 90 percent have been taken by one parent from another in a disintegrating family.

Are those children all at risk? Absolutely. But this is not the fear that grips most parents who let a child walk to school for the first time, who leave the children alone in the house, who lose a preschooler in the shopping center, who wait for a child to come home from school, and wait and wait. It is the strangers that we fear.

It is impossible to exaggerate the pain of those parents who have lost a child. It is incalculable, inconsolable. But it is easy to exaggerate the risk, and in these months, the fear has been fanned out of all proportion to the reality.

I think it's worth asking why. Why, now, is there such a receptive audience for this primal anxiety? It isn't just the misused statistics that causes an epidemic of concern. There must be some particular vulnerability in parents today.

The terror of losing a child is a staple of mythology as well as nightmares. Village folklore was full of stories about strangers who stole children. Gypsies were the vagrants and suspects. In those days, communities were tight enough that the only strangers were rootless outsiders.

Today, more and more of us are outsiders, strangers on our own streets. The cities are bigger, neighborhoods less stable. The ratio of strangers to friends, strangers to families, has changed dramatically. This is, I think, at the root of our insecurity.

In this same world, we routinely place our children in the hands of people we hardly know. The doctor at the clinic, the teacher at school, the swimming counselor, the bus driver. It is not a coincidence that the fear of child abduction is heightened at a time when more of us leave small children in day care outside their home and family than ever before.

When we tell our children—as we must—to beware of strangers, the number of people wearing that label is much larger than it once was. The more time they spend away from us, the more unknown their world, the more easily our anxiety can be tapped.

The victims of abduction deserve their priority, deserve all the sophisticated methods of discovery in our arsenal. But the victims of hysteria should wonder about the strangeness of our lives. Fear grows irrationally in a world without communities where we know the names of children only when they appear on a milk carton, on a tollbooth or on a poster in a supermarket.

JULY 1985

A GARRULOUS GIFT

WHEN OUR CHILDREN were little, my sister and I would occasionally use our own private language around them, a summer-camp lingo we called uppy-duppy. Our parents had a more sophisticated strategy to deal with us: polysyllabic words, telegraphed spelling messages. Their parents in turn had an adults-only language that had been imported from Europe.

What all three generations shared was a desire to keep some information from the young. There were subjects that came with an invisible label—Not in Front of the Children. Sometimes we applied it for their protection, sometimes for our privacy, but it separated stages of childhood and adulthood.

There was nothing unusual about us. There have always been ways for an older generation to shut out the younger, to block their access to information, to apply a rating system. Language is one, doors are another. Children have been routinely removed from the room during "grown-up conversations," or fights, or tears.

But it is different now. Our grandparents had a whole list of taboos: death, sex, c-a-n-c-e-r, m-o-n-e-y. Our own uppy-duppy era was much shorter and less serious.

Modern parents, after all, are much more open with their children. Or so we tell ourselves. Still, at times I wonder whether we haven't lost the power to screen the adult world for and from our children.

Last week, a friend tells me, the talk of the second-grade car pool was of Tylenol. They found out about the cyanide on the evening news. This morning, an eighth-grade teacher calls me in dismay to report the number of her students who have seen "adult" movies on cable TV or videos.

Last month, the space shuttle exploded before thousands of school children's eyes. No father broke the news, no mother framed the event, no grandparent translated the information. Young and old saw this together. The best that these elders could do was to react, to play catch-up, to help children understand what they had seen.

The adult screen has been virtually wiped out by the television screen.

There is a moment in Joshua Meyrowitz's *No Sense of Place,* a striking analysis of television's impact on our culture, when he describes how TV has blurred the lines between childhood and adulthood. "What is revolutionary about television is not that it necessarily gives children 'adult minds,'" he writes, "but that it allows the very young child to be 'present' at adult interactions.

"The widespread use of television is equivalent to a broad social decision to allow young children to be present at wars and funerals, courtships and seductions, criminal plots and cocktail parties. . . . [Television] exposes them to many topics and behaviors that adults have spent centuries trying to keep hidden from children." Death, d-i-v-o-r-c-e, or, as we say in uppy-duppy, "s-up-ex."

Perhaps the biggest secret that has been blown is about adulthood itself. When Meyrowitz analyzed programs as different as the 1950's *Leave It to Beaver* and the 1980's *One Day at a Time,* he found something similar: "They both reveal to children the existence of adult weaknesses and doubts."

Television lets children know what we are saying in the other language and what is going on behind the closed door. This exposure, he writes, "undermines both traditional childhood naivete and the all-knowing, confident adult role. . . ."

In the electronic age, the parent is less of a guide and more of a fellow traveler. We don't slowly expose our children to the world in a series of monitored field trips anymore. We don't control the flow of information into their lives. It comes through a garrulous and permanent guest who doesn't respond to the command, "Shh, the children."

As parents we are brought the questions raised in our children's minds by the set in the living room. It is both harder to protect those children and harder to pretend to them. When they ask us to explain what is happening in Manila or Dallas, we cannot speak in tongues.

Our own parents, certainly our grandparents, kept too much from us. Many kept themselves from us. As thoroughly modern parents of the electronic age, we comfort ourselves with the notion that we are choosing this "honesty" and, yes, "openness." I just hope that our own children aren't left more v-u-l-n-e-r-a-b-l-e.

A TALE OF TWO BABIES

I F THIS WERE Gilbert and Sullivan, we could be sure of a happy ending. Two babies switched at birth would be returned to their rightful place amidst a chorus of approval before the final curtain. We would leave the theater smiling.

But this tale of two babies is so unique, so layered in complex family histories, that it's hard to write a way out of its tragic outlines.

On December 2, 1978, a woman named Regina Twigg gave birth to a healthy baby girl in a Florida hospital. Somehow someone, in the first days of its life, switched that baby with another who had serious heart disease. The Twiggs loved and raised Arlena as if she were their own. Indeed she was their own by every test except the genetic one.

Only last summer, in preparation for a heart operation, did Arlena's parents learn from blood tests that she wasn't their biological child. When the girl died, the mourning family faced torturous questions about the fate of the other girl as well. Where was she? Who had her? What was her life like? These were questions made even more painful to Regina Twigg, who was herself adopted.

Now the Twiggs believe they have found that girl. The only other white baby born in the same hospital at the same time as Arlena lives in Florida with her father. But they want to know for sure.

So the Twiggs went to court this week to force another parent to test another nine-year-old. The petition they filed, not surprisingly, had the earmarks of a future custody suit. They claimed that the legal father "wrongfully retains custody." Moreover, they said, he has failed to provide "an ongoing stable home environment with the presence of a mother to love and care for her."

Indeed from the details, the life of this second child, whatever her genes, hasn't been easy. Her mother died when the child was three and a half. The father, who had been estranged, remarried soon after and then divorced the girl's stepmother. But this father also claims that the child is his. Though willing earlier to go through the testing, he now says the Twiggs have no right to intervene.

In some ways, this story is so unique as to make it a legal and journalistic freak show. But in another way, it resonates with us, because it raises a series of moral as well as legal questions about parents and children.

Do the Twiggs, however horribly wronged, have the right to pursue a child into another family's private world in search of bloodlines? What gives them that right? Their wounds? Their genes? Do they need proof that the child's home they would enter is not a happy one, not "ongoing, stable"?

On the other hand, does the legal father have the right to bar the Twiggs, who have suffered so much injustice, from knowing whether this child is theirs? What gives him that right? Possession of the girl? Protection of his family?

And is this a matter of parents' rights at all?

The Twiggs' petition says that the genetic testing (and presumably the custody claim) is in the "best interests of the child." If they are sure of that, the lawyers are far wiser than most of us. A child has many interests. An interest in knowing her biological parents? Yes, we have said that in adoption cases. An interest in a happy home? Yes, if you can define it. An interest in continuity? Maybe even an interest in being left alone? Sometimes these interests conflict.

It is morally outrageous to imagine that the Twiggs, victims of a terrible theft, could not win retribution. Surely they have rights. But just as surely there are times when you cannot right one wrong without the risk of creating others.

So there can be no truly happy ending for two families that have had such troubles. But is it too much to hope that these two families could get out of court and come to some private resolution?

If I were the father, I would agree to genetic testing if only because this daughter's name and face is unlikely to remain secret for long. Identity is not a thing to read about in the supermarket press. I would do it as well to squelch any unfounded suspicion that he was party to the swap.

If the girl proves to be the genetic offspring of the Twiggs, I would hope those good people, Regina and Ernest Twigg, would have the wisdom and control not to sue for custody but to become their daughter's extended family. I would hope both families could in some cautious way be available to her, and she in turn could be linked to both.

Courts deal in conflicts and this one is easy to exacerbate and very hard to settle. But if these were the two children swapped at birth, then these are also parents who learned the same remarkable truth.

They learned that you don't need the same bloodlines to love a child, to make it yours. Surely people who share that understanding could learn to share a child.

OCTOBER 1988

When the Children
Don't Leave Home

AT FIRST it seemed like an aberration. The political focus group that wouldn't. Wouldn't focus, that is.

Stan Greenberg, a political pollster, would gather a mixed group of strangers together in Michigan or Delaware or Iowa. His role was to foster an in-depth conversation about the country, the candidates and the campaign of 1988.

A typical evening might begin with one man introducing himself as a 48-year-old autoworker with two kids, 23 and 26, still living at home. The 42-year-old secretary next to him would then talk about her son, who had to leave the state to find work. The autoworker, only half in jest, would turn to the secretary, offering, "I'll give you mine."

Before the "real" discussion could even begin, the entire group was off and running on an animated, often humorous and deeply felt dialogue about kids: the adult kids who never left home, the ones who were having trouble getting a foothold into adulthood, an economic grip on independence. How can they afford an apartment? A marriage?

At first Greenberg, head of The Analysis Group, would try to get the conversation back on track. But after it had happened six times, twelve times, twenty-four times, he realized that this was the track, a track that led directly toward a center of strong anxiety.

Greenberg, who is not an entirely disinterested observer (he is the father of two college-age children), decided to add a question to two of his statewide surveys. How often, he asked, in one Midwest and in one East Coast state, do you get upset about kids who are not able to leave their parents' home and set up their own?

A full 50 percent said "frequently or very frequently." This was a startling figure, since nowhere near that number of people actually were suffering from the full-nest syndrome.

It turns out that this issue runs deeper through society than expected. It doesn't just exist in middle-aged swap fests of anecdotes about the younger generation—"My teenager has a ring through his nose" or "Oh, yeah, mine has green spiked hair." Rather, as Greenberg says, "Kids have become the idiom for a broad range of economic concerns." They are the way we talk about the future, the way we express our worries about an economy, even a world, that doesn't promise anymore that things will get better for us or for the next generation.

The oldest of the baby boom generation, parents who were independent at a young age themselves, are particularly conscious, even self-conscious, about the difficulties their young are having taking hold. The "idiom" they speak is often muddled, one part psychology, two parts economics.

"To parents, a 30-year-old at home may be seen as pretty visible evidence of failure," muses Greenberg. "Maybe they haven't succeeded in their parenting role helping these kids get out and on their own. Maybe they're unable to pass on what they've achieved."

But parents also talk with sadness about children who were forced to leave hometowns and home states to find work. "It is very perverse," says Greenberg. "We have people concerned about kids when they go off to get decent jobs and people concerned when they don't go."

These anxieties about the young even cloud the horizons of the elders who are doing well. The Analysis Group polled one state with only 2.5 percent unemployment and found that the majority nevertheless believed that "the country is on the wrong track." This sentiment correlated highly with concern about their kids' futures. In Michigan, even voters optimistic about themselves believed that "something is wrong with an economic contentment . . . that cannot be passed on to one's children."

What is coming home in all this information? More than the "children." We each know some young person facing the high price of a starter home and the low wage of a starting job. We know parents who give them what they can: a room. But most politicians have regarded the young as a small demographic sample whose problems wield little political clout.

What these anecdotes, these tales from the runaway focus groups, suggest is how powerful our generational links are, how deeply the anxiety about the future affects attitudes about the present. Our connections are ultimately, and politically, as real as the hallway that leads to a 27-year-old "child's" room.

JULY 1987

PAT ROBERTSON'S FAMILY POLICY

I WAS THE last in the crowd to snicker when Reverend Robertson forgot his anniversary date. After all, Pat and Dede were not the only couple in America to carry something new down the aisle along with their borrowed and blue. If they wanted to backdate the marriage prior to conception, that was their business.

In any case, what the good Reverend tried to hide from the public seemed less significant to me than what he bragged about to the public: the drama of the second pregnancy. When Dede Robertson was in her eighth month, Pat Robertson took off for an isolated island in Canada. She was left to care for their toddler, her pregnancy and their move to a new house. He went to commune with God. When she begged him to return, he replied: "This is God who's commanding me."

There is no public record of Dede's immediate reaction. It's bad enough being married to a doctor when a patient calls. A direct line from God is heavy-duty competition. But the point is that the Reverend told and retold this tale to explain how difficult the call from God was. For him.

Now it seems to me that if Robertson's God could stop a hurricane off the Atlantic Coast, he might have delayed Dede's due date. Robertson was still a seminarian at the time. Maybe he didn't have the megawatt power of televised prayer to help him communicate.

But this was long before he became a politician. Indeed, the most fascinating Robertson rewrite isn't his résumé but his autobiography. In the first edition, he says God told him not to go into politics. In the current edition, the commandment is edited out.

I would let all this lie, except for the fact that the genial, charming minister-candidate is now traveling about the country saying that Americans are having too few babies. Or, to be more accurate, that married middle-class Americans are having too few babies.

He has taken arguments about the "birth dearth" and used them in precisely the distorted way that could be expected from the Reverend van Winkle of the Republican Party. The man who, by the way, won nothing but unctuous welcomes from his opponents in the debate.

For the sake of the economy, Robertson says, we need to breed children to become workers and taxpayers: "How will a shrinking work force take care of the elderly? We must have more children to expand the work force." For the sake of foreign policy, we need to breed children, lest we see a worldwide population decline in "our culture and our values."

Robertson seems to regard the uterus as a national resource. This is a point of view not necessarily shared by those who harbor this part of the anatomy.

His entrepreneurial ideas about increasing American productivity in the human department are predictably chilling. One of the management tools he favors is a ban on abortion. Another plan would make birth control less available. As he said in Vermont last week, he'd veto any budget that gave "even one penny" to Planned Parenthood, an organization whose mainstay is offering contraception. This is one way to become a founding father.

The Robertson birth policy is even more retrograde when he makes plans for the mothers who actually produce the tiny taxpayers. He is opposed to one class of women at home with children: those on welfare. He is, however, happy to pay any middle-class married woman a tax-deductible reward to stay home with them.

Someone might tell Reverend Robertson that among those Western, democratic values that he is afraid will wither on an infertile vine are the values of individual choice. We don't have children for the Fatherland or the work force but for the love of family. Another Western, democratic value is equality.

Surely one of the reasons for the low birthrate is that women carry the larger burden of caring for children. Pat is not the only man of the traditional stripe who ever left at a crucial time. Today, this candidate's family policy is about as remote from the real world of pregnancy and child raising as that isolated island in Canada.

NOVEMBER 1987

DADDIES DOING IT ALL

THE FOLLOWING is a tale of two workers. One we will call Hugh, as in Hewlett-Packard. The other we will name Rock, as in Xerox. Hugh and Rock have been the stars of thirty-second vignettes at the cutting edge, as they say in Adspeak, of the conflict between work and family.

Hugh, when we first meet him, is in the shower. But is he humming his favorite tune? No, Hugh is thinking about business. Suddenly he turns off the water, wraps a towel around his toned torso, puts on his glasses, strides to the phone without even a side glance at the gorgeous woman curled up on his sofa and dials a colleague: "Y'know that electronic mail project for the bank? Well, I have an idea."

The not so subliminal message of this ad is that Hugh and his Hewlett-Packard are not the clock-watching nine-to-five types. As the voice-over says: "An idea can happen anytime. And when you work for Hewlett-Packard, you don't just sell business computing systems, you solve problems. So when you have an idea, you do something about it." Hugh is working all the time.

What about Rock? Actually, the real star of last year's hit commercial was Rock's daughter, Sarah. Sarah had her face up against the window, hoping that Daddy would get there in time for the birthday party. Rock had been working later and later.

As the happy ending of this ad implied, Xerox came to the rescue! The new office efficiency had "one very important side benefit. The birthday party his daughter never forgot." Rock is not working all the time.

There are differences between Hugh and Rock that go beyond the hours they keep. Hugh lives in an upscale urban apartment. Rock lives in a house with curtains. The only woman in Hugh's life is an elegant lady who glances up adoringly as he breezes past her to the phone: Isn't he cute when he's working? The woman in Rock's life, however, is Little Sarah: Isn't she cute when he isn't working?

But the biggest gap between these two models and role models is in the sales pitch. Hugh is being sold as the person you want to hire. Rock is the person you want to be, or at least marry. Hugh is the person you would want for your company. Rock is the person you would want for your family.

In real life, these two personalities may not stay as neatly segregated as they do in the thirty-second adworld. In real life, Total Worker Hugh may marry the woman on his sofa, start a family and become a Mixed Loyalty Rock. He may even ask for paternity leave.

In real life, Rock may instinctively search for a Hugh to get the office in shape so that he can make it to the birthday party. He may even demand that Hugh work overtime until the job is done.

In this same real life, most of us have personalities that are splitting all over the place. We want one thing from our employers and quite another from our employees.

A woman who has felt the demands of job and children for the past decade now manages a small business. Two of her own workers have been pregnant in the past year. Today, she confesses to me ruefully, her empathy is showing stretch marks. A friend was recently asked to speak at a weekend conference on balancing work and family. When this man, a father with two small children, said that he doesn't work weekends, the conference manager was wholly surprised and not pleased.

Stories like these are endemic. We want reasonable work hours for ourselves and the telephone number for plumbers who work nights. We want to be able to see our own kids' school plays and able to call our doctors out of their kids' plays. We want to get home early and to have the supermarket manager stay late.

We are all a part of the conflict between work and family, between the successful worker and the successful parent. We are its victims and its producers. To the papa Rocks go the happy children; the unencumbered Hughs get the glitzy apartments; and to the rest of us goes the schizophrenia.

What happens when we try to live by this split-screen message? We get stuck between a Rock, a Hugh and a very hard place.

POST-CHILD MOTHERING

IT'S BEEN twenty years since I lumbered gracelessly through my last pre-Mother's Day. Eight and a half months pregnant, my patience with the whole process was stretched as far as the skin over my stomach. If Someone in Charge had asked my opinion, I would have said that becoming a mother took far too long.

I see it differently now. Today I am the mother of an adult. By some peculiar trick of time and turn of phrase, I suppose this means I am a childless mother. It took nine months to have a child; it has taken nineteen years to become childless in a natural way.

Does that sound like some reverse orphaning, some tragic loss? I don't mean it that way. But in retrospect, the transition into motherhood came with such ceremony, with such obvious physical markers. The much longer transition to the first stage of childless mothering is far more subtle, and far less celebrated. There is no shower for a woman when she completes the trimester of her life spent as a full-time mother. There is no midwife to help that woman deliver a healthy adult.

The shelves of my library are full of books about how to raise babies. But there is only a meager handful of writings about the care and feeding of the relationship between mothers and their grown children.

Hundreds of psychologists have analyzed and itemized the symptoms that accompany the total-immersion experience of motherhood. They are eloquent about the anxiety, even panic, that accompanies the first discovery of infant dependence. But very few have identified and labeled the vertigo of self-image that comes as mothers let go and are let go.

In my newspaper this morning, the Mother's Day ads of 1988 are mostly pictures of mothers and babies. They are contemporary versions of the eternal mother and child. They are the primal images in our collective memory.

But in the real modern world, we spend about eighteen years as the mother of an official child and another twenty, thirty, even forty, as the mother of a designated adult. How we handle the transition to childless mothering may be as telling as how we handle the plunge into first mothering.

Generations ago, grown children, especially daughters, were symbolically given away—in marriage. Today we are more likely to send them to a dormitory. If our ties aren't severed, however, they are loosened. It's a much gentler and a much messier procedure.

I have a colleague whose mother told her to phone only with good news. I cannot imagine such a thing. Most of us provide a kind of crisis center, a hot line for our young, who then forget to tell us when the crisis is past. Our technically adult children, after all, need mothering at one time and resist it at another. They want nurturing and independence. Indeed, they want their independence nurtured.

It may be hard for mothers to respond to these mixed feelings, but it's harder still to admit to their own. The whole spectrum of family emotions, the management of distance and closeness, the desire for separation and symbiosis, emerge again at this turning point of parenting.

Most childless mothers don't want to be intrusive, and we don't want to be remote. We want to lead lives that don't depend on our sons and daughters and don't close them out. It's not at all clear how such terrain is managed.

Having entered motherhood assigned to the intensive care of our children, at some point we are placed merely, though crucially, on call. Not a few of us worry: Is the next stage waiting to be called?

As for myself, I remember one image of post-child mothering as it first happened to me. Almost three years ago, my daughter and I were in New York, each on separate missions. In the evening we met together at a coffee shop midway between appointments, sharing something sinfully chocolate, and exchanging the stories of the day.

This was not the scene you would find on most Mother's Day cards. It was something else, some rough mix of family and friendship. This, I said to myself then, is what it can be like.

The moment brought to mind a line that Lillian Hellman wrote in a wholly different context. Maybe it's too cool or too idealistic, but I still harbor this as one image for the long years of childless mothering. "In the end," she wrote, "they were together for the best of all possible reasons: the sheer pleasure of each other's company."

PART TWELVE

AT LARGE

The experts huddling around the cradle of the five billionth baby talk about "the carrying capacity" of Earth as if it were a plane instead of a planet hurtling through space. How many people, they ask, do we have room for? How many meals are there aboard, how many seats, how much fuel?

SALMAN RUSHDIE: TERROR
AND OTHER ISMS

I T IS PECULIARLY fitting that Salman Rushdie should have opened his novel with a terrorist fantasy. At the outset of *The Satanic Verses,* two Indian-born men are tumbling 29,000 feet from a hijacked plane that breaks apart over England.

In the real world, the jumbo jet has become a most familiar and symbolic target. The flying cocoon that allows us to pass over the turmoil of the world sipping wine and watching movies has made an easy hit for those who want to reach around the world and explode our sense of security.

Now Rushdie himself is a target for one of the great "isms" of the world that has rationalized its beliefs into terror-ism. The theocrat of Iran has sent a message across borders and cultures. He has put out a contract for the murder of the novelist as retribution for the crime of blasphemy. The leaders of Western Europe have responded by closing embassies, outposts of their civilizations, saying they do not deal with hit men.

If Rushdie were not at the terrifying epicenter of this furor it is the sort of event he might write about, even create: An Islam-born author condemned by Muslims who haven't read his novel and, indeed, refuse to read it. Riots in Pakistan that threaten a Radcliffe- and Oxford-educated prime minister because she doesn't join the call to kill the author. The unbelieving West in conflict with the true-believing Mideast. A cultural standoff.

There is more than a small irony to this most-talked-about, least-read novel. Rushdie's extravagant fantasy explores the conflicts between the values of belief and skepticism. He lays out the struggles between the comfort and rigidity of religious fanaticism, and the freedom and struggle of religious doubt.

The Satanic Verses wallows in just the kind of ambivalence that an author can explore only under the luxurious rules of tolerance. This ambivalence is, as well, the first victim of absolutists.

But the fine points of literary and cultural debate are lost in the current drama. It has become a much simpler story of life and death. Not a literary work but a potboiler starring a man of words threatened by an international gang of murderers. It's another moment when we see, crystal-clear, how vulnerable civilization is to violence, as vulnerable as the questing mind is to a bullet.

Our world is divided into haves and have-nots: Those who have and have not freedom of speech. Those who have and have not tolerance. Those who have and have not an abiding belief in the right to think for yourself.

The leaders of Iran are not the only ones who regard an open mind as a festering sore. We have had our own running arguments with those who define skeptics as heretics. There are more than a few Americans who would defend the Book by banning books. Ask about them at the library or the school board meeting.

Those who led the charge against the American film, *The Last Temptation of Christ,* were no less certain than the Ayatollah that their religion had been slandered. Nor were they more likely to have seen the movie than the rioters were to have read the book. But our laws and tradition protect the right to doubt in public, to air our imaginings, to question everything out loud.

How do we protect those cool rights in a world full of passionate beliefs? How do we defend the right to doubt when it is attacked by murderous, even suicidal, certainties? How do we protect civilization against its discontents. We've struggled with this issue on foreign tarmacs and airports and Lebanese apartments.

That is what's at stake in the Rushdie story. Swiftly and in rare unison, the heads of state in Europe isolated Iran. Even in America, where the government response has been late, the public reaction has been strong. The bookstore chains that took Rushdie's novel off their shelves have received more criticism for cowardice than praise for prudence. So have the publishers, far too slow to protest.

This is one of those moments of consensus about what is important to us. Salman Rushdie wrote extravagantly about the cultural crossfire of his life and then got caught in the real thing. As the target of fanaticism, he is making Western countries stand up with certainty for the right to doubt.

There is a moment in the novel when one of Rushdie's characters mimics the voice of the Ayatollah: ". . . If I was God, I'd cut the imagination right out of people." In that attempt, Iran has ignited a rare international incident in defense of something the West holds sacred: the freedom to imagine.

IN SEARCH OF FRESH
LUNGS

THIS IS NOT the best of times for the folks who make and sell cigarettes in America: The revenge of the nonsmokers is in full spring swing. An anti-smoking law just went into effect in New York. Northwest Airlines is about to ban domestic puffing. Lawyers in New Jersey are trying to prove that a company is liable in a smoker's death. Everywhere you look, the Surgeon General in full military regalia is promising a Smoke-Free America by the year 2000.

What is a poor beleaguered tobacco conglomerate to do? Pick up their little white sticks and go off in search of fresh lungs?

That's what's happening. The American market for cigarettes is shrinking and likely to go on doing so. Public smoking, like public spitting, is becoming a socially unacceptable habit. So the manufacturers are moving west, really west, all the way to the Far East.

Turn on television in Japan and you see spiffy, upbeat and very familiar advertisements for an American product: cigarettes. There is the liberated American woman selling her Japanese counterpart on Virginia Slims. There is the Camel man lighting up in his Jeep. Mixed into the Japanese messages are such familiar American words as *king-sized*.

How did this happen? We all know about trade barriers and government monopolies in the Far East. We heard Dick Gephardt talk about the $48,000 K car. But one of the little secrets of the trade story is that cigarettes have broken through. An American cantaloupe may still cost $10 in Tokyo, but a package of American cigarettes only costs about $1.60. As a consequence, we sold 32 billion cigarettes in Japan last year, up from 5 billion in 1981. Hold your applause, please.

The opening of Asian markets to American tobacco occurred with the help of the State Department, the building that houses that Treaty Room newly refurbished—with money from the tobacco industry—in its lovely tobacco-leaf motif. Cigarettes got the sort of trade priority other industries covet.

The government was persuaded in 1986 to launch an investigation into unfair trade practices by Japan and Taiwan against the cigarette companies. Jesse Helms of tobacco-laden North Carolina then put the arm on Japan's President Nakasone, writing that his "friends in Congress will have a better chance to stem the tide of anti-Japanese trade sentiment . . ." if he opened the door to cigarettes.

Nakasone folded. As a Japanese newspaper put it, he used tobacco "as a blood offering." The cigarette biz boomed. American cigarettes went from 2 percent of the Japanese market to 10 percent. Ah, the blessings of freer trade.

Now, as the irrepressible Greg Connolly, public-health activist and anti-smoking adviser to the World Health Organization, likes to say, "We're dumping cigarettes in the Far East. The United States government is actively involved in the promotion of world smoking."

Indeed, doing business in the Far East must be more fun these days. The Japanese don't have any of those sticky rules against TV advertising that we have. Their labeling laws are nothing short of wimpish. They warn: "For your health, don't smoke too much." And there is a ripe market for women. Though 63 percent of Japanese men smoke, a mere 12 percent of women do.

Is this what Americans have in mind when we talk aggressively about the balance of trade? A world in which they sell us Toyotas, we sell them Camels. They give us cars; we give them cancer.

Somehow I don't think so. Last year, R. J. Reynolds sent eight million packs of Winston Lights contaminated with the herbicide Dicamba into Japan. Not exactly a goodwill ambassador for future American products. Nor are the slower and subtler health effects of smoking. Says Connolly, "The number of deaths that will occur in the Far East from smoking may far exceed the number of deaths in the United States from illegal drugs." We, too, can export disaster.

The tobacco companies argue that cigarettes are legal. If Asians don't smoke our brands, they will smoke their own. It is an unconvincing argument from people who use advertising techniques abroad that would be outlawed at home.

The desire in America is to get rid of smoking, not send it overseas. The government used its clout for the wrong product. How much disease in the Far East will bring shame to the label "Made in America"?

APRIL 1988

SATURDAY NIGHT SNUBBIES

WHEN OLEN KELLEY got to work at a Silver Spring, Maryland, supermarket on Saturday, March 21, 1981, he found himself facing a Saturday Night Special. This was not, mind you, a sale on chicken wings. It was, rather, a Rohm Revolver Handgun Model RG-38S.

With this "snubbie," two robbers had convinced Mr. Kelley's staff to retire to the dairy freezer. They then persuaded him to turn over the cash. But when the manager was unable to also give them the combination for the safe, he was shot.

Mr. Kelley had already been the victim of five armed robberies, but this time he started looking for justice. The police went after the gunmen. He and his lawyer went after the gun.

Now, if you have been reading the literature of the National Rifle Association lo these many years, you have committed to memory the slogan: Guns Don't Kill People, People Do. This is true, but guns can be very helpful in a homicidal endeavor.

Last week, the highest court in Maryland decided that the Saturday Night Special, alias the snubbie, was altogether too helpful. They unanimously broke legal ground by ruling that anyone who is injured by such a weapon in the state of Maryland, from now on, can hold the manufacturer and the marketers liable.

The court said, "The manufacturer or marketer of a Saturday Night Special knows or ought to know that he is making or selling a product principally to be used in criminal activity." In one decision, they did what gun-control advocates have been unable to do in decades. They made it likely that in one state, and perhaps more, the most pernicious weapon will begin to disappear from the store shelves.

For those of you who have not personally met one of these weapons, the Saturday Night Special is the generic name for a short-barreled, lightweight, cheap gun that can be easily concealed. It is very, very attractive to criminals. It is also poorly made, inaccurate and unreliable, which makes it far less attractive to people who want guns for law enforcement or sport or even protection.

Indeed, the court quoted one salesman who pushed the sweet little snubbie on his daily round of stores this way: "If your store is anywhere near a ghetto area these ought to sell real well. This gun is most assuredly a ghetto gun."

Mr. Kelley's suit against the manufacturer and marketer of the weapon that fired into his body was admittedly somewhat unusual. It was legal to sell the gun fired at him. Moreover, the product was not defective per se; it worked in this situation precisely as it was supposed to. In an ordinary liability suit, a manufacturer wouldn't be responsible for the criminal use of a product.

But suits against third parties are more popular in our litigious world. In the past several years we have seen the victim of a drunk-driving accident successfully sue the bar where the driver got boozed up. We have also seen the victim of rape sue the landlord who hadn't secured her apartment. The bartender wasn't driving, the landlord wasn't the rapist, the salesman wasn't pulling the trigger. There has been a wider sense of shared blame. In this case the product was a big part of the problem.

I have qualms about the role of the Maryland high court in this case. It's an example of full-throated judicial activism. I would prefer that these handguns were controlled by legislatures than by lawsuits. Both federal and state legislators have singled out Saturday Night Specials as weapons with little legitimate purpose. But their limp attempts to deal with handguns have loopholes that look like canyon holes.

The NRA—perhaps the most powerful lobby in the country—will try to stop the spread of this precedent. But at the very least the decision should embarrass legislators. Why must we leave the legislative lobby and go into the judicial chambers to get rid of guns that serve no legitimate purpose?

If the manufacturer and marketer knows or should know, in the words of the court, that the snub-nosed gun has no legitimate purpose, so does and should the federal and the state legislatures. The Maryland court said that common law is "constantly searching for just and fair solutions to pressing societal problems." So, presumably, do legislators.

This pressing social problem is in the shape of a snub-nosed handgun pressed against an Olen Kelley on a very special Saturday night.

WHITEWASHING THE PAST

HE IS EVERYWHERE these days. Looking rested and tanned and sage. Dispensing advice and experience. In tiptop form. He even looks good on television now.

Watching Richard Nixon's speech before the American Society of Newspaper Editors in Washington, I could not decide whether to hold my nose or take notes. Confronted with full-page reviews of his book, I cannot decide whether to be intrigued or appalled.

If Nixon had been convicted of a felony, surely he would have been paroled by now. This is the case for rehabilitation. If, on the other hand, he is welcomed into the fold of respected elder statesmen, doesn't it neutralize wrongs into misdemeanors? This is the case for exile.

What is the relationship between forgiving and forgetting? I ask the same question when the ads come on my set showing Dow Chemical at its best. The young woman and her grandfather are walking together down a country road. As she talks about her work at Dow saving farms and farmers, my mind flashes back to the Dow products that were dropped on Vietnamese villages.

At times I wonder if I am to become a crazy lady in my middle age, one of an ever-diminishing band of people still yelling at the television set: "What about Watergate?" "What about napalm?" At other times I wonder if that would be better or worse than becoming one of those evenhanded people who say, "To be fair, we must balance the Watergate break-in and the China breakthrough, must balance napalm and Saran Wrap."

Do I want my moral compass to become a clock, so that wrongs are diminished with time? If not, do I want to be tied to a clock that stopped? Do I, do any of us, know when and whether to let go of past wrongs?

Most of us have faced dilemmas like these, even in everyday life. I have been a witness to marriages where one partner did in the other on the way out the door. His or her behavior was "unforgivable." We all said so. Yet almost all were at some time, to some degree, forgiven.

Indeed, the partner who remains publicly wronged, timelessly bitter, is almost inevitably criticized because he or she hasn't, we all agree, "moved on." When are we supposed to move on and when are we supposed to stand sentry, witness to personal and public history?

The classic moral example—too uniquely evil to have wider meaning—is the Holocaust. Our fear of forgetting is such that we put up memorials and are appalled if the swastika reappears as some pop emblem. Yet even here, we expect the grandchildren of Holocaust survivors to be allies with the grandchildren of Nazis.

Times change. People change. The person who carried the candle of a cause for one generation can be disparaged by the next for carrying a grudge. The sixties still argues about "Hanoi Jane" Fonda, while the eighties identifies her as the star of an exercise tape. There comes a generation that knows not Sacco and Vanzetti, Joe McCarthy, and then Watergate. Some forty-two million Americans have been born since Richard Nixon was forced to resign from office.

Underlying much of the resistance against rehabilitation, against forgiving, is the fear that our old enemy, the old wrongdoer, will be able to claim victory after all, simply by outliving the rage. He or she will have gotten away with it, whether the "it" is a personal or public wrong. Our memories are short, our sense of history is slight, the infamous and famous alike get homogenized into that morally neutral category called "Celebrity."

But it seems to me there is a criteria, though imperfect, for rehabilitation. It's something quite old-fashioned that I would call confession or repentance.

An admission of guilt, an expression of sorrow, may be better standards by which to judge a friend or corporation or an ex-President than mere time or punishment. Without repentance, a new image may be nothing more than a PR job. Without repentance, forgiving can mean forgetting. This can whitewash the past, prove that what happened wasn't so bad if it wasn't worth remembering.

I am not one of those people who measure cardiovascular health by how fast their pulse returns to normal when Richard Nixon appears on a television screen. But how does he describe his attack on the Constitution that we call Watergate? "Apart from the fact that it was wrong, it was stupid . . ."

That is just not enough. Not enough to buy my vote for admission into the circle of elder statesmen. Not enough, Mr. Ex-President.

APRIL 1988

THE BOMB THEY CALLED
"LITTLE BOY"

T HE FORTY-YEAR-OLD newspapers on my desk chart the terrible
plot line, day by day, toward its horrific climax.

On June 20, 450 planes drop 3,000 tons of incendiary bombs on three
Japanese cities, leaving behind "one solid mass of flames."

On July 27, 350 planes drop 2,200 tons of firebombs on cities with popula-
tions of 377,000.

On July 29, 550 planes drop 3,500 more tons of firebombs.

Finally, on August 6, 1945, a single plane drops a single bomb, the bomb they
call "little boy."

In the dry words of *The New York Times* news summary, "One bomb hit
Japan . . . but it struck with the force of 20,000 tons of TNT. Where it landed
had been the city of Hiroshima; what is there now has not yet been learned."

It is hard for those of us, raised in the nuclear age, to imagine what Americans
thought when they read the news forty years ago. I have asked my elders, elders
who were younger then than I am now. One, a bombardier who flew over
Europe, struggles to remember: "I just thought it was a bigger bomb." Another,
a Marine in the Pacific waiting to invade Japan, answers: "I thought, well, I guess
I'm going to live."

Still others who read the papers on that distant summer day, with eyes glazed
by years of war news, must have turned from the news to the ads that bordered
it: "Looking forward to fall and a fine fall suit? Come to our third floor and
select, in air-conditioned comfort, the wool suit you'll need."

The casualties may have sounded less awesome after four years of death statistics. World War II had already smudged the lines that distinguished soldier from civilian, front line from city. Some 40,000 Britons had died in the Blitz, 135,000 Germans in the firebombing of Dresden, 70,000 Japanese in one night's firebombing of Tokyo.

The 130,000 killed those first minutes in Hiroshima may have been more numbers to those already numbed. We did not yet know about skin that peeled off and faces that melted, about radiation sickness and the silent leukemia that struck years, even generations, later. We hadn't yet heard the stories of the *hibakusha,* the survivors.

In the first days of the atomic age, the scientists talked about their accomplishment and the military about cost-effective killing. A colonel said at a press conference that since the bomb had done the work of two thousand planes, "That makes atomic energy far cheaper than any other way of bombing."

Yet in this seamless daily flow of history, there was also an abrupt awakening, an immediate, often subliminal, understanding that the atomic bomb had changed everything. Dailiness couldn't dull the early rumblings of existential dread.

The sounds of it were there in Truman's dramatic announcement: "The force from which the sun draws its power has been loosed against those who brought war to the Far East." They were in the solemn cadences in the Vatican's lonely moral judgment: "The last twilight of the war is colored by mortal flames never before seen on the horizons of the universe from its heavenly dawn to this infernal era." They were in the rush to proclaim that this bomb could be a force for good, could portend a new dawn of energy or, at least, a "club for peace."

But now the newspapers have yellowed. Even the microfilm is hard to read. We have learned in intimate detail what happened on the ground at Hiroshima and Nagasaki. Yet in mad competition with the Soviets, we collectively produced some 50,000 bombs that do indeed make the first seem like a "little boy."

The etiquette books tell us to give rubies for a fortieth anniversary. But we have given far more than that in this bondage of two generations. We have given the wealth of nations to the bomb. We have sacrificed peace of mind.

On this August 6, in Washington and Moscow, men will get up, eat breakfast, kiss their families good-bye and go to the office, to spend the day at nuclear-war games. Diplomats will argue: How many bombs are enough? Who has more?

And all across the world, people who may not be able to explain fission, people who cannot imagine an argument that would justify extinction, will for a moment think about Harry Truman's "rain of ruin" and nuclear winter. They'll remember that the mushroom shape of their deepest fears first rose forty years ago over a place called Hiroshima. They will surely wonder why, in all these years, those who lead the superpowers have done nothing, absolutely nothing, to still that fear.

AUGUST 1985

MERCY DYING

THE SCENERY from the taxi window fits perfectly onto the familiar London palette: A gray, green and brown cityscape marks the route to the collection of medical buildings known as St. Christopher's.

I have traveled here because St. Christopher's was the first modern hospice. It was opened twenty-one years ago to give more than tender, loving care to the dying; it promised to give medically skillful loving care.

I have also come here because we read and hear so much about two alternatives for the terminally ill: suffering and suicide, merciless medicine and mercy killing. Many in America now believe that medicine is more concerned with prolonging life than preventing pain.

This beacon of the modern hospice movement offers a very different model. A place where medicine and humanity can ease the way to death without technological heroism or its horror stories. A place where death is allowed its normalcy.

In the director's office, with its requisite portrait of Queen Elizabeth resting casually against the windowsill, a ruddy and energetic Dr. Tom West calculates that eight hundred people a year are patients at St. Christopher's, nearly all of them cancer patients. "Here we receive people because they are dying *and* in pain," says Dr. West.

The hospice doesn't artificially prolong life, nor does it shorten life. Indeed, talking with Dr. West about some of the mercy-killing stories fresh in my own mind, he makes clear distinctions between the hospice and euthanasia movements.

"The pro-euthanasia community feels that if you can't cure a patient with cancer and can't control the symptoms, you should offer the patient a chance of opting out of life. Hospice is saying you *can* control symptoms and, having controlled symptoms, it is amazing to see how much use patients and families make of that extra time. I have seen so many situations that it makes me sweat to think I might have cut the life short."

Dr. West adds his own beliefs into the equation carefully: "I happen to think we are not meant to shorten our time. I also happen to think we are not meant to suffer." The widespread perception of these as the only choices comes, he believes, out of mainstream medicine's ignorance about painkilling drugs and from the reluctance of doctors to use them.

"Every patient that every doctor has is going to die. But if you look at the curriculum of medical schools, symptom control is just not there." If he has a goal, it would be to carry the message of hospice, particularly about the control of pain, back into the world of mainstream medicine. To see the line between hospice medicine and traditional medicine blurred.

Today, however, it's the hospice movement that is growing. St. Christopher's, founded by Dame Cicely Saunders, a physician who is still very much a presence here, is now one of 200 hospices open in England. It also has a large home-care program. There are some 1,670 hospices with widely different programs in America where more than 170,000 Americans died last year.

If these hospices have anything in common, it is their patient-centered approach. Dr. West's definition of hospice care begins with the management of mental as well as physical pain, and goes on to put an emphasis on communication with patients and their families. "The commonest list of things I tell patients are these: You will not run out of painkillers. You will not be abandoned."

On the day of my visit, there is a birthday cake being wheeled into one patient's room and a band for the staff party is assembling downstairs. I walk with Dr. West across the hospice grounds, past the day-care center for community children, to a room set aside for the steady stream of professionals who visit St. Christopher's.

Remember, he tells them this afternoon, a movement was founded here twenty-one years ago. That's just one generation. We are now taking what we've learned into the second generation.

This modern hospice, the entire movement, was created in response to the impersonal technological and frightening excesses of medicine. But it doesn't reject modern medicine; it says that we can use medicine carefully and humanely.

Today, the glare of publicity is regularly focused on a patient who faced a choice between prolonging suffering and cutting life short. It's focused on a husband or wife who faced the options of merciless medicine or mercy killing. But here at St. Christopher's, for twenty-one years, they have been learning and teaching that there's a third and a better way.

DECEMBER 1988

THE CRAYOLA DEFENSE

UNTIL I SAW the commercial, I had no idea that Star Wars was so simple, even a kindergarten child could understand it. I thought you needed physics when all you really needed was Crayolas. The regular box of Crayolas, not even the giant size.

The thirty-second television spot, brought to me courtesy of the Coalition for the Strategic Defense Initiative, changed all that. It opened with Crayola figures of mom, dad, child and Spot. (I think it was Spot, though it might have been a small brown horse without a mane—hard to tell.) There was also a black Crayola house and a yellow Crayola sun.

While the school piano tinkled in the background, a little girl narrated her wonderful tale of ten Crayolas in search of national security. "I asked my daddy what this Star Wars stuff is all about," she began. "He said right now we can't protect ourselves from nuclear weapons and that's why the president wants to build the Peace Shield."

As she reported this, a white line appeared in a huge arc that covered the house, family, horsedog and even the sun. This was the Crayola Peace Shield. The young narrator went on to explain how "it would stop missiles in outer space so they couldn't hit our house." On cue, little brown Crayola missiles bumped up against the white Crayola shield and were destroyed.

The girl concluded, "Then nobody could win a war and if nobody could win a war there's no reason to start one." With that, the shield turned into a rainbow and the sun smiled.

Frankly, I always liked coloring, not to mention story hour at school. This tale had just enough truth in it to be especially appealing. Creating a "Peace

Shield" isn't really much harder, after all, then drawing a gigantic white line around the sun. The real sun. In fact, instead of financing the Pentagon's efforts at Star Wars, I think we should commission the artist Christo to wrap the United States the way he wrapped that island in Florida. It would be cheaper.

What is so artistic about the pro-SDI spot isn't just the coloring. It's the timing. The thirty-second commercial has already been seen in Washington and the conservative coalition is planning to air it nationally in the next pre-summit days. It is just a small—child-sized—part of the campaign to convince the American public that a Star Wars defense is too important to bargain away for something silly like nuclear-arms reduction. After all, it doesn't matter how many nuclear bombs there are if we all have our white Crayolas handy.

This isn't the first cartoon rendition of Star Wars. The network news shows SDI working with astonishing regularity. They continually offer some artist's concept of an incoming missile being blown up. The artist never misses. The "visuals" contribute to the notion that SDI not only exists (it doesn't), but that it can work.

Nor is this the only commercial. The Defense Department has carefully orchestrated a series of "tests" under the Strategic Defense Initiative Organization. They are really what MIT physicist Kosta Tsipis calls "an unchallenged advertising campaign."

One by one, we have been treated to ever-so-successful reports of engineering tests, complete with dramatic "blow-'em-up" film footage straight out of a video game. They purport to show a new defensive technology in the making. But in fact, as Tsipis and his colleague, Philip Morrison, who have analyzed the tests, report, they were "mainly simulations of progress, orchestrated and widely reported for public effect."

In fairness, the Reagan administration needs all the Star Wars ads it can muster. If, in fact, Star Wars becomes the sticking point in summit negotiations, the public doesn't share the president's consuming commitment. We remain convinced that any new U.S. weapons program will be inevitably matched by the Soviets in a never-ending arms race.

In the latest ABC–*Washington Post* poll, 74 percent of us would trade the fantasy of SDI for a substantial reduction in nuclear arms.

With a summit around the corner, we can count on a beefed-up advertising campaign to sell Ronald Reagan's Star Wars. Perhaps a few more spiffy "tests" from the Defense Department, certainly a spate of these thirty-second sagas from the coalition. We're off to Never-Never Land. Clap if you believe in white Crayola Peace Shields.

NOVEMBER 1985

AFRICAN AND AMERICAN

I CANNOT TRACE my roots very deep. I run out of names and places quickly. Of my eight great-grandparents, only two were born in America. The others, whose names I do not know, came from all over Europe, mostly from towns that were German one year, Polish the next, Russian the third.

Some were kicked out of those towns, still others chose to emigrate. They came and married each other—sometimes against their families' wishes—and begat. They became Americans. To trace my ancestry back through even such a short history to one set of ancestors in one town in one country would mean cutting out the others the way Alex Haley did when he chose Kunta Kinte from his lexicon of forebears.

Like most third- and fourth-generation Americans, then, I am a genetic melting pot, the product of nationalities that spent centuries trying to murder each other. If there is an ethnicity that makes any sense at all it has been expanded from a country to an entire continent. European American.

It is from this personal vantage point that I witness the movement of some of my countrymen and women to name themselves after a different mother continent: Africa.

Twenty years ago, the civil-rights leadership told its followers to drop the names that white Americans had given them. They were no longer colored, no longer Negro, but black. Black and proud, black and and powerful, black and beautiful.

Now there is an impulse to turn from a name that promoted unity on the basis of color to a name that promotes unity on the basis of origin. To turn from a title that describes people in contrast to others, whites, to a title that describes people in connection to their own ancestry. African American.

"We are not just former slaves living in the United States," says Ramona Edelin, the head of the National Urban Coalition, who raised the issue at a recent meeting of leaders, "We are African Americans."

"To be called African American has cultural integrity; it puts us in our proper historical context," says Jesse Jackson, speaking for himself and others who have urged the use of a title that until now has been mainly used by academics.

At first, as an American who regards her ties to the mother continent Europe with great distance, I regarded the phrase *African American* with great skepticism. After all, what is in a name? Does this one promise to be more precise? If *black* is a word used to describe a huge range of skin color that rarely resembles ebony, then African is a word that covers countries as different as Ethiopia and Kenya. It covers cultures as diverse as the Kikuyu and the Bakuba.

Does this name promise unity? How do you find unity identifying with Africans when Africans themselves, like Europeans and Asians, are often in deadly conflict with each other? When the Americans in question may trace their strongest roots to the Caribbean, or may indeed trace much of their genetic heritage to Europe?

Does this name make some symbolic point? Trace back 100,000 years and all humans are descendants of a single African "Eve." Go forward far enough from the mother country to the mother continent and we are people of the mother earth.

But that line of reasoning is far too abstract, too starry-eyed. The question, it seems to me now, isn't whether this name change makes genetic or ethnic sense, but whether it makes emotional sense. And it does.

A change of name is a serious business. A name is identity, a handle on consciousness, a public and collective description of who you are. It may be especially important for those who still carry the surnames of slaveholders.

The name *black* emerged out of confrontational politics of the civil-rights movement. But now the toughest battles are not against segregation but against violence and drugs, the destruction of family and community and culture. Today among the leadership you hear less talk of rights and more of values.

In this context of change, African American sounds right. It's a name that resonates of cultural history, a name that reflects the real desire to teach children that "I am Somebody." A name that reaches back past slavery and out past the limits of an embattled city block for that lesson.

"Who are we if we don't acknowledge our motherland?" asks Ramona Edelin. "We are really adrift if we are just former slaves." She adds, "When a child in a ghetto calls himself African American, immediately he's international. You've taken him from the ghetto and put him on the globe."

The black leadership of today has turned inward, toward internal healing, toward self-help. It is a fitting impulse to choose a name that looks backward in order to move forward.

JANUARY 1989

FERGIE'S FAMOUS HIPS

WHAT ELSE was to be expected? It was a romance that began after all when Sarah threw an ice cream puff at Andrew while watching a polo match. What fun these Brits are, falling in love over a food fight! Wap goes the puff! Zing go the strings of his royal heart!

Fergie must have reminded him of the guys in the Navy. A regular sort. A hoot as they say in the States. Even at boarding school, she was remembered as the girl who put salt in the sugar bowl, led the cream-pie fights and organized the illicit midnight feasts in her dorm.

Is it any wonder then that such foodie origins would lead the press to focus directly on her hips? The British tabloids—the comics as they call them—spent the wedding week speculating madly about Sarah. Not about her wedding dress, mind you, but about the size of the bridal hips lurking under it.

Ever since the British press went on twenty-four-hour Fergie watch, certainly since Sarah and Andrew were engaged, they have dug up every adjective along the rounded continuum from curvaceous to Rubenesque to describe the 26-year-old Sloane Ranger.

This, however, was enough to test the patience of her family motto: "Out of Adversity Comes Happiness." Her father finally blurted out: "She'll be whatever weight she wants to be. . . . If that's not what the media want, then it's too bad. . . . The point is that Andrew fell in love with her the way she is. . . ."

Of course, that barely slowed the comics down. If just one reporter could have gotten a tape around Sarah while she and Di were in Annabel's dressed up as police officers, he would have been given a front-page scoop, a regular stop-the-presses event. As it was, the Hip Brigade had to settle for taking her measurements vicariously. Reporters on the Fergie beat actually measured the model in Madame Tussaud's wax museum when it arrived the week before the wedding.

Forty-four inches reported the *Daily Mail!* Forty-two inches reported the *Daily Express!*

Now, I for one have no idea whether Madame Tussaud's artists were keeping up-to-date with Sarah's size. But the reporters were certainly up-to-date with current mores. The only thing that is remarkable about royal matchups these days, the only thing that widens the eyes of a jaded public, is when a prince marries a size twelve.

Consider the facts. Sarah has what an older generation of Englishmen used to call "a past." This is not a reference to the fact that she is descended from King Charles II and his mistress Lucy Walters, although even that might have been a bit racy for Andrew's great-great-great grandmother Victoria.

Sarah, rather, had a romantic past. She had previously lived with two men. So had Wallace Simpson, of course, but she had made the mistake of marrying them. Divorce is still a problem for the Windsor family. At Buckingham Palace divorce is enough to get a servant booted. But among the public, Sarah hardly got a raised eyebrow. After Prince Andrew's dalliance with the X-rated Koo Stark, Fergie rated a PG.

It was her size that caught the eye of the public. In the season of sticks, Andy chose curves. In the era of minimalism, he picked a Rubens. As Papa Ferguson said, "The point is that Andrew fell in love with her the way she was." The point is that here is a prince worthy of the surname Charming.

With this marriage, the second son of the House of Windsor officially reverses the Cinderella myth. He is the first prince in modern memory who hasn't scouted the land for a woman with the smallest size slip. Sarah is the first commoner who hasn't squeezed her way into royalty. Theirs is a storybook marriage for every woman who ever hesitated before writing the word *full-figured* in her ad for the personals column.

Maybe Sarah will follow the lead of her sister-in-law. Maybe she'll turn skinny on us. But my wedding wish is a simple one: May her happiness spread. May she broaden the image of women. Even, verily, unto a size fourteen.

So here's to the happy couple. Throw me an ice cream puff. Raise it to the ceiling. Let's give Sarah and Andrew a proper cheer: Hips, Hips, hooray.

JULY 1986

CAN WAR BE PASSÉ?

T HE TWO MEN have now come down from the summit. For three days we lived off the heady air of their high-altitude politics. But such an atmosphere can dissipate as quickly as helium from a balloon.

With pomp and circumstance, Reagan and Gorbachev cut 2,000 weapons from the nuclear arsenal. But on the plains of reality, we still live with 48,000 more, acres full of redundant annihilators. Even if the START agreements succeed, we will have more than 30,000 nuclear weapons.

The real high of the summit didn't come from these modest cuts. It came rather from the sudden openness to new possibilities, the glasnost to change.

Suddenly, a whole category of weapons is to be removed. Suddenly, we can go into each other's forbidden zones to verify. Suddenly, the terms of what we "need" for national security are rewritten. Assumptions are shifting and questions that were considered hopelessly naive are again forming on our lips.

At the end of the line of these questions are perhaps the only ones worth asking. Might it be possible, finally, to eliminate war? Or is there a heart of darkness in human beings that makes war inevitable and all our efforts futile?

These are not questions arms controllers like to ask. Serious people are supposed to crunch numbers; wondering is left for philosophers. Yet our beliefs about the nature and behavior of human beings inform our attitudes about arms policy.

Nuclear weapons have already altered the nature of war. For most of history, great powers fought to become top dog or top turtle in the imagery of Dr. Seuss. That sort of war is no longer a rational option. It is a war without winners.

A series of "smaller" wars have gone on under the nuclear umbrella. Korea,

Vietnam, Iran-Iraq, Afghanistan. But not one has ended in victory as it was once defined. These, too, have been wars without winners.

Now some say a reduction of nuclear weapons would only "make the world safe for conventional war" between superpowers. If indeed we build up conventional forces, we could fall into a disaster that mimics the opening of World War I. But our knowledge of a nuclear ending makes a deliberate move incredible.

Nuclear weapons have created a new concept of limited war. Brutal and without victory. And perhaps even archaic.

Randall Forsberg, a hard-headed idealist who founded the Freeze movement and now heads a disarmament think tank, shares a hopeful belief that, "Nuclear weapons are teaching us how not to be violent. We have learned that you don't use everything you have. You choose not to. It's only in the nuclear era we have begun to practice this, not just in terms of nuclear weapons but in conventional war."

Forsberg makes a controversial but intriguing case that violence—both interpersonal and cultural—is slowly diminishing. "The ability to be violent exists in all of us," she cautions, but it isn't uncontrollable, inevitable. In human relations we now regard violence as aberrant behavior. We may eventually regard violence between nations as equally aberrant.

"I think this society has developed a dual standard in this half century," she says. "We have a very strong ethic that there's only one situation in which it's legitimate to use violence. If you're defending yourself against aggression. That works at every level: for me personally, for society at large, for the international system.

"The other standard is that might makes right, realpolitik, power politics backed up by force. It exists, but it's become archaic."

It's not a coincidence that, after World War II, after Hiroshima and Nagasaki, we changed the name War Department to Defense Department. The next question is whether in concert with the Soviets we can reduce our arms—nuclear and conventional—to a truly defensive posture.

Nuclear arms symbolize our inability to end war. We don't know how. We doubt human nature, worry about that heart of darkness. We have to scare each other out of war. Yet it's also possible that we have begun a long, uncertain, fragile and not at all inevitable process of ending war.

In 1946, Albert Einstein said that the atom bomb "has changed everything except our way of thinking." The best legacy of the summit of 1987 is not in the provisions of this modest treaty, but in the hope it raises that we may, at last, be changing our way of thinking.

DECEMBER 1987

BIRTHDAY PARTY FOR A PLANET

THERE WAS NO official birth announcement. No television crew recorded the event. No one pinpointed the place of birth or whether the baby was a boy or girl. But if the calculations of The Population Institute are right, sometime on Monday, a baby was born who brought the total number of human beings on Earth to a new record: five billion.

Such a record doesn't hold very long, not even for a minute. By the weekend, the five billionth baby will have been joined by another million. By the end of the year there will be eighty five million more people sharing a planet that will not have grown by a single inch. We cannot add acres to the Earth's surface, the way we add rooms to a house, to accommodate new members of the human family.

It took all of recorded time to reach a population of one billion in 1830. It took eleven years to reproduce the latest billion. There may be three billion more of us by 2021. And we still don't know precisely how many people this planet can sustain.

The experts huddling around the cradle of the five billionth baby talk about "the carrying capacity" of Earth as if it were a plane instead of a planet hurtling through space. How many people, they ask, do we have room for? How many meals are there aboard, how many seats, how much fuel?

They debate the limits of Earth's "resources." They ask how humans can use them to sustain our species. We have learned, after all, how to turn a desert, acre by acre, into fields and an ocean, ounce by ounce, into drinking water. We can harvest the coal inside of mountains and the oil inside the earth for our own purposes. What are the limits? How far can we push them?

But from my vantage point at this birthday party, I wonder about this whole point of view. I suspect that this press of population has influenced our attitudes toward the place that humans should occupy in the world.

When we talk about the "carrying capacity" of the planet, it is as if Earth were here strictly to support us. We talk about "resources" as if mountains and oceans and animals were ours to use. There are so many of us now that we think about the world increasingly as the private property of our own species.

Even in our country, where there is no longer a population explosion, it is remarkably hard to find someplace that doesn't have a human stamp on it. Nature is no longer our everyday habitat. We visit it, vacation in it. Even as tourists to nature, we queue up for a raft trip down the Colorado, we drive into our National Parks.

If we did not pave Paradise, we put up a parking lot next door and pay admission. When we save nature, it's in carefully designated preserves and tree museums.

I once passed a stretch of land in North Dakota, untouched by the plow. It was so unique that it was protected and pointed out as virgin prairie. In California last month, I visited a park of giant redwoods, saved decades ago from lumberyards. On a trail well-tended and well-trod in Muir Woods, I had to imagine what it was like to be alone in a thousand-year-old grove without a rented car and a refreshment stand.

It is rare to feel like one of many species on Earth. Rare when we experience a sense of belonging to the landscape. Rare when we come to nature not to own it or develop it but to be in it. We are so many, so dominant that the other species are present in our everyday lives as pests and pets . . . or food.

We have also used the Third World, as our resource, our raw material. Now, with the relentless pressure of its own people, this world turns to its own development. It's the "developing world" that hacks Brazilian forest into farmland and subdivides African plains into suburbs. There is less sentiment for sharing space, more need to use space. As the numbers grow, people think less about living in concord with the Earth and more about working it.

A species that has controlled its death rate can still control its birth rate. The experts ask whether Earth can support five billion people. A much harder question for this birthday is whether five billion people can support Earth.

JULY 1986

PART THIRTEEN

GENERATION GAPS AND TIES

It is odd enough for any member of a massive youth generation to ride over the line into the world of Oldies. But who would have thought that once they got there, the postwar babies would reopen the generation gap from the other side?

When a Baby Boomer
Meets an Oldie

THE MORNING it came home to him, my friend was taking his daily bike ride to nowhere. Up on the exercycle, earphones in place, he was twirling the dial, trying to find some decent traveling music on the airwaves.

At precisely 7:45 A.M., just when the digital readout hit his aerobic rate, he had located it: a great station. The hits kept coming and my friend kept bicycling. Then, suddenly a woman with a youthful voice interrupted his biking high to make this announcement: "Good morning. You're listening to Oldies 103."

Oldies? Had his discovery been the oldies station? The very notion was enough to give him a coronary if, of course, he wasn't in such great shape for his age. Oldies were Frank Sinatra, not the Rolling Stones. Oldies were his parents, not him.

My friend (I will call him Bruce Babyboomer) was a member of the birthing class of 1946, and husband of Betty, circa 1948. He was not unaware of middle age. Indeed Bruce had received the bike for his fortieth. But he had never felt quite so pushed into the next generation until now. Oldies.

His mind began to race through other evidence that he had come of age. There was a man of exactly his years who was being considered for the U.S. Supreme Court. There was a man younger than he running for President of the United States.

Just recently, his wife had pointed out how young the women in the Oil of

Olay ads were these days. Why would somebody only 30 worry about wrinkles?

If that were not bad enough, the Vietnam War, his war, had been resurrected and reduced to a weekly program. To college students it was, he imagined, like a World War II show. Oldies.

Cycling away, he started to think about another sign of aging. Had his generation begun behaving like any other older generation, bashing the young?

The jokes making the rounds among his friends since the stock crash had all carried that edge. They were jokes about 22-year-old arbitragers who had it coming. Jokes about know-it-all 25-year-old brokers. About the younger generation. About Kids Today.

A friend of Bruce and Betty's had spent the weekend with teenage nephews and come back aghast. These teenagers didn't know who Gene McCarthy was, what happened at Woodstock, where the Ho Chi Minh Trail was.

"They aren't getting the same education we had," complained the uncle, who was born in 1951. Culturally illiterate, the trio of Babyboomers all agreed. But now my friend wondered whether the boys were culturally illiterate or just young.

Bruce began to mentally list some of the changes that were occurring as his postwar cohorts came into mid-life. In the schools where they teach, the movement is toward "structure" for the young, and back to "basics" for their education. In the courts where they practice, the pendulum has swung from expanding students' rights to supporting authority.

The colleges they liberated are once again being pressured to act as parents. The legislatures now routinely vote higher drinking ages with their blessings. Everywhere among his peers, there is aging, and with it a bit of youth-bashing, a touch of youth-squashing.

Is this just a mid-course correction for a society that had adulated youth? he wondered. Or is his generation, the baby-boom generation that took power in its youth, consolidating it in mid-life? Are the new "oldies" tightening the reins?

My friend is at the early edge of this massive population that has moved through society flexing its numerical muscles, demanding attention by its sheer size. Youth ruled when he was young. Middle age rules now that he is middle-aged. Is that a coincidence?

There came a generation that knew not Spiro Agnew, Walter Cronkite, parietal hours—that only knows "Jumpin' Jack Flash" as an Oldie.

It is odd enough for any member of a massive youth generation to ride over the line, even on a stationary bicycle, into the world of Oldies. But who would have thought that once they got there, the postwar babies would reopen the generation gap from the other side?

NOVEMBER 1987

WHEN WE WERE YOUR AGE

THE CONVERSATION BEGAN, as many of them do, with the following phrase: When we were your age . . .

The group around the dinner table were women, two generations of them. The topic was relationships and pretty soon we came to the edge of the generation gap.

When we were your age, a single woman couldn't get birth control.

When we were your age, abortion was illegal.

When we were your age, sex was a very risky business.

When we were your age, all of our friends were thinking about marriage.

The four younger women in their college garb of sweaters and pants leaned forward to listen. It was late and we had met them in the city for wine and pasta. But suddenly, it was as if these young women were in nursery school and we were the adults who came to tell them a story they'd never heard.

One of the older women wondered gently if this was what the experts meant by cultural illiteracy. Her guests were women born during the years just before and after Bobby Kennedy was shot. On a pop quiz, they couldn't identify Da Nang, or name a member of the Nixon Cabinet, or define "Clean for Gene." All they knew of pre-sexual-revolution America was what they had seen in *Dirty Dancing.*

The other woman was sure her young dining companions had heard all this before, but it just hadn't registered. What is it that they say about sex talks between adults and children? Answer what is asked, no more, no less. The young will find out what they need to know. In their twenties, these young finally needed to know about then and now. When we were their age.

But as the evening wore on from wine to coffee, it became apparent to both of the delegates from the older generation that we were talking from one vantage point and they were listening from another. We were telling tales from the bad old days. They were listening with nostalgia. We were sure that they had much more freedom than we'd had. They were not.

I have thought about this exchange more than once since that dinner. Thought about the new realities of these young lives. About the brief blip of freedom—for better and worse—that can be seen receding. About what it's like to be twentysomething.

We were denied access to birth control by the law. Their access is now limited by anxiety. The pill that eased so many minds of short-term worries about pregnancy now comes with a set of long-term worries about breast cancer.

Legal abortion assured women that their lives would not be changed irrevocably by a single accident or error, one act of passion or victimization. Now that, too, is at risk. In the morning paper, there is a pro-choice ad that says: "After 16 years of safety, time is running out."

Sex and safety do not come in the same package. What does it mean to be twentysomething in the AIDS era? What does fear do to sexuality? Some women find it easier to say no than to say "condoms." Others wake up the morning after wondering not if they are pregnant, but if they are infected.

As for young marriages, it is an article of faith among my generation that it is better to wait than to end up, as we often did, divorced. It is an article of faith among mothers that their daughters should start careers first rather than wake up, as we did, unskilled.

But the pressure on the women to plan their lives with split-second timing and an eye on the biological clock begins younger and younger. At twentysomething, they look ahead, as we did not, and see their thirtysomething sisters who are often stressed or lonely or in line at the fertility clinic.

From their vantage point, an early marriage may seem less like a risk than a shelter. Even in this age, they are the keepers of sexuality and fertility who feel many of these pressures more than the men in their lives.

Does this all sound too worrisome? If the quartet we dined with are any example, the younger generation of women is more self-confident, stronger, far more introspective than mine. They don't take much for granted. They don't live by a set program.

But it is not an easy time. Not at all. And sometimes I wonder how this generation, more pressured than you might imagine, will fill in the blanks as they tell their own children, "When I was your age . . ."

UNDERSTANDING MADONNA

S O YOU MADE a commitment when you were young that you would never, ever, become the sort of adult who turned purple at the sight of Elvis's pelvis. Nor would you ever ask a Beatle, "What do you call that haircut?" You would stay cool. You would, at any cost, understand.

Up to now, all things considered, you've done pretty well. When your daughter bought the $30 ripped T-shirt, you didn't cut off her allowance. All you said was, "Do you think that's your best color?"

When your son came home with a pierced ear, you didn't go into your mother's fainting routine. You offered him rubbing alcohol and then stayed awake all night trying to remember which ear meant gay.

And when the tenth-grade English class you taught went punk, you didn't ban the Mohicans. You went ahead teaching *Romeo and Juliet* to the girl in the front row, just as if she didn't have pink hair and a safety pin in her left nostril.

Indeed, at no time did you ever utter a threatening or humiliating word to a skinhead, although you practiced your yoga breathing a good deal. You and your friends would tell each other that behind every mace bracelet on the street was a fragile adolescent ego searching for identity. The worst thing you ever did was utter the parenting mantra of the child psychologists: "I love you, but I don't love what you are doing."

So what did it get you? What was your reward for all this understanding? I'll tell you what it got you. Madonna.

Madonna of the belly button. Madonna of the "virgin" T-shirts. Madonna of the blonde hair and black roots. Madonna of the black lace bras under see-through shirts. Little Madonnas to the right of you and the left of you.

Now you ask me, where did you go wrong? Well, don't look for an answer in the stars. Look for it if you must, where I found it, in the movie *Desperately Seeking Susan*. I promise you that this is not a demented teen film. It's a terrific farce about a bored housewife, Roberta, who fantasizes herself into the amoral, anarchistic, sleazy life of Susan. Susan—if you live beyond the circulation of the Planet Earth—is played by Madonna, who is actually playing herself.

This movie is more than a vehicle for the rock star; it's a subtext for the whole Madonna phenomenon. The heroine, Roberta, feels about Susan the way a groupie feels about Madonna, which is the way a middle-class adolescent feels about the rebel. She is in awe. Are you beginning to get it?

Roberta, standing in for every good girl, is the delayed adolescent whose naughtiest act is finishing a birthday cake after her husband tells her not to. By contrast, Susan/Madonna is pure ego, unencumbered by guilt, family, conscience, and certainly unencumbered by class, middle or otherwise.

If you study this subtext, Madonna's black lace bra and white lace stockings become the 1985 female version of Brando's leather jacket and Ringo's bangs and Elvis's bumps. The middle-class life that's being mocked is updated (in this movie, boring adults star in their company's television ads and slip copies of *I'm O.K., You're O.K.* onto the night table), but the theme is an adolescent classic: one generation rebelling against its elders.

This is where you find the truth about the plague of Wanna Be's, those Madonna groupies now playing to highly critical reviews in your neighborhood. The same old adolescent need to rebel has run up against an escalating adult wall of tolerance. The more accepting the adults, the more outrageous the young until you get the Wanna Be's. These are the freaks who evolve when you raise the freak-out threshold.

I mean, think about it. Think about how hard it is for kids to shock the sort of elders who once played in college productions of *Hair*. Imagine rebelling against today's parents who accept rebellion as a normal stage of life. Try being outrageous in front of a teacher who refuses to notice that you have waxed your eyebrows off and are wearing black lipstick on the upper lip and white on the lower.

The results of all this are that you are left to grind your teeth and suppress your horror while the terminally tacky young talk like helium addicts and wear black lace training bras to the breakfast table. The one thing you misunderstand is how the young long to be misunderstood.

So, the next time you see a girl jiggling her belly button down the street, take my advice. Stand still, look her straight in the eye and scream. Go ahead, fake it if you have to. It's all for the sake of the children.

JUNE 1985

VACATION TIPS

Lo, it is winter vacation and the fledglings have come home to roost. These are not just anybody's fledglings. They are ours, the very same ones who emptied the nest, not to mention the nest egg, on their way to college last September.

How we felt their absence! How we now feel their presence!

Parents who had months of total access to their own cars (including the dial on the radio) are now struggling to readjust to the wonders of time-sharing. Parents who had control over the contents of their refrigerators are being led on a daily magical mystery tour of leftovers. Will the milk disappear? Will the cheese stand alone?

It is not that we don't deeply love our children and welcome them eagerly into the bosom of family. But in their months at college they have developed the life-style of a roommate rather than a family member.

Locked into the college youth ghetto, most have lost the knack of living with anyone over twenty-four. Their parents may regard their reappearance as the invasion of the life-style snatchers.

For this reason, to facilitate a smooth winter break, a family vacation that leaves no broken ties or limbs in its wake, I feel compelled to offer a vacation tipsheet. The following answers the age-old questions facing college students who come home for the holidays: What is the difference between a parent and a roommate?

1. Biorhythms. For reasons that are inexplicable, the biorhythm of a student undergoes a radical change upon entering college. The average college day

begins at roughly 11 A.M. and runs until at least 2 A.M. This is not always understood by your parents, who may be misled by the appearance of a nine o'clock morning class on your registration card.

Parents, you should remember, stopped sleeping at the birth of their first child. By now, due to such mundane considerations as work and late-night anxiety attacks about your future, they have entirely lost the trick. They tend to go to bed at the shank of the evening, which is to say midnight.

Remember: Roommates can engage in deep conversations about the meaning of life at 1 A.M. Parents cannot. On the other hand, parents think you look sweet when you are sleeping. Unless it's noon.

2. Music. The high-rise dorm you left behind, Babel East, undoubtedly contained more sound equipment than people. Roommates appear to function best in stereophonic sound, their every conversation and action, even reading, comes with its own sound track. By now, quiet may make you nervous.

Parents, on the other hand, grew up somewhere between Chuck Berry and John Lennon, but decidedly before Sony. They regard music as something to listen to. They actually turn off the radio when they leave a room. They do not accept it as the permanent accompaniment. Do not try to discuss your incomplete in physics or your desire to spend the summer in Tibet to a hard rock beat.

3. Telephone usage. The telephone company has made its greatest inroads with your generation. Roommates regard Alexander Graham Bell as the one truly significant founding father, far surpassing Thomas Jefferson. Roommates do not consider it unusual if you direct-dial cross-country in order to get the telephone number of a friend across the street.

Parents, on the other hand, tend to get nostalgic about letter-writing, especially when they get telephone bills. One of the very first genes lost in the aging process is the one that understands how urgent it is to call the friends you just left at the airport in another area code.

4. Miscellaneous manners and matters: Roommates don't care if you sit through a whole dinner. Roommates do not care if you come home when you said you would. Roommates do not call the police with your license number if you decide on the spur of the moment to stay over at a friend's. Roommates do not assume that you are lying on the side of the road. Parents do.

Finally, remember to be kind to your elders. After all, you are going through a stage of life together. You are learning how to be a part-time family.

P.S. There's one other difference between roommates and parents. You can always get another roommate.

DECEMBER 1987

GENERATIONAL WARFARE?

THERE ARE, in life, small moments of recognition that produce a click, a glottal stop of consciousness. Finally, once and for all, you know something is out of whack.

Maybe it happens when you read the statistics again and, at last, it sinks in. Today a child in America is six times more likely to be poor than an elderly person.

Maybe it happens when you notice a line on Form 1040. Everyone over sixty-five, no matter what income level, is entitled to a second personal exemption.

Or maybe it happens because you know someone young and struggling who is paying Social Security taxes, and you know someone old and wealthy who is getting benefits.

For me, it happened as I read a tale of the joys of aging written by Sheilah Graham. The Hollywood gossip columnist wrote about a house in Palm Beach and pleasure trips abroad. Almost incidentally, she added: "This is a small matter, but it gives me satisfaction to pay half-fare on buses and trains and only $2 at the movies." Click.

It's not that I begrudge Ms. Graham her "satisfaction," nor do I know the bottom line of her bank account. But somehow I do not think she is the person we had in mind when we thought of bus subsidies and senior-citizen discounts, or when we established social programs and tax policy.

Something has gone out of whack. We have looked at the elderly too long as a single class. By and large, they are no longer the "ill-clad, ill-housed, ill-nourished" population that Franklin Delano Roosevelt described. The country has done a remarkable job of changing that portrait and so have the elderly themselves. Today, the rate of poverty among those over sixty-five is lower than among the rest of Americans.

We've made these changes at a cost that we find easier to calculate than to remedy. This year, the working population will pay $200 billion in Social Security taxes. Those benefits have increased 46 percent in real terms since 1970, while the real wages of those who pay them have declined by 7 percent. Over half of the money from all the social programs go to the 11 percent of Americans who are elderly.

"The transfers from the working-age population to the elderly," Samuel Preston of the University of Pennsylvania explains, "are also transfers away from children, since the working ages bear far more responsibility for child-rearing than do the elderly."

This isn't a time for elder-bashing nor do I have the stomach for generational warfare. We can't replace the stereotype of the impoverished old with a new stereotype of the entitled old. But it is important to update policies to match the new reality. As Preston says, "If the main purpose of social programs is to help people who are poor have more resources, it doesn't make sense to use age as an indicator of poverty."

There is already some pressure to right the imbalance within and between generations using the tax structure. We now tax half the Social Security of elderly couples with incomes over $32,000 and put that money back into the Social Security Trust Fund. There is, at least, talk of extending that tax and of awarding future cost-of-living increases on the basis of need.

As for Medicare, some reformers recommend raising money from the 40 percent of elderly who pay income taxes and using it to lower Medicare premiums for low-income people. Other politicians, from Moynihan to Reagan, want to raise the personal tax exemption for all but the highest income brackets to $2,000 as an aid to families with children.

These are nibbles and not complete answers. There are few politicians who want to raise the hackles and the opposition of their older constituents by raising issues like the one posed by Paul Hewitt of AGE (Americans for Generational Equity): "Everybody in the country agrees that it's a good idea we aren't providing student loans for families with $100,000 incomes, and yet we are doing it with Social Security."

Only 38 percent of the voters in the country live with children. It is an article of faith among politicians that the elderly will think of themselves first. But I am not so sure or so cynical. In that same article, Sheilah Graham wrote, "As

an older person, I don't have to worry about the future. I am in the future."
But then she talked of giving something to her grandson.

This is the other model that older Americans respect: the family. In the family, when it works right, we do not send our children to summer camp while our parents are without food. Nor do we send our parents to Florida while our children need clothes for school. We make adjustments; we balance the checkbook according to need. It is time to re-balance that checkbook now—not by a standard of age alone, but using the calculator called fairness.

APRIL 1986

IN LOCO PARENTIS

TO A SURVIVOR of the sixties, the story was familiar: a student rally, a beleaguered dean, a full-throated protest. But the pickets carried a cryptic message: "Say Yes to Guests."

Guests? What had mobilized the students on the sprawling urban campus of Boston University was a new policy banning overnight and late-night visitors to the dorms. Starting next January, no one except a relative of the same sex, or a prospective student, can be in a dorm room after 11 P.M. on a weeknight or 1 A.M. on the weekend.

For the first time in many years an administration at a major university decided to limit dormitory hours. "We are simply saying that we must have an environment in which students have the right to sleep and study," says Dean Ronald L. Carter.

The rights to sleep and study have been sorely battered indeed since student residences were transformed into Liberty Halls. Many dorms today resemble crowded subway trains where the loudest music box dominates the environment. The biorhythms of the entering freshmen undergo a wrenching change to fit in with the sleep cycle of dormitory action. There are more than a few horror stories about a roommate's lover who becomes a permanent lodger.

B.U.'s focus on regulating "guests" has led students to believe that the new rules are less about bedtime than about bed partners. Dean Carter insists these are not anti-sex rules, especially in coed dorms, but rather rules for a livable community.

Even so, the university's decision provokes a new set of questions. Is this university, are many universities gradually returning to their role as parent? Is it about time? Or is this an inappropriate role for educators who deal in young adults?

At some point during the late sixties, eighteen became the age of total emancipation. Since you could be drafted at eighteen, the reasoning went, you should be able to vote at eighteen, drink at eighteen and live as an independent adult making your own decisions. Colleges that had been parents since colonial families sent their young teens to school basically stopped overseeing the social and moral lives of students.

Dr. Ernest Boyer, president of the Carnegie Foundation for the Advancement of Teaching, says that by the early 1980s, "Campuses were dramatically divided. They had rigid academic requirements. But they said nothing about what it meant to be a good citizen on campus. On some campuses there was a low-grade decadence with no guidelines that could be debated intelligently."

When Dr. Boyer asked college presidents about this, they squirmed. They felt they were not in charge of student life, but were held accountable when trouble happened.

Now, public attitudes about young adults have gradually changed and so have collegiate ones. The drinking age was raised in most states and the campuses followed suit. Indeed, it is worth noting that nobody at the B.U. rally protested the new restrictions on alcohol in dorms.

Colleges are pulling back from the sort of freedom that set undergraduates adrift, the freedom that seemed a lot like neglect. But that doesn't mean they should retreat to the old rules of paternalism, regulating student life from the dean's office.

Dr. Boyer repeats the ambiguous words of a student he once interviewed: "We don't want the university involved IN our lives, but we want someone to be concerned ABOUT our lives." That is a subtle distinction that any parent of a college student has to recognize. And so does any administrator.

What B.U. has done under its combative president, John Silber, is to reassert institutional authority. It never engaged students in revising the code for communal living. It just laid down a new law. Guests out by 11. No overnight visitors. B.U. behaved like an authoritarian parent and the students rebelled at being treated like children. It was utterly predictable.

In the passage to full adulthood, college students want guides, not overseers. They need the sense that there are community standards and older adults who uphold them. But they also need to feel like substantial and welcome participants in the community, and not like subjects.

So, at Boston University these days, even those undergraduates who find Liberty Hall a noisy and disruptive place are raising the banner for the dubious right to "say yes to guests."

SEPTEMBER 1988

REUNION OF THE
UNGENERATION

THIS IS WHAT you get for your twenty-fifth reunion: The license to wear a silly school hat in public. The right to park your car in Harvard Square (but not Hahvahd Yahd) without fear of the meter police. And the obligation to think about how you got from there to here.

The class of 1963 reassembled this week under clear June skies. We are four parts Harvard, one part Radcliffe, and jointly a class without claim to membership in any officially recognized generation. The people here began college at the end of the Eisenhower years and graduated before President Kennedy's assassination.

As a group, we don't belong to the fifties or to the sixties. We are too late to be members of the silent generation, too early to be campus radicals. We were destined to be transitional, at the end of something old or the cusp of something new.

But individually, who were we twenty-five years ago? Looking around these reunion events, at more or less completed versions of the people I knew, I wonder how these lives really got made. How any life gets made.

My reunion report, thick and juicy, is fundamentally as incomplete on this subject as a résumé. So are my memories. Twenty-five years ago I graduated from college. Two weeks later I was married; twelve weeks later I had my first job. Five years later a child. Now a second husband, a grown child, a career, friends, home: in short, a life. However directed that path looks in the polished prose of reunion retrospectives, it seems to me that I just put one foot in front of the other.

I say this because I am stumped when asked by the current generation of college students for some formula, some five-year or twenty-five-year plan to help them create their lives. I am not a passive person; my classmates are by and large people who were ambitious for themselves and/or their world. But looking back on it, I think most of us subscribed to the Woody Allen School of Philosophy: 80 percent of life is showing up. Day by day, year by year, we were presented with choices and made them. We showed up. And up. And up.

It is dangerous to speak for others. Perhaps I was a peculiarly unintrospective 22-year-old. But it seemed to me that, in 1963, what you did when you left school was to simply get going. Start living the life that would eventually become yours.

I don't think it's the same for the class of 1988. I think that the eighties students are having trouble getting going, taking hold. Maybe they aren't as welcome in the world, maybe there isn't as certain a place for them. But many of them also have an exaggerated, perhaps paralyzing, sense of the importance of early decisions. They seem to have a passion for certainty combined with a strong fear of making mistakes. And a belief that the first mistakes could be fatal. Sometimes they get stuck at the starting gate.

This is true in their professional lives. It's true in their personal lives. The young people I have met on campuses these last years spend much more time worrying about the future than we did. Some are paralyzed by choices. Others rush to a pre-professional shelter simply to relieve that anxiety. But there is much uncertainty about the decisions that start narrowing options, whether career options or love options.

Would the Class of '88 be reassured if they leafed through the 1963 reunion book? In our less cautious, less introspective way, we wrote the opening paragraphs, the first drafts of our lives with a great deal less angst.

The twenty-fifth reunion reports are full of our "mistakes." The very mistakes younger graduates want to avoid. Our lives are littered with mid-course corrections. A full half of us divorced. Many of the women have had career paths that look like games of Chutes and Ladders. We have changed directions and priorities again and again. But our "mistakes" became crucial parts, sometimes the best parts, of the lives we have made.

As a writer, I believe that a blank slate is very much overrated. It's terrifying. It's easier to get some words down, to just get rolling, than to wait for the perfect ones to come to mind. You can always rewrite.

I suppose that's the sort of advice you would expect from a member of the ungeneration. How do you make a life? Put one foot in front of the other. Make some choices. Take some chances.

It's not very lyrical. It doesn't soar. But what else would a new college graduate expect from those middle-aged people in those silly hats?

JUNE 1988

BACK TO THE FUTURE

I MUST HAVE BEEN sixteen or seventeen before I wondered about my parents. I mean wondered about them as separate people with their own pasts and psyches. I had heard stories of their childhoods before that, of course. But it took a greater leap of imagination than I could manage to "see" them as they had been at ten, to truly believe that they had once been my own awkward age of thirteen or fourteen.

Only toward the end of the lengthy transition from child to adult did I begin to know them in their own context, in terms of their own histories, as people who had lives before and beyond my own. Now, I am the parent of a teenager and I find it equally awkward to transmit whole the younger image of myself.

I thought about this when I spent a muggy night last week going *Back to the Future*. For once a movie was as advertised, a film for the whole family. Or maybe a fantasy for whole families.

This time science fiction was the tool of psychology. The story touched lightly, whimsically, on some of the dramatic chords of family life. The son in this movie, Marty, drives a car back into the past. He finds himself a peer of his parents. He faces them as they really were, not as they remembered or pretended.

The plot is out of Psych I or Greek Mythology. What more primal fantasy for a boy than to discover that his father was a kick-sand-in-his-face wimp and that his mother, young, beautiful and sexy, prefers him. But Marty is in a position more awkward than that of Oedipus. Having interrupted the flow of history by his time-machine visit, he must be the matchmaker for his parents to assure his own birth.

The rest is a midsummer night's fun, wacky and delightful. But I was most touched by the final scene. Marty returns to his own 1985 home to discover a family transformed by his tinkering with their past. His parents' sterile marriage is now a loving one; their thwarted ambitions and emotions fulfilled. And maybe this is the greatest fantasy of all.

For every teenager who would use one wish to satisfy his curiosity, to see his mother and father as they were in an old rerun, there must be two who would use that wish to fix things. The fantasy that somehow you could straighten out your family if you could only go back and find the key, that you could make it all work out right this time, belongs to every child of an unhappy parent.

To a certain degree, the fantasy is a power trip not unlike the one that fueled this movie son back to 1955. Today, children are routinely portrayed as smarter and more worldly than their elders. In the 1955 media world, television was black and white, and father knew best. In 1985, the colors are more vibrant and the roles are reversed.

I can't name a film or a television family—with the exception of Bill Cosby's—where the parents take their rightful place. The burden of that premature power must be as exhausting in real life as it is in the cinema.

But it's striking that this movie son uses his power to rewrite the script of his parents' lives, and give them all a happy ending. It symbolizes the moment in a child's life when he realizes his own vested interest in the happiness of these people who are his parents.

I have seen that understanding, as most of us have, among legions of children who have been through divorce and wish for repair. I have seen it, too, among children whose parents, like Marty's, have stayed miserably locked together. Even as adults, many carry the cost of parental self-sacrifice and the burden of their elders' unhappiness.

We know this, or most of us do. But in the last hazardous tunnel to adulthood, when teenage kids tug and pull their way to separation, it's easy to forget what this movie remembers: Our children wish us well.

AUGUST 1985

ROLLING STONES NO
LONGER

"**W**HAT IT COMES DOWN to is this," says Peter Hart, reading from the data in front of him. "These people did a lot, regret very little, and don't want their kids to do any of it."

Hart is generalizing about a generation. "These people" are Americans who range in age from nineteen to forty-four, the ones he surveyed in great depth for *Rolling Stone* magazine.

The profile that emerges is one of people who are isolationists, economically anxious, politically inactive. And more than that. They are a generation that has changed an extraordinary number of our social mores while leaving one almost untouched. Like their own mothers and fathers, they are conservative toward their children.

Two thirds of the generation in this poll has had premarital sex. Almost half have used drugs. Thirty percent have lived with a member of the opposite sex. Only eight percent regret either premarital sex or smoking marijuana. Indeed, the only regret that ranges into the double digits was for having driven while drunk.

From the attitudes tallied up, this *Rolling Stone* generation doesn't appear to feel that their own lives were critically impaired by their behavior. They weren't permanently derailed by the demons of sex, drugs and rock 'n' roll. Nevertheless, they are much less confident, much more worried, about the next generation. As worried perhaps as their own parents had been about them.

When the pollsters asked the very people who had used drugs—and without regrets—how they felt about their children using the same drugs, virtually all of them disapproved. Most of them disapproved strongly.

When asked whether the permissive attitudes toward sex—*their* generation's attitudes toward sex—were a change for the better or for the worse, a full 59 percent of all respondents said this change was for the worse. Among parents, two thirds thought it was for the worse.

What are we to make of this? Is social conservatism a genetic trait that lies dormant in many, only to emerge in the hormonal imbalance of childbirth? Or is there in this generation a realistic fear that the risks are growing greater, the threshold of disaster lower than before? Or are we just living in a time when people's values are often out of sync with their behavior?

Parents are, I suspect, congenitally more protective of their children than of themselves. Stephen King couldn't compete with the horrific fantasies that we can create when a child is late coming home from school or from a date. The same parents who remember the escapades of their own youth with humor get chills anticipating those of their children.

For these reasons, the casual, unregretful marijuana smoker of the past may worry as much as any other parent about the possibility of a child getting trapped by the drug culture. The 35-year-old who was sexually active in college or between marriages may think more of the pain than pleasure that sex could bring their young.

At the same time, the outside reality has indeed changed enough to warrant anxiety. Drugs have become more frightening in the crack era, and extramarital sex riskier in the AIDS era. Even the older and unregretful members of this sample have largely learned over time, this time, to say no.

But something else is apparent in this huge middle generation. Their behavior is less traditional in many ways than their values. They are carrying two mind sets into adulthood, especially with regard to family and children.

Consider their conflicting attitudes about divorce. A majority of this generation applauds the social changes that make it less important to keep a bad marriage together for the sake of the children. And yet two thirds of them regret the fact that there are more single parents today. They are a lot less certain about change and a lot more traditional when they think of the children than when they think of themselves.

This is the thread that runs through many lives. This vast middle generation of adults describe themselves as more family oriented than they expected. As individuals they were risk-takers, experimentalists. But as members of a family, they have become more traditional, more conservative.

Not surprisingly, they have even now adapted one of their parents' favorite sayings. They want their children to do what they say, not what they did.

THE SIXTIES: LOVE IT OR
LEAVE IT?

THE SIXTIES have taken another curtain call. Abbie Hoffman is making his last appearance on the cover of *People* magazine. The dates there mark his birth and death: 1936 to 1989. But the photo of Abbie in his American-flag shirt is vintage 1968.

It is no surprise to this observer that the eulogies for Abbie have also been obits of an era. Some people are like that: so identified with one moment, or one movement, that everything they do becomes symbolic, wrought with meaning.

What does it mean to the counterculture if a Jerry Rubin becomes a capitalist? What does it mean to the women's movement if a Gloria Steinem wears a miniskirt? What does it mean to the radicals if Abbie Hoffman commits suicide? It is a struggle to see the individual when a life becomes a public statement.

But the postmortems of Hoffman have an edge to them that has become uncomfortably common among people when they talk about the sixties. The cover line on *People* puts it succinctly: "He was the madcap firebrand of '60s protest, but when times changed, he didn't."

The not-too-subtle message of the headline writer was that the icon had become the anachronism. The message in that message is that a person's politics must evolve or become extinct. The cautionary tale in this obit is that people either leave behind the sixties—its values as well as its excesses—or get trapped.

This modest round of sixties-bashing over the cremated body of a man who called his place of residence "the Woodstock nation" may be particularly unseemly. The activist and supreme clown was more a victim of his own body chemistry than the times. But it fits the popular image of "sixties people" that has emerged in the eighties.

"There is some idea that they are all either Mercedes-drivers or manic-depressives," says Todd Gitlin, author of *The Sixties*. There is the notion that the activists of that decade are now either successful Yuppies who trimmed their politics to fill their bank account or failed Yippies who let it all hang out until they couldn't get it back together. Either cop-outs or burn-outs.

If this reading of the sixties legacy has an aura of revenge, a tinge of I-told-you-so, that's to be expected. Americans have yet to sign a domestic treaty about the Vietnam War. The civil war over values that was the "sixties" is equally unresolved.

Today many an old adversary is there to take, as Gitlin says, "the revenge of the conservative culture on those who were rebellious." They find vindication in the belief that the sixties "kids" have either come home to tradition, prodigal son and daughter, or have been lost.

It is a serious and smug misreading. The eighties are not the sixties. To behave as if they were would be as absurd as to go on petitioning the Pentagon to stop the war in Vietnam.

At the same time, values are not trendy items that are casually traded in. Those whose values were warmed in the cauldron of the sixties don't see Yuppie and Yippie as two choices of the eighties, but as two warnings. They are warnings about the importance of growing up and the dangers of giving up. Warnings about the difficulty of living a daily life that is both moral and practical.

"Everyone who is 'out of the Sixties,' " says Gitlin, "has a struggle finding a way to live that is suited to someone who has a stake in society and is continuous with what they were when they were young.

"These people wrestle with questions: How do you raise kids, spend money, what do you do about politics. For them, everything becomes an ethical question, a political question."

You can see the wrestling matches everywhere: in the latest comics where the quintessential sixties kid, Doonesbury, worries whether his duty as a breadwinning father means he should take a job making cigarette ads. In the supermarket and over the kitchen table where decisions are made about gasoline brands, disposable diapers and politics. And in community work, where they are carrying on.

Abbie Hoffman said in an interview that he wanted to die with his integrity intact. Many of the people who once laughed with him are trying to live with their integrity intact.

Don't write their obits yet.

APRIL 1989

PART FOURTEEN

SURVIVING THE EIGHTIES

Words that had become archaic, words like "greed," have apparently returned to vogue. If there is greed, can avarice be far behind? Life-styles of the rich and famous may yet become exposés of the rich and avaricious.

AT LAST! TOO RICH AND
TOO THIN

CAN IT BE a mere six years since the Reagan crowd became the "in" crowd, toasting their takeover with the sort of sentiments embossed on glasses in the Horchow catalog? You remember: Living Well Is the Best Revenge. You Can Never Be Too Rich or Too Thin.

It was never clear exactly what living well was the best revenge for. Some imagined childhood slight? Years of hardscrabble and put-downs? Or was it just a defensive way of justifying the high life?

The other slogan seemed a whole lot more obvious. There was a certain psychic, or maybe psychotic, balance between a fat pocketbook and a lean body. It was the balance between self-indulgence and self-denial. The key word being *self,* as in *self-centered.* The end result of all this was a clique of real-life women who wore $1,500 dresses in size fours.

The poor in the eighties might starve on macaroni and garbage-can cuisine, but the rich in our society also had to starve, albeit on radicchio leaves and caviar. The working class did manual labor, but the rich did aerobics. These were the visual messages of the Reagan clan's democracy. Don't be jealous, folks; there's no ease on easy street.

Now, we are in something that has been dubbed the "post-Reagan" era. My colleagues date this transition from the elevation of Howard Baker to the role of regent. For my own part, I prefer to use a cultural landmark. I will date it from a headline in a super-trendy, New York monthly called *Spy* that announced: "You *can* be too rich and too thin."

In Manhattan, according to the author, where all things are measured in terms of real estate, "there is an inverse relationship between a woman's dress size and the size of her apartment." The gap has grown to cavernous dimensions: size-two women in fourteen-room apartments.

The article goes on to name names, and cite statistics of the richest and thinnest: Carolyn Roehm, five-foot-nine, size six, owner of a $5.5 million Park Avenue apartment; Nan Kempner, five-foot-nine, size four, whose husband is CEO of Loeb Partners Corp. Annette Reed, five-foot-five, ninety-eight pounds, size two, with her four sisters worth over $365 million.

The entire list of yesterday's fashion "musts" is viciously attacked by this revisionist: bony hands, chicken necks, thin hips. The author says, right out loud, that, "The line between elegance and anorexia is, well—oh, all right—extremely thin."

This was not the first article to report that flesh was coming back in fashion. There have been quotes here and there from doctors and designers. Bosoms are no longer relegated to the *Sports Illustrated* swimsuit issue. One fashion magazine this spring included a section on stately sizes.

There are even hints that fashion folk, alarmed by the AIDS epidemic (called the slim disease in Africa), are subconsciously looking for fleshier images. But more notable is the fact that the women in the *Spy* article are defensive about their size, or lack of it, and even deny dieting. The too thin are now apparently too embarrassed.

So much for too thin. What about too rich? No one has yet done a similar piece, with names and numbers saying that the line between rich and too rich is, well—oh, all right—filthy. We don't criticize having money so much as the collecting and spending of it.

Nevertheless, in the wake of the Wall Street scandal, words that had become archaic, words like *greed,* have apparently returned to vogue. If there is greed, can avarice be far behind? Life-styles of the rich and famous may yet become exposés of the rich and avaricious.

All of this leads to the notion that the extremism of this era is on the way out. For six years, the gap grew between rich and poor. The rich got richer, and the rest of the country waited to see what would trickle down. What we got was as useful as a size-four designer gown.

Now middle-class America is making a comeback. Middle-size, middle-weight, middle-income America. Who would have believed it? The wealthy are coming down a peg or two. The fashionable are going up a size or two. Outliving the Reagan era is the best revenge.

MARCH 1987

A POSTSCRIPT FOR THE
POST-YUPPIES

AFRIEND OF MINE, a man who chases the cutting edge of change the way his Gallic ancestors once pursued the holy grail, tells me that he is now "post-Yuppie." This isn't a formal announcement, mind you. That isn't necessary.

I already knew that Yuppiedom was passé. In selected urban areas, women have burned their bow ties, begun leaving their running shoes at home and grown defensive about ordering white-wine spritzers. Men are increasingly secretive about owning VCRs and embarrassed to have the espresso machine right out there on the kitchen counter.

It was inevitable that my friend, who along with two others are probably the reigning troika of trends (I suspect they have a *New York* magazine reporter permanently assigned), would be early in and early out of Yuppiedom.

So what struck me was not the fact that he was in a post-Yuppie phase. It was the fact that he was using a post-Yuppie phrase.

With nary a warning from the traditional trend spotters, it appears that the post-war babies of the post-industrial society have begun placing their favorite prefix all over the American scene. These are the four little letters—p-o-s-t— which once meant "after," as in post-operative. But now they are being used to write premature political postmortems.

Consider the academic who recently drew a profile of middle-class young American voters. They were, he told a reporter, "post-ideological."

The implication was that these voters had already been through the heavy philosophical stuff. They were not hostile to ideology, they were beyond it. Perhaps they'd taken it freshman year. Now ideology was a bit like a Betamax. It was okay, but they wouldn't want to get stuck with it when something better came along.

Last year, the big phrase was post-feminist. Any young woman who had not personally signed up for Radical Feminist Cell 16 was called a member of the post-feminist generation. The label managed to wear-date the women's movement so that it seemed unfashionable. Feminism itself was described as something the country had outgrown, like a singed training bra.

Putting the four-letter *post* before the right sort of word is the kiss of datedness. The word becomes a Perrier gone flat in the marketplace. But it does this in the most apparently benign, nonjudgmental, neutral sort of way.

Consider the man I heard on the radio talking about the needs of Americans in the post-civil-rights era. The what? Separation of church and state, and free speech, he went on flatly, were all splendid ideas, but well, what do we need now, for the 1980s?

Then there are the commentators who talk about the Reagan post-welfare state, instead of what they mean: the anti-welfare state. There are even sociologists talking calmly about a post-literate world and a post-verbal generation. Once a 35-year-old described himself to me as a post-peacenik. I did not at that moment have the nerve to ask him whether he currently was "into" war.

I suppose there might be some modest value in this post-age. I think it would be amusing to be post-young instead of middle-aged. Reformed smokers could become post-smokers. Atheists could choose to be post-theists. Vegetarians could be post-carnivores. Retired citizens, post-workers. Divorce, post-marriage. The rest I would leave to post-erity.

But I am wary of linguistic tricks. *Post* is being sprinkled through the political language more generously than the dreaded *neo* ever was.

If my friend wants to be post-Yuppie, good luck to him. In his trendy troika the Yuppie has gone the way of the Babbitt and the Preppie. I don't care if he stops serving shitake mushrooms the way he once quit on kiwis. There is hardly any social judgment to be made between shitakes and chanterelles. No one really cares if we live in a post-kiwi world (except, I suppose, the kiwi grower).

But I get uncomfortable when we turn ideas into trends, when we trivialize concepts and values into games of "ins" and "outs." When ideology, literacy and civil rights are treated like racquetball, nouvelle cuisine and new-wave music, it's time to write a post-script to the era: Label it post-cerebral.

JULY 1985

THE FAVORITE

GRANDFATHER

BY NOW there is a pattern to it. The President holds a press conference. He makes a couple of mistakes, a misspeak or two, and a passel of stumbles. His aides stand in the wings looking nervous, occasionally stricken.

When the questions have ended, the members of the media stand around checking their notes and impressions with each other. One is puzzled. Another nonplussed. Metaphors abound. The ship has lost its rudder. The reins have slipped.

Calls go back to the office. Editorial conferences are held. Is it time for another piece, segment, show on this? Do we ask again the questions about Reagan the non-manager? Is it time for a Gipper-grasp update? Anybody got a new way to handle the delicate issue of age and slippage?

Somebody in the conference groans, "Old news, we've done that piece." Somebody else insists, "But you're talking about the President of the United States." The segment, piece, show gets done somewhere. It includes some stumble clips, some reactions and careful commentary.

Next come the pollsters, who send their questions out over the phone lines and come back with the reactions of the public. The bottom line is: They think the President is doing a good job.

This scenario—run after the first Mondale debate, rerun during the winter of Iran revelations—was recycled yet again in the past week. As the economic summit broke up, the President rambled through his Venice press conference. He could not remember the name of United Nations Security Council. He didn't know that the Germans had already decided to try hijacker Mohammed Ali Hamadei. He forgot that his policy was to stabilize the dollar.

Details, details. The shovel brigade came out in full force. There was a media event at the Berlin Wall. There was a TelePrompTer speech from the Oval Office. And all is quiet in public opinion.

By now I have developed a theory about this silent majority. I don't think Americans are unaware that the presidential grasp of information, the presidential performance, has diminished over the past seven years. I think something else is going on in the public mind.

Call it the Favorite Grandfather Theory, if you will. If the analysts are right, many Americans have regarded Reagan as a father figure or a grandfather figure. The young in particular voted for him in droves. The majority have been— there is no other word for it—fond of the man.

But as he slides through his late seventies, under the enormous pressure of office, their respectfulness is also sliding . . . into protectiveness.

A friend and Reagan supporter tells me that watching the President perform without a script makes him anxious. It's not exactly like watching his child at a piano recital, waiting for the fingers to slip. It's more like watching an elder—a mentor, yes—a favorite grandfather, losing his powers in public. My friend closes his eyes and turns off his TV at the scary parts.

I find in myself a similar and unfamiliar reaction. When my colleagues press the President, I subconsciously hold my breath: Will it happen now, is this going to be embarrassing? I don't want to see the man lose his dignity. I don't want to watch him dodder.

This is tough stuff to talk about. But I think these squeamish feelings are widespread. Lesser fans of Ronald Reagan than I find themselves perversely hoping that he'll just get through the next press conference, the next summit meeting—the rest of the term—and retire happily to his ranch. This hope mutes our criticism. Mutes our demands. Mutes us.

The Favorite Grandfather Factor is not something that people share with outsiders, certainly not those outside the family. Certainly not to pollsters. Families have the instinct to protect their patriarchs, save their pride, and Ronald Reagan has elicited family feelings from millions in this country.

So it goes on. By some unwritten agreement, the President is protected and the public protected from acknowledging his decline. Every once in a while there comes a press conference, another handful of mistakes. Questions about his performance resurface. And then they pass and, for a little while longer, we are spared the discomfort of confronting what we already know: The President of the United States is past his prime.

THE RETURN OF THE
CONDOM

ONE OF THE remarkable twists in the plot of "The Return of the Condom" is that it's making the biggest hit among women. A covering that can only be worn by men is being discussed by, marketed to and even bought by the opposite sex.

In the 1940s and '50s, this condom was part of the rite of passage of the sexually anxious male. In the 1980s, it's becoming part of the paraphernalia of the sexually anxious female. Thirty years ago, the condom made an impression in the wallets of insecure men. Today it's finding a place in the purses of nervous women. Then, it was used for birth control; now, for AIDS-control.

I saw my first ad directed at women just a few months ago in *Ms.* magazine. The message began with a woman saying the obvious: "I never thought I'd buy a condom." She went on to describe sex these days as "a risky business" and to end with the pitch, "So why take your fears to bed?"

Since then, I have noted condoms in pastel containers bearing names that are less reminiscent of warriors and more of women's pages, e.g., life-styles. I have also seen the most dramatic pitch to women, saying bluntly: "I'll do a lot for love, but I'm not ready to die for it."

According to loose industry estimates, 40 percent of the condoms are currently bought by women. Use some armchair calculations, factor in booming sales in the gay community, and it seems likely that, among heterosexuals, more women are buying condoms than men.

Does this matter to anyone but a market researcher? With the possibility of AIDS behind each new sexual encounter, we care less who buys condoms than that they get used. But I am still struck by the idea that, here again, women are being urged to be "responsible," women are the ones who are both self-protective and other-protective.

In the original version of "The Condom," men were more likely to be charged with birth control. If boys carried that promise of sexual adulthood in their wallet, at least adulthood was associated with responsibility. Fathers of teenage boys, never long on intimate sexual talk, did offer one perennial and charming warning not to get some girl "knocked up."

Later, in the confused course of what we call the sexual revolution, women took on the role of contraceptor. Many were eager for this power. They thought it was safer and even fairer since "women are the ones who get pregnant."

But many also became uncomfortable in their newfangled inequality. Fathers stopped delivering even cursory warnings to their sons; mothers gave them to their daughters. Men found it easier to stop worrying about pregnancy; women wondered if men found it too easy to stop worrying about them altogether.

At the turn of the eighties, as an amateur sociologist, I once conducted a totally unscientific study of the relationships of my women friends. We figured out together that, on the whole, men who asked women whether they were using birth control before they had sex were more caring and better prospects for the long run than those who didn't.

What then of this *Ms.*-directed pitch for condoms? Why has safety become more of an issue among women than men? Only women may get pregnant, but AIDS is an equal-opportunity disease. Perhaps men are greater gamblers, or more afraid to appear afraid. Perhaps women simply talk more among themselves, expressing their fears and sharing advice.

Mostly, I suspect that this gap in the behavior of men and women facing the same sexual epidemic is the legacy of the past generation of change. Women have kept watch over the exigencies of their sex lives. They have been the caretakers, the calculators of risks. They have continued this role. In this new day, so-called men's magazines still portray sex as a sport, while women's are full of messages about health.

In the final analysis, though, condoms are used by men. Even when women are persuaded or frightened into buying them, it's men who wear condoms. The man who is reluctant to protect himself and his partner is probably not—in an updated version of my sociological study—a good prospect.

At this moment, when AIDS has turned the sexual revolution upside down, one of the tricks of social policy is to get men to take the initiative again. The much-heralded "Return of the Condom" must also be a return to mutual responsibility.

MARCH 1987

WALL STREET AND MAIN STREET

I N THE WEEK of the crash, Arthur Kane was not the only one in
America looking desperately for the culprit. The demented man, who
walked into a Merrill Lynch office in Florida with a six-shot .357 Magnum
in his briefcase, blamed his own stockbrokers for the debacle. But the
shooting didn't clear up the economic mystery.

Who dunnit? What dunnit? A cast of experts, not one of whom predicted
the crash, has spent the past days playing detective. They have produced an entire
lineup of suspects. The deficit dunnit. The computer dunnit. The interest rates
dunnit. The trade-imbalance dunnit. Somewhere there's probably a contrarian
who insists that the miniskirt dunnit.

But the best and brightest of those seeking clues have said it was "psychology"
that killed the bull market. "This summer while the market was rising," re-
marked John J. Phelan, Jr., the man who chairs the New York Stock Exchange,
"I'd never seen so many people so antsy in my life."

In the days since October 19, most financial analysts have turned psychoana-
lysts. The study of the market has become a study of the collective mind. A study
of antsy-ness. Have we gone from morning in America to the morning after?
From optimism to pessimism about the future?

Traveling west last week while the market was tumbling south, I kept
encountering perfect strangers on airplanes who talked freely, and with a good
deal of black humor, about how much money they had lost. The veil of privacy

that normally surrounds the subject was lifted. Money had suddenly become a shared, public property.

I met no one who claimed prescience. Only Donald Trump obnoxiously gloated to the public of his street smarts, his Wall Street smarts. The man next to me on a Northwest flight out of Minnesota was typical of the irony I heard. With self-deprecating wit, he explained to me how he had prudently kept out of the market until exactly two weeks before the disaster.

At the same time, in all my travels, I encountered no one who was fundamentally surprised. Shocked, yes, but surprised no. It was in the "psychology" of the thing. Everyone more or less thought it was coming. Maybe, in a peculiar way, they thought they had it coming.

One traveling companion who had lost three years of profits in eight days put it this way: "I hate losing money, but it was just paper money. I never thought it was real. I never really earned it."

I don't want to put too much stock in psychology at this volatile moment. It's not good for the portfolio. But along with the optimism that's a part of the American character, there is also a puritanical streak. Especially about money. Especially about money that hasn't been won by labor. To Rosabeth Kanter, at the Harvard Business School, "there has always been this psychological tension between Wall Street and Main Street." It's one that exists inside our own heads: a tension between "honest hard work" and "getting rich quick."

To many the market came to look like an unseemly racetrack frequented by a pin-striped crowd of high-rolling gamblers. Even those who were winning weren't necessarily comfortable with the crowd. Or the climate. They kept an eye on the exit.

In the past few years many of the "haves" in this country have come to wonder if they "have" it too easy. We have grown uncomfortable with the gap between rich and poor, uneasy with the realization that we're living it up on credit, personally and nationally. And downright queasy about a bull market in the face of all that.

Peter F. Drucker, the 77-year-old professor of the Claremont Graduate School, used a blunt analogy for the Wall Streeters of this era: "The last two years were just too disgusting a spectacle. Pigs gorging themselves at the trough . . . you know it won't last." For the most part, we did know it wouldn't last. Not surprisingly, the one solace in the down market was the plight of bewildered 28-year-old former hotshots, Drucker's "pigs." The young hustlers had become a symbol of the disorderly upside-down world of the boom. No one was sorry for them. "What do you call a Yuppie stockbroker?" went the joke. "Hey, waiter!"

So if psychology dunnit, if it's psychology behind the downward spiral of the past weeks, it's the puritanical side of our nature coming back to the fore. Not just uncertainty, but old-fashioned discomfort about the funny money and the funny economy that helped push the bottom out of the market. And as the poet Joseph Brodsky said when he won the Nobel Prize last week: "Life has a good deal up its sleeve."

OCTOBER 1987

COMMERCIALS IN THE

CLASSROOM

L ET ME BEGIN by saying that I do not think Chris Whittle is a capitalist pig. Honest, Chris. Some of my best friends are entrepreneurs. If I were to characterize the genial and creative head of Whittle Communications (and after our several conversations, I think I am entitled to), I would describe him as one of those people who want to do well by doing good. Like the pop business manuals say, he thinks of a crisis as an opportunity.

The crisis at hand is the miserable state of education. To talk to Whittle is to hear the term *cultural illiteracy* sprinkled like crumbs along a path of reasoning he wants you to follow. He talks earnestly about teenagers who think the Holocaust is a Jewish holiday and Geraldine Ferraro is a talk-show host.

The opportunity, as he sees it, is to produce and beam a national news program right into the schools. He would provide color TV monitors, VCRs, satellite dishes and ten minutes of fairly zippy daily news. In return, the schools would provide a guaranteed teenage audience for two minutes of commercials.

The test run of this trade-off is a program called Channel One that will begin on Monday in schools in Kansas City, Detroit, Knoxville, Cerritos, California, Billerica, Massachusetts, and Cincinnati. If all goes well, Whittle hopes that Channel One will be broadcast in eight thousand high schools, which means that more teenagers would see this than any other program except the Super Bowl. Commercial heaven.

Whittle likes to talk about this—indeed likes to think about this—as "an enlightened partnership between the business community and the educational community." It's an entrepreneur trying to take some of those juicy advertising dollars and transfer them into schools while making a profit along the way.

All of which makes it harder for him to understand the opposition. Peggy Charren, head of Action for Children's Television (ACT), calls this a "Great Big Gorgeous Trojan Horse." If the schools go for this trade-off, she says, "they might as well auction off the school day to the highest bidder."

Arnold Fege of the National PTA also calls this a "pernicious trade-off." Imagine, he says, students being required by the schools to watch Pizza Hut commercials. "The prime intent is to use the public schools to sell a product."

This classic standoff makes Channel One look more like a wrestling match than a news show. The entrepreneur describes his work as an example of the "private sector getting involved in the public sector." It's private enterprise creating (profitable) solutions for public problems.

Public-interest advocates point to this as a blatant example of the "privatization of the public world." The school day, like a national park, is being leased, minute by minute, acre by acre, to private industry.

If the schools allow advertising on television, says Charren in high dudgeon, what's to stop them from having advertising in a textbook? If those ads mean that the schools could afford twice as many books, says Whittle, let's hear it for the ads.

This argument about values is likely to be replayed throughout the 1990s as strapped communities try to get more bang for their diminished tax bucks. The schools want business involved in partnership. The business community has a vested interest in an educated work force and citizenry.

But it is one thing when business is interested in young people as students. Quite another when they are interested in students as consumers. It is one thing when the marketplace supports the schools. Quite another when the schools become a marketplace.

Channel One—at least in its prototype—is a slick if rather lightweight daily news hit. It will sorely tempt any school principal to trade a captive student audience for some video equipment.

But schools are expected to teach students values rather than deals. How does a principal explain this commercial exchange? That he sold his students, literally? Must the teachers enforce required viewing of messages from Nike or McDonald's?

At the very minimum, the schools become the sponsors of commercials. This is a deal they can refuse. The schools are not commercial turf. They are the marketplace for ideas.

MARCH 1989

SCIENCE AND THE STARS

OKAY, so it was funny. After all, few of us had associated the Age of Aquarius with the Reagan Ascendancy. We thought of Ron as more Old Values than New Age, more Stars and Stripes than Stars and Planets.

We worried about the influence of Elliott Abrams not Mars, about Jesse Helms not Jupiter. Sure, the guy came from Hollywood where people ask your sign the way they ask your profession in the East. But that was history, like his union work.

So when the news about astrology in the White House came out, it was played for the chuckles. Voodoo economics and lunar foreign policy. I looked in Linda (no relation) Goodman's *Love Signs* to find out why Don Regan the Archer would tell on Nancy Reagan the Cancer. It turns out they were always as different as Day (Nancy) and Night (Don).

As usual, the President and his inner circle managed to laugh with us, having learned that there's nothing like a self-deprecating chuckle to turn away ridicule. The motto of this administration has often been, "Just kidding, folks." I could see Nancy Reagan polishing up her act for the next Gridiron Club musicale.

But at some point in the hilarity, *McNeil/Lehrer Newshour* did one of those earnestly evenhanded debates about astrology, and I lost it. My humor, that is. There was Jeremy Stone, president of the Federation of American Scientists facing off Darrell Martinie, the astrologer known fondly in these parts as the Cosmic Muffin.

As far as I'm concerned, getting your horoscope read is on a par with getting your colors done. (I'm an Aries and an Autumn.) It's like reading your personality profile on the place mat chart in a Chinese restaurant. But a serious public debate on the validity of astrology? A serious believer in the White House? Two of them? Give me a break.

What stifled my laughter is that the image fit. Reagan has always exhibited a fey indifference toward science. Facts, like numbers, roll off his back. And we've all come to accept it.

This time it was stargazing that became a serious issue for the sober *McNeil/ Lehrer*. Not that long ago, it was Reagan's support of Creationism that resurrected a more prolonged and disruptive debate. Creationists actually got equal time with evolutionists. The public was supposed to be open-minded to the claims of paleontologists and fundamentalists, as if the two were scientific colleagues.

Before that it was Star Wars, the most costly "science" fantasy in the Reagan constellation. The President just plain old believed in an impenetrable shield around the United States. While a galaxy of scientists protested, he clapped for this Tinkerbell and we paid $12 billion.

It's been clear for a long time that this President is averse to science. He treats the scientific method as one of a range of interesting tools for problem-solving, just a notch or two below intuition. (Where is Bill Bennett when we need him?)

In general, these attitudes fall onto friendly American turf, because most of us today share not only a touch of superstition but a bushel of scientific skepticism. We've seen "facts" come and go. We've seen the evidence and experts shift. Few of us bow before experts or footnote every idea with comedian Elaine May's old line: "And that man's a doctor!"

But at the outer edges, this skepticism about science easily turns into a kind of naive acceptance of non-science, or even nonsense. The same people who doubt experts can also believe any quackery, from the benefits of laetrile to eye of newt to the movement of planets. We lose the capacity to discriminate, to make rational—scientific—judgments. It's all the same.

No, I don't think the Chief Aquarian made crucial world decisions by a celestial calculation that's as accurate as the measurement of the flat earth. But this astrological news is in keeping with his fuzzy approach to science. On a pop quiz, would he really know the difference between physics and metaphysics?

How much worse, you ask, could the last seven years have been if there had been an astrologer in the Cabinet? Would the wisdom of the Zodiac have been less valid than the wisdom of Oliver North? Well, I will allow a small chuckle. But for the next eight moons, cross your fingers, don't step on any cracks, and wish upon a star.

MAY 1988

SEX EDUCATION: A
CURRICULUM OF FEAR

IT APPEARS that schools and families may finally break the logjam of silence about sexuality. Not to tell our children about the pleasures of sex but, rather, about its terrors. AIDS, of all things, may be the tragic impetus to bring frank and explicit talk about human sexuality to the young.

On Wednesday the Surgeon General reported, "Many people, especially our youth, are not receiving information that is vital to their future health because of our reticence in dealing with the subjects of sex, sexual practices and homosexuality." The silence, wrote C. Everett Koop, must end. It was a thought that might have been uttered at a convention of sex educators. It was a line that might have brought down on them the wrath of the right. But not today.

As the Surgeon General said, "The threat of AIDS should be sufficient to permit a sex-education curriculum." And he's probably right. AIDS has brought terms like *anal intercourse* on to the network news. AIDS has brought descriptions of condoms and explanations of "safe sex" onto the pages of family newspapers. Now AIDS may "permit a sex-education curriculum."

How much easier it will be to get a public consensus for a message about sex, when the message is that sex can be lethal. How much easier it is to convince parents to talk to their children when the motive is safety.

I read in Dr. Koop's expected and measured words an ending to that hybrid creature we mislabeled the sexual revolution. It ends in a deadly and communicable disease that is making no final distinction between homosexuals and heterosexuals.

For most Americans, the sexual revolution was not a vast national orgy of swingers. There was never widespread approval of adultery or promiscuity. The revolution—*evolution* is a better word—appeared rather as a massive questioning of the double standard and the sexual constraints we grew up with.

Through this time of change many Americans held to the belief that there was only one moral form of sexual expression: between husband and wife. But more, especially in the baby-boom generation, evolved a more liberal and complicated moral view.

In current life patterns, when there is a gap of ten or even fifteen years between puberty and marriage, we no longer expected celibacy or condemned premarital sex. There grew up what has been called conditional approval of sex. The notion runs something like this: Sex is okay *if* our children are eighteen, an age at which they are no longer legally our children. Sex is okay *if* it is in the context of a caring relationship. Sex is okay *if* they are responsible, careful to avoid pregnancy. Sex is okay *if* no one gets hurt.

This morality was riddled with our own upbringing and uncertainty. It demanded, among other things, that our young behave maturely, perhaps even more maturely than we. Many of us found it difficult to communicate this message to our sons and daughters. Like our own parents, we were slow to share experiences and suspicious of what others, even sex educators, told our young.

Now AIDS has come along. This disastrous disease has already killed fifteen thousand Americans, mostly homosexuals and intravenous drug users. But now it is reaching into the heterosexual community. The last condition of our tentative shaky approval—"sex is okay *if* no one gets hurt"—has been summarily removed.

How quickly parents and society can retreat to a one-word warning: Don't. Give parents a choice between protecting their children and exposing them to risk, and we will opt for protection every time. You can count on it.

Indeed Koop is counting on it. In his candid report on AIDS, he urged that education begin "at the lowest grade possible" and that it be "reinforced at home." Wisely he didn't say precisely what parents and schools should teach. The next controversies will break out between those who want to deliver a moralistic message and those who want a medical message—between no sex and "safe" sex.

It will be ironic enough if it's AIDS that paves the way for thorough sex education in the schools. It will be more ironic if the generation of parents who struggled out of one sexually repressive era find themselves anxiously ushering in another. Add one more sad entry onto the list of AIDS side effects: We may once again teach our young to be afraid of sex.

OCTOBER 1986

A PRIVATE FOREIGN
POLICY

I F I HAD to choose just one thing to remember from the Iran-contra mess, it wouldn't be the Swiss bank account number. It wouldn't even be the snow tires skimmed off the patriotic traveler's checks. What I would choose to remember is how easily, how comfortably, how casually, a group of wealthy people in America purchased a private foreign policy.

The millionaires who testified last week weren't just the pigeons of those can-do fund-raisers, Ollie North and Carl Channell. The trio of adventure capitalists—Ellen Garwood, William O'Boyle, Joseph Coors—regarded the chance to build a nice little army in Nicaragua like the chance to build a hospital wing in their hometown or a college library at their alma mater.

The fund-raisers presented them with a catalog of goodies to pick and choose from, everything from planes to boots, complete with price tag. A truly generous contributor might get a plaque on the plane bearing his or her name, the way hospital elevators proclaim their donor. The supergenerous were even offered a chat with the President. The only items missing from the catalog were mug shots of contra targets with price tags so that donors could pick their own victims.

Was it not stirring how Ellen Garwood's heart and purse strings got plucked by the anxiety that supplies to the contras would languish "much as supplies . . . to feed the starving people of Ethiopia . . . were left on the docks and rotted"?

But I don't want to remember these adventure capitalists and their charity as simply bizarre. In reality, they are not weirdos. They are, rather, the logical extension of the Reagan era's rule by the rich.

This an era that began in 1980 when angry candidate Reagan demanded to get his way at the New Hampshire debate because "I paid for this microphone." From that day until the day of the trio's testimony, there has been a single connecting ethic. You can do anything you want as long as you pay for it.

One of the precious things the rich can buy in America is "out." If people have enough money, it appears, they can buy out of consensus-building, buy out of community, buy out of compromising, buy out of, around or over the common will.

Consider what it is that people who have money—not super-money, just regular money—do with it. The first thing they buy is independent movement, a car to replace mass transit. The next thing they buy is independent space: a house to replace an apartment. And then they buy a larger house. And then a second house in the country.

One of the rules of the road to riches is that the more money you have, the more you own by yourself and the less you have to share. Indeed, the less you learn about sharing.

In upwardly mobile homes, the process of compromising, taking turns or making group decisions is increasingly circumvented by buying . . . out. The more upward, the more likely it is for children to have their own bedrooms, their own domains, their own doors to shut. Rather than hassling over the TV, the family gets a second. Rather than coming to terms with teenagers over the telephone, the teenagers get their own.

At the most rarefied level of limousines, helicopters, corporate empires and vast personal estates, the whole process of buying out gets vastly exaggerated. The very rich negotiate less and decide more. They don't have to arrive at a consensus among their employees: they tell them what to do. The man who pays for the microphone gets to make the rules; the person who owns the plane decides where it should fly. If you have the money, you can do it. Whatever it is. For many, that is the point of getting rich.

I am not suggesting that people go directly from buying a second television set to buying private planes for the contras. Nor that every wealthy person is incapable of community. It is far more subtle than that. But the very rich, whether they are on Wall Street or in Washington, whether in public or private life, are susceptible to impatience with process, impatience with community constraints. With the Congress. With the law.

The Reagan administration, rife with the attitudes and emblems of these rich, regarded the congressional "no" to supplying contras as a traffic jam they could fly over. The adventure capitalists, for their part, sprung for the planes. They bought out of the system.

And for a while in America, the rich had not only their own private estates. They had their own private foreign policy.

MAY 1987

GHOSTWRITERS IN THE SKY

THE STATE OF THE UNION ADDRESS did not carry a line of credits to Bentley T. Elliot and all the guys at the White House. It will go down in history as the words of the Great Communicator, not the Great Communicator's speechwriters.

There is no surprise in this, no cause for scandal or even a lifted eyebrow. It is not just the actor-politician who says what others have written. Few of our leaders write their own words these days or these decades.

The ghostwriter was surely a shadowy figure when the word first appeared in the 1880s—someone who "unknown to the public does literary or artistic work for which another gets all the credit and most of the cash." But now the ghostwriter is an official speechwriter or even a coauthor.

What was once done in secret is now done in a half-light. The hired political pen, or hired word processor of the 1980s, is at least known to those in the know. It was Peggy Noonan who wrote the eloquent words delivered by the President after the shuttle disaster. Anthony Dolan gets the credit or debit for the "evil empire" speech. Josh Gilder copped the Clint Eastwood phrase, "Go ahead, make my day."

Even the State of the Union address comes with its behind-the-TelePrompTer gossip. It was patched uneasily, or so they say, by a quilting bee of arguing writers and policymakers. The end result sounded for all the world like a generic speech right off the political supermarket shelf. "America is on the move. . . . Americans are striding forward to embrace the future."

The rhetoric reminded me of the comedic theme of George Lee Walker's crackling new novel, *Doodah.* In his fantasy of corporate life, a speechwriter (not unlike Walker himself) finally breaks down and babbles that everything they write for the chairman boils down to "Doodah, doodah. . . ."

Today, we are not only more open about the role of these shadow figures, we are also more accepting. No pol is embarrassed to have writers. The demands that events and the media make for something new can't be stated by one person. Writers have become another group of specialists, word specialists, who put political ideas on paper the way a draftsman might shape his client's idea of a house.

But I think we have become too accepting. This week, the top three books on the national best-seller lists—*Iacocca, Yeager, Elvis and Me*—were not written by Lee or Chuck or Priscilla. They were written by William Novak and Leo Janos and Sandra Harmon. Yet it is unabashedly, predictably, Iacocca, Yeager and Presley who stand up when the talk shows call "Author, author."

In politics as well we reverse the theatrical rules. The audience assigns authorship to the person who delivers the lines, rather than the person who writes them. We know what the President "said" today when, in fact, he may have only read it today.

I don't suggest that writers are putting words in the mouths of puppet Presidents. As Anthony Dolan has said, "Speechwriting in the White House is plagiarizing Ronald Reagan." The boss is both the primary source and the final editor. Yet some of those famous Reaganisms are Noonanisms or Dolanisms. There is a gap between speech and speaker.

As a writer I may be prejudiced, but I am convinced that the very process of writing is one of struggling with ideas and making a commitment to them. Someone who does not write his own "stuff" may skip the stuff of thinking. Someone who doesn't craft his own lines can more easily treat them as a store-bought commodity readily replaced by a new, improved product.

This may be one answer to the grand mystery of the Reagan administration, the President's ability to say absolutely anything, to misspeak time and again, and pay no price in the public mind. We don't hold him to his word. We have become so conditioned to the separation of speech and speaker over the years that words themselves may have lost their importance. Even those of the Great Communicator.

When speech is divorced from speaker and words from meaning, what is left is just ritual, language as ritual. This is the state of the disunion: "America is on the move! . . . Americans are striding forward to embrace the future." Doodah. Doodah.

FEBRUARY 1986

LIFE-STYLES OF THE

GREEDY

WHEN IT BECAME KNOWN on the Street that Martin Siegel had pleaded guilty to selling insider information, one of his bewildered friends said to a reporter, "He didn't need the money." It was, by all normal accounting systems, a classic understatement.

In 1985, Siegel legitimately earned $1.7 million. In the past few months, he was able to scrounge up $9 million as part of his deal with government prosecutors. At thirty-eight years old, he had a Connecticut estate, a million-dollar condominium in Manhattan, a family and a reputation as the best and the brightest of the new breed.

Yet on a number of occasions, this articulate, educated, "secretary of defense" in the takeover world stood in a public place in New York City waiting for a courier like an ordinary drug dealer. He gave the password and got the cash. Eventually, before his anxiety or his conscience got a grip on him, Siegel had taken more than $700,000 in cash from the godfather of this story, Ivan Boesky.

Why did he do it? This is what intrigues people about the latest star of the Wall Street scandal. Why does anyone who is already rich risk it all for a bit more? Even those who can't spell "arbitrageur," those who can't explain the inner workings of a takeover, reach for an explanation of the inner workings of the psyche.

The question will be asked again before this story is over. The public curiosity about the lives of the rich pales beside our curiosity about the crimes of the rich. The profiles of Boesky pointed to an insatiable egomaniac. But the stories about Siegel are much more ambiguous. Words like *handsome, self-confident, creative* are attached to his name. So are words like *compulsive* and *insecure*.

In the retrospective psychoanalysis we favor, it is said that the mid-life bankruptcy of the father left this son with a permanent, unquenchable fear about his own financial future. He dipped into his suitcase of cash for spending money to avoid dipping into his capital. He apparently rationalized it by calling the payoff his "consulting fee."

If you prefer group analysis, then we are told that Siegel lived in the rarefied and immunized world of Wall Street deal-makers. Vast amounts of money rode on the sort of knowledge Siegel specialized in. Stocks rose and fell on news of a takeover. Information was the admission card to play the game with the big boys. It was too seductive finally for him, and for the others, to hold the admission card and not play.

But the analysis of parents or peers doesn't respond fully to his bewildered friend's comment: "He didn't need the money." The suggestion in this querulous remark is that money, enough money, protects people from temptation. In the bewilderment at the crimes of the rich, there lurks the belief that money should provide a buffer against the desire for money.

It doesn't always work that way. For some people, the sense of need always stays ahead of their balance sheet. There is no "enough," especially in a business where money is the product. There are people we all know who start out wanting "enough" to pay their bills, and having gained that, enough to pay for college, and then a second house, a vacation. Having acquired all that, they want enough money to live the same way without working, and then enough for their children to live that way.

People who begin comparing themselves to the Joneses may end up comparing themselves to the Trumps. They go on wanting money. It is said that Siegel, whose own home was described as a Gatsby estate, was awed in turn by the Boesky estate. What is a few million dollars compared to $33 million?

The new breed of deal-makers, a friend tells me, operates with the morals of the limo crowd. Siegel went one better: He commuted by helicopter, above the crowd. He must have also assumed he could hover above the law.

This is not, mind you, some Greek tragedy. Although we are intrigued by the distance of the fall, Wall Street is hardly the turf of the gods. If the rich are different from the rest of us, it's because they commit crimes with more digits.

Why did he do it? Why does someone who is rich risk everything for a little more? They do it for the money. In following these Wall Street stories, I am reminded of what Emerson wrote: "There are three wants which can never be satisfied; that of the rich wanting more, that of the sick wanting something different, and that of the traveler who says, 'Anywhere but here.'"

CELEBRITY MOMS

WITH ALL DUE apologies to Amy Irving, I think it's time for a moratorium on heartwarming stories about the rich, the famous, the unwed and the pregnant.

It's not that I wasn't tickled to read the profile in *McCall's* on the upcoming debut of her baby, who is "a Steven Spielberg production."

It's not that I didn't understand Amy's impatience with tacky questions about marriage: "We're so married in our hearts it seems redundant to think of wedding now. We're just enjoying being pregnant together."

It's not even that I doubt Steven's commitment: "Amy has managed to hold my attention for almost eight years now."

The problem is that I read this charming neo-domestic vignette right after finishing the full-scale drama about children and poverty. According to two government reports that were published last week, it seems that the child-poverty rate is at the highest level in this country since the mid-sixties. More than one in five American children live in families below the poverty line, and most of them live there with one parent, their mother.

The figures proved that the absolute easiest way to be poor is to be born out of wedlock to a young woman. If you need a statistic to memorize, try this one: 92.8 percent of all children in black, single, female-headed families where the mother is under thirty and did not complete high school, are in poverty. There are more of these children who are "missing"—missing a decent life in America—than we can ever feature on a weekly allotment of milk cartons and transit posters and toll tickets.

This is not, I hasten to add, Amy Irving's fault. Nor is it the fault of Farrah Fawcett or Jessica Lange or Jerry Hall or, for that matter, Ryan O'Neal, Mikhail Baryshnikov, or Mick Jagger. (Can you match the bio-mates? Sure you can.)

If poverty, as they say, is due to a lack of money, we have more poor because we have been cutting back the real dollars we spend on the children's programs since 1969. But if the favorite route to poverty, through unwed births, has been clogged with newcomers during these years, that, too, is part of the price tag.

There are as many theories about the increase in unweddedness as there are study grants. They range from biology to morality to economics. A current favorite holds that there are just too few men—especially minority men—who are "marriageable," which is to say, gainfully employed. An old standby is that teenage girls need to see some positive alternatives, some "reasons why" to postpone motherhood.

Today, with a copy of the Amy Irving profile on my lap and Jerry Hall's autobiography on my desk, I think it's worth wondering about role models. Or about role modeling if you belong to the "interfacing," "accessing," "networking" school of verbing.

In the best of all possible worlds, girls would choose Clara Barton, or Eleanor Roosevelt, or Sally Ride as a role model. But there are probably more teenagers who want to trade places with Trudie Styler, the unwed mother of Sting's baby, Michael, than with Sally Ride. Eleanor Roosevelt's U.N. speeches raise fewer goose bumps among the teen set than Jerry Hall's description of unwed conception with Mick: "We were out in Connecticut when I conceived, on a rainy day after riding horses." Like wow.

The problem is that many teenagers are better at fantasy than figuring. It takes a while for them to realize that there's more than hair that separates Farrah Fawcett's unwed motherhood from theirs. There are, for starters, fifteen or more years and a healthy bank account. In the case of Mommy Irving, there's also a child-support contract with Daddy Spielberg.

What is distilled from these life stories as they are boiled down into one exhilarating, glamorous view, is the celebrity of unwed motherhood, and the unwed mother as celebrity. The more positive this role model is for young women, the more negative the results.

To Amy, Jessica, Farrah, Jerry, et al, I offer a blessing on their various and sundry offspring. But motherhood isn't an easy role, and they aren't exactly models. Their tales, impregnated with the ecstasy of being impregnated, ought to at least come with a disclaimer: This story may be hazardous to minors.

The truth of unwed motherhood is in the statistics, not in the stars.

MAY 1985

EXIT RON REAGAN:

STAGE RIGHT

HE GOES the way he came in. With a smile and a softshoe, and a script. This most extraordinary man, more at ease with himself than any President within memory, less plagued by doubt than any world leader within range of a camera, said farewell the way he said hello. Full of stories. Feeling good.

The tempo he set for his time was upbeat. The backdrop was a flag. The motto was "Morning in America." And not surprisingly, before he moves west, Ronald Reagan let us know again what he cares most about: the American spirit, the national pride, "the new patriotism."

The warning this President left was not about the terrible possibilities of war, nor about the perilous state of the environment, nor the cancerous pockets of poverty. It was about the danger that the good "feeling" could fade. "I am warning," he said, "of an eradication of the American memory that could result, ultimately, in an erosion of the American spirit."

The American memory? The Great Communicator has always been an Indifferent Historian, his memory as selective as his myths. This pitch for patriotism was no belated boost for history lessons at the dinner table. To the very end, this man of Hollywood and Washington preferred a story line of anecdotes and images to a time line of facts and figures.

Reagan called on parents and teachers to "remember" what it means to be American—as he defines America. The America to which boat people come pursuing freedom and yelling, "Hello, American sailor—Hello, Freedom Man." Not the America to which other boat people came in chains.

The America that is a "magnet for all who must have freedom, for all the Pilgrims from all the lost places who are hurtling through the darkness, toward home." Not the America of the homeless who do not "choose" the streets.

His country is made of earth and celluloid, of fact and fiction, created by the soldiers of Omaha Beach and the moviemakers of Culver City. It is no wonder that he worries how we will adhere to this patriotism when he is no longer at the center of the stage leading the salute.

When Ronald Reagan is retired, I will remember the man who comforted a country when the *Challenger* exploded in midair. I will remember the leader who changed his lines, dropping the "evil empire" when he got a new Russian costar playing a new role. I will remember, with awe and wonder, his supreme self-confidence.

But I will also recall, with much more mixed emotions, the "new American spirit" that he takes such pride in.

If anything, this President led us into an era of feel-good patriotism. His American spirit was not a call to action but to emotion. He required little more from us than from fans. Applause, a standing ovation, up, up for America. All we were expected to do for the country was to feel good about it.

In his farewell speech, Reagan talked much about freedom and not at all about justice, the twin pillar of our ideal structure. Freedom is something you have; justice is something you have to work for. But the "new" patriotism is an easy, even lazy, one.

"Younger parents," said the departing President, "aren't sure that an unambivalent appreciation of America is the right thing to teach modern children." I am one of those parents. Alternately proud of our successes and troubled by our failures. Conscious of the gap between history and myth.

We want our children to be proud and to be aware. To be neither paralyzed by national self-doubt, nor lulled by a smug belief that "We're Number One." We don't want them to just revel in our ideals but to make them a reality. We want them to do more than cheer for America.

"If we forget what we did, we won't know who we are," said the President. My sentiments exactly.

So, as the credits start to roll on his last hours in office, this is the Reagan I take away: A man who followed and recreated a great American story line. A man who thought of us as an audience rather than a citizenry. A man who elicited goose bumps more often than action. He projected an image on the screen to make us feel as good as we did at a Saturday matinee, when everybody knew the good guys from the bad and the good guys always won. The End.

JANUARY 1989

A Price Tag on Ethics

THE ETHICS CHARGES came with a price tag on them. I was waiting for that. After all, Americans like to price things, even our values. Numbers, dollars and cents act like the magnetic sensors they use in department stores. They set off a public alarm.

The specific prices attached to the charges leveled against Speaker Jim Wright add up to $145,000 in improper gifts. That's 69 charges, or an average of $2,101.44 per charge.

I do not know whether this price tag is a fair one. But as a somewhat mathphobic observer of ethical debates and debacles, it strikes me that our culture is much more comfortable weighing people's personal ethics than their political ethics.

We are at ease with a moral judgment made against someone's private sin—lust or greed. We are much less comfortable judging someone's public ethic—those decisions that can lead to such outcomes as aggression, the abuse of the environment, the neglect of the needy.

After all, not far from the Capitol where Jim Wright's deeds were being added up, Oliver North's brass was being tarnished in the final days of his trial. The hero of the summer of '87 was less damaged by admissions of lying or defying Congress than by the petty stuff. The petty cash that is.

The prosecution portrayed him to the jury as a loose rudder on his own foreign-policy course. But the charges that came home to the jury of public opinion were those that pictured his hand in a till. This time the price tag in dispute was on a GMC suburban van. Whatever the costs of a covert operation in terms of life and legitimacy, they were less impressive to many than the source of a $3,000 payment on a private van.

So, too, when the Michael Milkens of the world come to grief, accused of insider trading, it is less the system's abuse of the economy that's excoriated in public than his greed. His memorable price tag: $550 million in income in 1987.

If it isn't money, then it is often sex that sets off the righteousness alarms. It happened with Gary Hart. It happened with Jimmy Swaggart and Jim Bakker. People are more likely to judge—harshly—the ethics of intimacy than those of public policy.

What toppled John Tower were not concerns about what effect the military-industrial complex might have on his judgment. It was concern about the effect of alcohol on that judgment. In Alaska, Captain Joseph Hazelwood may be responsible for the ruination of an entire bay, but he has only been accused of drinking when he should have been driving.

At times it seems that our ethical verdicts are barely related to the most egregious behavior. They are as out of kilter as the charges that jailed Al Capone for the least heinous crime in his career: income-tax evasion.

We seem to reserve the accusations of unethical behavior for the simple, direct, everyday misdeeds. The hand in the till. The body in the wrong bed. Corruption. Infidelity. Drunkenness. Thou Shalt Not Steal.

We are much slower to discuss, let alone decide, the ethics of governing and managing. What kind of ethics are behind the decisions to build bombers or housing? What value judgments can be made about the choice to develop land or conserve it? How do we decide which governments to support? How do we determine our Third World friends and enemies?

These are harder and more divisive questions. We prefer to put them in the utilitarian realm of practical politics, to keep them out of the heated atmosphere in which values are discussed. We risk being accused of naïveté for questions that sound like clichés: How do you make a choice between swords and plowshares? Yet these are also in the realm of ethics.

I am not suggesting that we turn down the concern over personal ethics, although at times it can be a distraction, even a cover. I think rather that we should expand the attention, the circle of light, to a much wider arena. We are comfortable talking about the ethics of politicians. We should be equally comfortable discussing the ethics of politics.

Here, too, there are prices to be paid.

APRIL 1989

FOR THE BEST IN PAPERBACKS, LOOK FOR THE

In every corner of the world, on every subject under the sun, Penguin represents quality and variety—the very best in publishing today.

For complete information about books available from Penguin—including Pelicans, Puffins, Peregrines, and Penguin Classics—and how to order them, write to us at the appropriate address below. Please note that for copyright reasons the selection of books varies from country to country.

In the United Kingdom: For a complete list of books available from Penguin in the U.K., please write to *Dept E.P., Penguin Books Ltd, Harmondsworth, Middlesex, UB7 0DA.*

In the United States: For a complete list of books available from Penguin in the U.S., please write to *Dept BA, Penguin*, Box 120, Bergenfield, New Jersey 07621-0120.

In Canada: For a complete list of books available from Penguin in Canada, please write to *Penguin Books Ltd, 2801 John Street, Markham, Ontario L3R 1B4.*

In Australia: For a complete list of books available from Penguin in Australia, please write to the *Marketing Department, Penguin Books Ltd, P.O. Box 257, Ringwood, Victoria 3134.*

In New Zealand: For a complete list of books available from Penguin in New Zealand, please write to the *Marketing Department, Penguin Books (NZ) Ltd, Private Bag, Takapuna, Auckland 9.*

In India: For a complete list of books available from Penguin, please write to *Penguin Overseas Ltd, 706 Eros Apartments, 56 Nehru Place, New Delhi, 110019.*

In Holland: For a complete list of books available from Penguin in Holland, please write to *Penguin Books Nederland B.V., Postbus 195, NL-1380AD Weesp, Netherlands.*

In Germany: For a complete list of books available from Penguin, please write to *Penguin Books Ltd, Friedrichstrasse 10-12, D-6000 Frankfurt Main I, Federal Republic of Germany.*

In Spain: For a complete list of books available from Penguin in Spain, please write to *Longman, Penguin España, Calle San Nicolas 15, E-28013 Madrid, Spain.*

In Japan: For a complete list of books available from Penguin in Japan, please write to *Longman Penguin Japan Co Ltd, Yamaguchi Building, 2-12-9 Kanda Jimbocho, Chiyoda-Ku, Tokyo 101, Japan.*